MECHANICS
M1 for Edexcel

George Lane
David Rayner

Elmwood Press

First published 2006 by
Elmwood Press
80 Attimore Road
Welwyn Garden City
Herts AL8 6LP
Tel. 01707 333232

All rights reserved. No part of this publication may be reproduced, stored in a retrieval system, or transmitted, in any form or by any means, electronic, mechanical, photocopying, recording or otherwise, without permission in writing from the publisher or under licence from the Copyright Licensing Agency Ltd. Further details for such licenses may be obtained from the A.L.C.S., 74 New Oxford Street, London WC1A 1EF.

British Library Cataloguing in publication Data

Elmwood Press
The moral rights of the author have been asserted.
Database right Elmwood press (maker)

ISBN 1 902 214 692

© George Lane, David Rayner

Typeset and illustrated by Domex e-data Pvt. Ltd.
Printed and bound by WS Bookwell

Contents

	Page

Part 1 Kinematics of a particle
1.1	Equations of motion	1
1.2	Vertical motion under gravity	8
1.3	Velocity-time graphs	12
1.4	Displacement-time graphs	18
Examination Exercise 1		21

Part 2 Basic Vectors
2.1	Vectors and Scalars	24
2.2	Representing vectors	24
2.3	Multiplying a vector by a constant	26
2.4	Adding vectors in **i-j** notation	27
2.5	Subtracting vectors in **i-j** notation	27
2.6	Equal vectors	27
2.7	Parallel vectors	28
2.8	Finding a unit vector parallel to a given vector	28
2.9	Obtaining a vector given its magnitude and direction	28
2.10	Vector representation	29

Part 3 Forces – Types of force
3.1	Force	35
3.2	Weight	35
3.3	Normal Reaction	35
3.4	Tension	35
3.5	Thrust	36
3.6	Friction	36
3.7	Driving force	36
3.8	Force diagrams	36
3.9	Drawing force diagrams	37

Part 4 Statics
4.1	Resolving forces into components	42
4.2	Which component uses $\cos \theta$?	42
4.3	Resultant of two or more forces	44
4.4	Equilibrium of forces	53
4.5	Friction and the coefficient of friction	62
4.6	Forces on an inclined plane	69
	4.6.1 Resolving weight	69
	4.6.2 Greatest and least friction force	70
	4.6.3 Forces acting along the plane	71
	4.6.4 Horizontal forces	72
	4.6.5 Force at an angle to the plane	75
Examination Exercise 4		82

                                                                    Page
Part 5 Dynamics of a particle moving in a straight line
5.1   Force and Newton's laws of motion   87
5.2   Applications of Newton's second law   90
      5.2.1   Horizontal and vertical motion   90
      5.2.2   Horizontal motion with friction   92
      5.2.3   Motion on an inclined plane   98
      5.2.4   Connected particles   104
      5.2.5   Connected particles over pulleys   111
      5.2.6   Connected particles over a pulley on an inclined plane 119
      5.2.7   Application of vectors   128
Examination Exercise 5   130

Part 6 Momentum and impulse
6.1   Momentum and impulse   136
6.2   Change in momentum   136
6.3   Impulse   137
6.4   Conservation of momentum   140
6.5   Conservation of momentum for bodies colliding   140
6.6   Conservation of momentum for bodies separating   144
6.7   Jerk in a string   145
6.8   Momentum and impulse in vector form   147
6.9   Further momentum and impulse questions   148
Examination Exercise 6   153

Part 7 Moments
7.1   The moment of a force   156
7.2   Sum of the moments of more than one force   156
7.3   Uniform and non-uniform bodies   159
7.4   Equilibrium of parallel forces acting on a body   160
7.5   Tilting   165
      7.5.1   Overlapping plank   165
      7.5.2   Plank on two supports   165
7.6   Non-uniform rods   168
Examination Exercise 7   171

Part 8 Applications of vectors to mechanics
8.1   Addition of vectors   175
8.2   The displacement vector   175
8.3   Relative displacement   176
8.4   The velocity vector   177
8.5   The acceleration vector   177
8.6   Constant velocity   178
8.7   Least distance between two particles   179
8.8   Collision of two particles   180
Examination Exercise 8   186

Specimen M1 papers   190

Preface

This book is for the first Mechanics module, M1, for candidates working towards the Edexcel AS/A2 modular examinations in mathematics. It can be used both in the classroom and by students working on their own. There are explanations, worked examples and numerous exercises which, it is hoped, will help students to build up confidence. The authors believe that people learn mathematics by doing mathematics. The questions are graded in difficulty throughout the exercises.

The authors feel that it is important to develop the ideas relating to statics and dynamics and to leave more abstract ideas on vectors until later. So although it is important to understand the vector nature of velocities and forces etc., the work in part 2 could well be deferred.

Regarding accuracy of answers, Edexcel (examiners report July 2004) encourage an accuracy of 3 significant figures in questions where approximate answers are to be given. In problems where $g = 9.8 \, \text{ms}^{-2}$ has been used, answers to 2 or 3 sf. are accepted.

Edexcel encourage candidates to draw good clear diagrams, where appropriate, and to present work in a neat ordered fashion, so the candidate benefits by clear thought processes.

Thanks are due to Edexcel for kindly allowing use of questions from their past examination papers. The answers are solely the work of the authors.

G. Lane
D. Rayner

Part 1

Kinematics of a particle

1.1 Equations of motion

If a particle moves in a straight line with constant acceleration a, then we can use certain formulae which connect its initial velocity u, its acceleration, its displacement s and the time taken t.

Consider the velocity–time graph shown below.

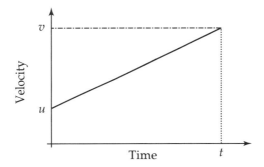

The gradient of this line is the acceleration a. This is constant and so the line is straight.

From our definition of acceleration it follows that $a = \dfrac{v - u}{t}$ (1)

From (1) we obtain $v = u + at$ (2)

The area under the velocity–time graph represents the displacement and so we see that

$$s = \frac{1}{2}(u + v)t \tag{3}$$

If we substitute (3) into (2) we obtain

$$s = \frac{1}{2}(u + u + at)t$$

$$s = \frac{1}{2}(2u + at)t$$

$$s = ut + \frac{1}{2}at^2 \tag{4}$$

Alternatively from (1) we have $t = \dfrac{v - u}{a}$.

1

Now substituting for t in (3),

$$s = \frac{1}{2}(u+v)\left(\frac{v-u}{a}\right)$$

$$s = \frac{v^2 - u^2}{2a}$$

and so $\quad v^2 = u^2 + 2as \qquad (5)$

In summary we have the following formulae which should be memorized.

$v = u + at \qquad s = ut + \frac{1}{2}at^2 \qquad v^2 = u^2 + 2as$

$s = \frac{1}{2}(u+v)t$

Distance travelled and displacement

(a) Suppose a car travels 5 km from O in a straight line. The distance travelled is 5 km and the final displacement of the car is 5 km from O.

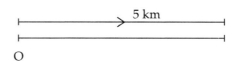

(b) Now suppose the car travels 5 km from O along the same straight road and then turns around and travels 3 km back along the same road. Here the distance travelled is 8 km but the final displacement of the car is 2 km from O.

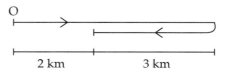

(c) In the equations of motion the symbol s stands for displacement. If the direction of motion of a body does not change, then the distance travelled and the displacement are equal.

Example 1

A car moving along a straight road accelerates uniformly from a speed of $5\,\text{ms}^{-1}$ to $25\,\text{ms}^{-1}$ in a time of 10 seconds.

Find (a) the distance travelled

(b) the acceleration.

(a) List the quantities

$u = 5$
$v = 25$
$t = 10$
$s = ?$

$$s = \left(\frac{u+v}{2}\right)t$$
$$= \left(\frac{5+25}{2}\right)10$$
$$= 150$$

Distance travelled = 150 m

(b) $u = 5$
$v = 25$
$t = 10$
$a = ?$

$v = u + at$
$25 = 5 + a \times 10$
$a = 2$

The acceleration $= 2\,\text{ms}^{-2}$

Example 2

A car starts from rest and moves on a straight road with a constant acceleration of $1.6\,\text{ms}^{-2}$ until its speed is $72\,\text{kmh}^{-1}$.

Find (a) the time taken

(b) the distance travelled.

(a) It is usual to work with metres and seconds so the speed should be converted into units of ms^{-1}

$1\,\text{km} = 1000\,\text{m}$

$1\,\text{hour} = 60 \times 60 = 3600$ seconds

$$72\frac{\text{km}}{\text{h}} = 72 \times \frac{1000}{3600}\,\text{ms}^{-1}$$
$$= 20\,\text{ms}^{-1}$$

we have $u = 0$
$v = 20$

3

$$a = 1.6$$
$$t = \text{?}$$
$$v = u + at$$
$$20 = 0 + 1.6t$$
$$t = 12.5$$

Time taken = 12.5 seconds

(b) $\quad u = 0$
$$v = 20$$
$$a = 1.6$$
$$s = \text{?}$$
$$v^2 = u^2 + 2as$$
$$20^2 = 0^2 + 2 \times 1.6 \times s$$
$$s = 125$$

Distance travelled = 125 m

Example 3

A particle starts at a speed of 8 ms^{-1} and has a constant acceleration of 4 ms^{-2}, over a distance 640 m. Find the time taken.

$$u = 8$$
$$a = 4$$
$$s = 640$$
$$t = \text{?}$$
$$s = ut + \frac{1}{2}at^2$$
$$640 = 8t + \frac{1}{2} \times 4 \times t^2$$
$$640 = 8t + 2t^2$$

This simplifies to
$$t^2 + 4t - 320 = 0$$

Factorising
$$(t + 20)(t - 16) = 0$$

Time is positive $\Rightarrow t = 16$

Time taken = 16 seconds

Example 4

A train travelling at 20 ms^{-1} is brought to rest with a uniform deceleration of 2 ms^{-2}. Find the distance travelled.

$u = 20$

$v = 0$

$a = -2$ 　　(notice the negative sign for a deceleration)

$s = ?$

$v^2 = u^2 + 2as$

$0 = 20^2 + 2 \times (-2) \times s$

$s = 100$ m

Distance travelled $= 100$ m

Example 5

A ball thrown 5 m vertically upwards is then caught by the thrower.

Find　(a) the distance travelled by the ball
　　　(b) its final displacement from its initial position.

(a) distance travelled $= 5 + 5$
　　　　　　　　　　 $= 10$ m

(b) displacement (a vector quantity)
　　　　　　　　　　 $= 5 - 5$
　　　　　　　　　　 $= 0$ m

Example 6

A particle is moving in a straight line with constant acceleration. It passes points A, B and C on the line at times $t = 0$, $t = 2$s, $t = 4$s respectively. If the distance $AB = 14$ m and $BC = 30$ m,

find　(a) the acceleration
　　　(b) the speed of the particle at A

```
A                        B                        C
├─────────────────────────┼─────────────────────────┤
t = 0                    t = 2                    t = 4
s = 0                    s = 14                   s = 44
u = ?
                              ─────────► a
```

In this type of question it is best to consider motion from A to B and A to C, because the speed at B is unknown.

Motion from A to B	Motion from A to C
$t = 2$	$t = 4$
$s = 14$	$s = 44$
$u = ?$	$u = ?$
$a = ?$	$a = ?$
$s = ut + \frac{1}{2}at^2$	$s = ut + \frac{1}{2}at^2$
$14 = u \times 2 + \frac{1}{2} \times a \times 2^2$	$44 = u \times 4 + \frac{1}{2} \times a \times 4^2$
$14 = 2u + 2a$	$44 = 4u + 8a$
$7 = u + a \quad \ldots (1)$	$11 = u + 2a \quad \ldots (2)$

Solving the simultaneous equations (1) and (2) gives $a = 4$ and $u = 3$.

The acceleration $= 4$ ms^{-2} and the initial speed $= 3$ ms^{-1}

Exercise 1A

In each question state which of the following formulae you are using:

$$v = u + at \quad s = ut + \frac{1}{2}at^2 \quad v^2 = u^2 + 2as \quad s = \frac{1}{2}(u+v)t$$

In Questions **1** to **4** all symbols are given in S.I. units.

1. If $u = 10$, $v = 20$ and $a = 2$, find the value of t.

2. If $s = 200$, $u = 40$ and $v = 10$, find the value of t.

3. If $u = 7$, $a = 2$ and $s = 5$, find the positive value of v.

4. Given that $u = \sqrt{10}$, $v = 5$ and $a = 3$, find the value of s.

Questions **5** to **7** are about a particle moving along a straight line with uniform acceleration from A to B.

5. initial velocity $= 2$ ms^{-1}, final velocity $= 10$ ms^{-1}, displacement $= 12$ m. Find the time taken.

6. initially at rest, time taken $= 10$ s, final velocity $= 30$ ms^{-1}. Find the acceleration.

7. initial velocity $= 40\,\text{ms}^{-1}$, final velocity $= 50\,\text{ms}^{-1}$, acceleration $= 10\,\text{ms}^{-2}$. Find the displacement.

8. A man accelerates at a constant rate from $6\,\text{ms}^{-1}$ to $12\,\text{ms}^{-1}$ over 5 seconds. How far does he run?

9. A car is travelling at $20\,\text{ms}^{-1}$ and then accelerates at $3\,\text{ms}^{-2}$ for 4 seconds. How far does it travel as it accelerates?

10. A train is travelling at $30\,\text{ms}^{-1}$ and then accelerates to a speed of $35\,\text{ms}^{-1}$. If it covers a distance of 160 m, find the acceleration.

11. A particle accelerates from $5\,\text{ms}^{-1}$ to $8\,\text{ms}^{-1}$ over two seconds. Find the acceleration.

12. A car is travelling at $15\,\text{ms}^{-1}$ and then accelerates at $2\,\text{ms}^{-2}$ over a distance of 50 m. What is its speed after travelling 50 m?

13. A particle travelling at $7\,\text{ms}^{-1}$ accelerates at a constant rate until it reaches a speed of $11\,\text{ms}^{-1}$. If it travelled 12 m as it was accelerating, find its acceleration.

14. A particle is travelling at $4\,\text{ms}^{-1}$ and then accelerates for two seconds at $3\,\text{ms}^{-2}$. Find how far it travelled as it was accelerating.

15. A cyclist is travelling at $5\,\text{ms}^{-1}$ and then decelerated at $1\,\text{ms}^{-2}$ over a distance of 12 m (he did not ever come to rest and change direction). What was his speed at the end of the 12 m and how long did he take to cover this distance?

16. A model boat is travelling at $5\,\text{ms}^{-1}$ and then accelerates at $2\,\text{ms}^{-2}$. How long does it take the boat to cover 24 m and what will its speed be after it has covered this distance?

17. A car accelerates for four seconds at a constant rate. Over the four seconds it travels 104 m. It covered 58 m in the last two seconds. Find the speed at which the car was travelling before it started to accelerate and the rate of acceleration (in ms^{-2}).

18. (a) Express a speed of 72 kmh^{-1} in ms^{-1}.

    (b) Express a speed of 180 kmh^{-1} in ms^{-1}.

    (c) Express 5 ms^{-1} in kmh^{-1}.

    (d) Express 12 ms^{-1} in kmh^{-1}.

19. A car A travelling at a constant speed of 72 kmh^{-1} overtakes a car B travelling at a constant speed of 54 kmh^{-1} in the same direction. At the point when A overtakes B, A begins to accelerate at $0.25\,\text{ms}^{-2}$ and B accelerates at $5.25\,\text{ms}^{-2}$.

    (a) Find expressions for the distances travelled by A and B in time t after the point when B overtakes A.

    (b) Hence find how long it takes for B to overtake A.

    (c) At what speed will B be travelling (in kmh^{-1}) when this happens?

20. Three points A, B and C lie a straight line in that order such that AB is 15 m and BC is 12 m. A particle leaves B at $t = 0$ heading at 6 ms^{-1} in the direction of C and subject to a force which causes an acceleration of 1.5 ms^{-2} towards A. In other words the particle begins to move away from A, comes to instantaneous rest and then travels towards A.

   (a) Find the time at which the particle changes direction.

   (b) Show that the particle just reaches C.

   (c) After how much longer will the particle reach the point A?

   (d) What is the total distance the particle has travelled in its path from B to A?

21. A car accelerates at a constant rate (not from rest) for six seconds. It travels 36 m in the first 2 seconds and then 108 m in the next four seconds. Find the initial speed of the car and its acceleration.

1.2 Vertical motion under gravity

When a body is falling under gravity we adopt a model in which the body is a particle and air resistance is ignored so that the acceleration is uniform. The acceleration of the body is approximately 9.8 ms^{-2} and is often referred to as g, the acceleration due to gravity.

In problems it is important to state the direction, either upwards or downwards, which is taken to be positive. A useful shorthand is to draw an arrow such as ↑ +, for upwards positive, or ↓ +, for downwards positive.

Example 1

A ball is thrown vertically upwards with a speed of 16 ms^{-1}. Find:

(a) the maximum height reached

(b) the velocity after 1 second and after 2 seconds.

(a) Take upwards as positive. (↑ +)

$u = 16$

$a = -9.8$

$v = 0$ (at the highest point)

$s = ?$

$v^2 = u^2 + 2as$

$0 = 16^2 + 2 \times -9.8 \times s$

$s = 13.1$

The maximum height reached = 13.1 m.

(b) $+\uparrow$ $u = 16$ $+\uparrow$ $u = 16$
         $a = -9.8$ $a = -9.8$
         $t = 1$ $t = 2$
         $v = ?$ $v = ?$
         $v = u + at$ $v = u + at$
         $v = 16 - 9.8 \times 1$ $v = 16 - 9.8 \times 2$
            $= 6.2$ $v = -3.6$

The velocity after 1 second is 6.2 ms^{-1} and after 2 seconds is -3.6 ms^{-1}.

Notice that after 1 second the ball has a positive velocity and so is going upwards and after 2 seconds it has a negative velocity and so is coming down.

Example 2

A ball is thrown vertically upwards from a point 2 m above the ground with a velocity of 18 ms^{-1}.

Calculate   (a) The speed with which the ball hits the ground
               (b) The time of flight.

(a) Take the positive direction upwards. Consider the whole flight,

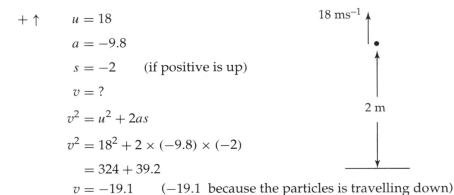

$+\uparrow$ $u = 18$

        $a = -9.8$

        $s = -2$ (if positive is up)

        $v = ?$

        $v^2 = u^2 + 2as$

        $v^2 = 18^2 + 2 \times (-9.8) \times (-2)$

           $= 324 + 39.2$

        $v = -19.1$ (-19.1 because the particles is travelling down)

The ball hits the ground with a speed of 19.1 ms^{-1}.

(b) $+\uparrow$ $u = 18$

           $a = -9.8$

           $s = -2$

           $t = ?$

           $s = ut + \frac{1}{2}at^2$

           $-2 = 18t + \frac{1}{2} \times (-9.8)t^2$

           $4.9t^2 - 18t - 2 = 0$

This can be solved using the formula for quadratic equations.

Time of flight = 3.78 seconds

Example 3

A ball is thrown vertically upwards with speed 15 ms^{-1}. It hits the ground 4 seconds later. Find the height above the ground from which the ball was thrown.

Take the positive direction upwards

$+\uparrow$ $u = 15$

$a = -9.8$

$t = 4$

$s = ?$

$$s = ut + \frac{1}{2}at^2$$

$$s = 15 \times 4 + \frac{1}{2} \times -9.8 \times 4^2$$

$$= -18.4$$

The displacement s after 4 seconds is -18.4 m.
The ball was thrown from a height of 18.4 m.

15 ms^{-1}

Ground

Example 4

A stone is thrown vertically upwards from ground level with speed 10 ms^{-1}. Find the time for which the stone is above a height of 2 m from ground.

The stone has a displacement of 2 m when it is going up and when it is coming down. Take the positive direction upwards.

$+\uparrow$ $u = 10$

$a = -9.8$

$s = 2$

$t = ?$

$$s = ut + \frac{1}{2}at^2$$

$$2 = 10t + \frac{1}{2} \times -9.8 \times t^2$$

$$2 = 10t - 4.9t^2$$

$$4.9t^2 - 10t + 2 = 0$$

Using the formula to solve quadratic equations, $t = \dfrac{10 \pm \sqrt{100 - 4 \times 4.9 \times 2}}{2 \times 4.9}$

Solving gives two times

$t_1 = 1.18$

$t_2 = 1.82$

Time required $= 1.82 - 1.18$

The stone is above a height of 2 m for 0.64 seconds.

Exercise 1B

Take g as 9.8 ms^{-2} and give answers to 2 significant figures where appropriate.
In each question state which of the following formulae you are using:

$v = u + at \qquad s = ut + \dfrac{1}{2}at^2 \qquad v^2 = u^2 + 2as \qquad s = \dfrac{1}{2}(u+v)t$

1. A marble falls from a table 1.2 m high.

   (a) How long will it take to hit the floor?

   (b) How fast will it be travelling when it does so?

2. A tile falls vertically from a height of 4 m. At what speed will it hit the ground?

3. A man throws a ball vertically upwards so that it just reaches a height of 30 m above him. How fast did he throw the ball?

4. A ball is thrown vertically upwards with speed 12 ms^{-1} and is caught at the same height. For how long is the ball in the air?

5. A tennis ball is hit vertically upwards with speed 20 ms^{-1}.

   (a) At what times does the ball have a displacement of 3 m?

   (b) Hence calculate for how long the ball will be above a height of 3 m.

6. A particle is projected vertically from the ground with speed 35 ms^{-1}. What will its speed be when it is 40 m above the ground?

7. A particle is thrown upwards with speed u ms^{-1}.

   (a) What height will it reach (in terms of u and g)?

   (b) How long will it take before it reaches its initial height again (in terms of u and g)?

8. A bag is dropped from a hot air balloon which is rising at 6 ms^{-1} and is 120 m above the ground. How long will it take the bag to fall to the ground?

9. A stone is dropped from the top of a building 100 m high. A second stone is dropped from half way up the same building. Find the time that should elapse between the release of the two stones if they are to reach the ground at the same time.

10. A ball is dropped from the top of a building and at the same time a second ball is thrown vertically upwards from the bottom of the building with a speed of 15 ms^{-1}. They pass each other 2 seconds later. Find the height of the building.

11. A ball is dropped from a height of 20 m. One second later a ball is thrown downwards from the same point with speed 16 ms^{-1}.

    (a) How long after the first ball is released will they be at the same height?

    (b) How far from the ground will they be at this time?

1.3 Velocity–time graphs

The velocity–time graph illustrates the motion of a body which accelerates uniformly from a speed u to a speed v in a time t.

The acceleration a is defined as the rate of change of velocity.

So $a = \dfrac{v - u}{t}$ which shows that the acceleration is equal to the gradient of the line AB.

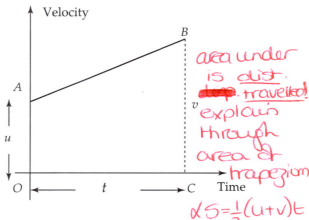

Also for this motion we have $s = \left(\dfrac{u + v}{2}\right)t$ and we see that the area of the trapezium $OABC$ is also $\left(\dfrac{u + v}{2}\right)t$. This shows that the area under a velocity–time graph is the distance travelled.

Remember:

> 1. Gradient of velocity–time graph = acceleration
> 2. Area under graph = distance travelled.

Example 1

A van starts from rest and accelerates uniformly at 1.5 ms^{-2} for 10 seconds. It then maintains a steady speed for a further 20 seconds before decelerating uniformly to rest in 6 seconds.

(a) Sketch a speed–time graph for the motion of the van.

(b) Find the maximum speed of the van.

(c) Find the deceleration.

(d) Find the total distance travelled.

(a)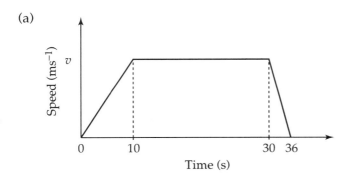

(b) Acceleration = Slope of graph

$$1.5 = \frac{v}{10}$$

$$v = 15$$

Maximum Speed = 15 ms^{-1}

(c) Deceleration = $\frac{15}{6}$

= 2.5 ms^{-2}

(d) Total distance travelled = area under the graph

$$= \left(\frac{1}{2} \times 10 \times 15\right) + (20 \times 15) + \left(\frac{1}{2} \times 6 \times 15\right)$$

$$= 420 \text{ m}$$

Example 2

A car travelling at a constant speed of 30 ms^{-1} passes a stationary motorbike. Six seconds later the motorbike starts off and accelerates uniformly at 4 ms^{-2} until it reaches a speed of 40 ms^{-1}. It then maintains this speed until it reaches the car.

(a) Sketch a speed–time graph for motion of the car and the motorbike.

(b) Find the time taken for the motorbike to reach the car.

(a)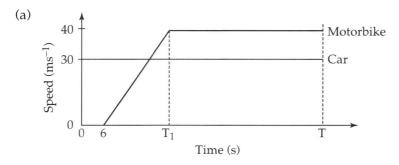

(b) Acceleration of motorbike = gradient of graph

$$4 = \frac{40}{T_1 - 6}$$

$$T_1 - 6 = 10$$

$$T_1 = 16$$

When the motorbike reaches the car they will have travelled the same distance so the areas under the two graphs are equal.

$$30\,T = \left[\frac{1}{2} \times (16 - 6) \times 40\right] + 40(T - 16)$$

$$30\,T = 200 + 40\,T - 640$$

$$T = 44$$

The motorbike reaches the car after 44 seconds.

Example 3

Draw the acceleration–time graph that corresponds to the following velocity–time graph.

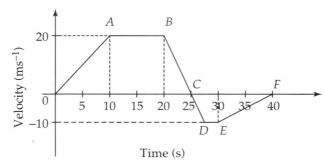

Acceleration $OA = \dfrac{20}{10} = 2$

Acceleration $AB = 0$ (constant speed)

Acceleration $BCD = \dfrac{-20}{5} = -4$ (deceleration)

Acceleration $DE = 0$

Acceleration $EF = \dfrac{10}{10} = 1$

The time at $D = 27.5$

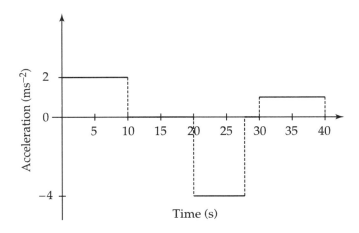

Exercise 1C

1.

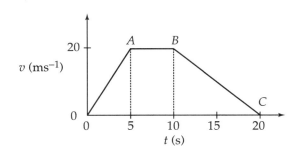

The velocity–time graph shows the motion of a particle along a straight line.

Find (a) the acceleration during OA
(b) the deceleration during BC
(c) the total distance travelled.

2. A car is uniformly accelerated from a velocity of 10 ms^{-1} to a velocity of 30 ms^{-1} in a time of 5 seconds. Draw a velocity time graph and find the acceleration and the distance travelled by the car in 5 seconds.

3. A car is moving with a velocity 20 ms^{-1} when the brakes are applied and it decelerates uniformly to rest in a distance of 40 m.

   Sketch a velocity–time graph and find,

   (a) the time taken to stop

   (b) the deceleration of the car.

4.

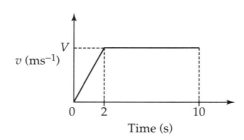

The velocity time graph shows the motion of a sprinter in a 100 m race. Find V.

5. Sketch the acceleration–time graph that corresponds to the following velocity–time graph.

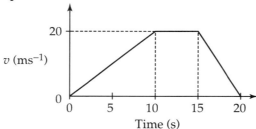

6. The acceleration–time graph illustrates the motion of a particle moving in a straight line.

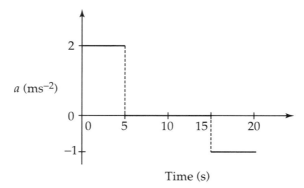

At $t = 0$ the particle is at rest.
Sketch a velocity–time graph for the particle's motion.

7. A tram starts from rest at stop A and accelerates uniformly to a speed of 20 ms^{-1} in 10 seconds. It maintains this speed until it is 120 m from stop B at which point it slows down uniformly to a stop at B. Given that A and B are 2 km apart, find

   (a) for how long the tram is moving at constant speed

   (b) the total time to travel from A to B.

8. A lift starts from rest and moves vertically upwards a distance of 40 m. The lift initially accelerates with a constant acceleration for 1.8 s until it reaches a speed of 4 ms^{-1}. It moves at this speed for T seconds before slowing down with a constant deceleration for 2.2 seconds before coming to rest.

   (a) Sketch a velocity–time graph for the motion of the lift.

   (b) Find the value of T.

   (c) Sketch an acceleration–time graph for the lift.

9. A train starts from rest at station A and moves along a straight horizontal track. Initially the train accelerates uniformly at 0.8 ms^{-2} up to a speed of 20 ms^{-1}. It moves at a constant speed of 20 ms^{-1} for T seconds and then slows down for 20 seconds before coming to rest at station B, which is 4 km from A.

   (a) Sketch a speed–time graph for the motion from A to B.

   (b) Find T

   (c) Sketch an acceleration–time graph

10. A particle is moving in a straight line. It is initially moving with a speed of 20 ms^{-1} when it is subjected to a deceleration of 4 ms^{-2} for 7 seconds.

    (a) Sketch a velocity–time graph for the motion.

    (b) Find the change in displacement.

    (c) Find the distance travelled by the particle.

11. A car moving at a constant speed of 30 ms^{-1} passes a motorbike. The motorbike sets off immediately and accelerates at 4 ms^{-2} until it reaches a speed of 40 ms^{-1}. It then maintains this constant speed until it just catches the car.

    Sketch a speed–time graph for the car and the motorbike and find the time taken for the motorbike to reach the car.

12. A runner running at a constant speed of 5 ms^{-1} passes a cyclist, who is at rest. The cyclist immediately sets off with a constant acceleration of 1.5 ms^{-2} for a time of 6 seconds. The cyclist then continues at a constant speed until he catches the runner.

    (a) Find the greatest speed attained by the cyclist.

    (b) Sketch a speed–time graph for the motion of the runner and the cyclist.

    (c) How long does it take for the cyclist to catch the runner?

17

13. Two cyclists A and B are going in the same direction along a straight horizontal road. Cyclist A is moving at a constant speed of 6 ms^{-1} when he passes cyclist B, who is at rest. 5 seconds later cyclist B sets off with a uniform acceleration of 2 ms^{-2} for a time of 4 seconds and then continues at constant speed until he catches cyclist A.

Sketch a speed-time graph for the two cyclists.

How long does it take for B to catch A?

1.4 Displacement–time graphs

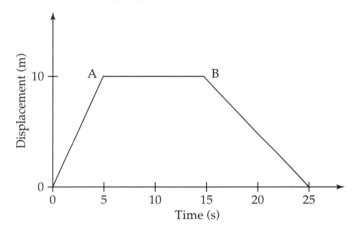

The graph shows how the displacement of a body varies with time.

$$\text{Velocity} = \frac{\text{change in displacement}}{\text{time taken}}$$

so the gradient of a displacement–time graph gives velocity.

The above graph shows a body which moves 10 m in a time of 5 seconds, remains stationary at 10 m for 10 seconds and returns to its starting position in a time of 10 seconds.

From O to A the velocity $= \dfrac{10}{5} = 2 \text{ ms}^{-1}$

From B to C the velocity $= \dfrac{-10}{10} = -1 \text{ ms}^{-1}$

This velocity is negative because the direction is reversed.

The total displacement $= 10 - 10 = 0$ m

The total distance travelled $= 10 + 10 = 20$ m

Exercise 1D

1. The following displacement–time graphs refer to a particle moving in a straight line.

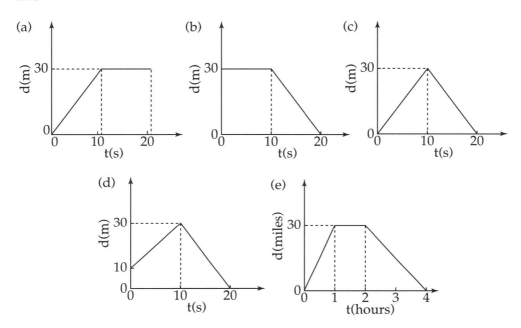

Find in each case the speed of the particle at each stage and the total distance travelled.

2. The displacement – time graph is for the movement of a particle in a straight line.

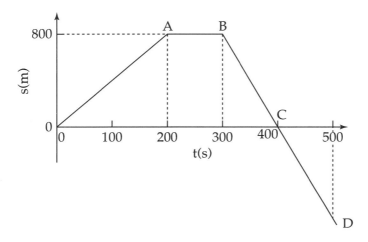

Find (a) the final displacement of the particle
(b) the total distance travelled
(c) the average speed

3. The displacement s(m) at time t(s) is given by

$$s = 6t\mathbf{i} \quad \text{for} \quad 0 \leq t < 4$$
$$s = 24\mathbf{i} \quad \text{for} \quad 4 \leq t < 6$$
$$s = (36 - 2t)\mathbf{i} \quad \text{for} \quad 6 \leq t \leq 8$$

Draw a displacement time graph to represent this motion.

Find (a) the final displacement after 8 seconds

(b) the total distance travelled

(c) the average speed

4. A woman takes 20 minutes to walk at constant speed along a straight road to a shop 2 km away. She spends 10 minutes in the shop and then returns at constant speed in 30 minutes.

(a) Sketch a velocity–time graph for this motion.

(b) Sketch a displacement–time graph for this motion.

5. A woman walks at constant speed to a shop 0.8 km away in a time of 10 minutes. She spends 8 minutes in the shop and returns at a constant speed in 12 minutes.

(a) Sketch a displacement–time graph.

(b) Find her speed as she walks to the shop in kmh^{-1}

(c) Find her average speed for the whole period in kmh^{-1}

Examination Exercise 1

1.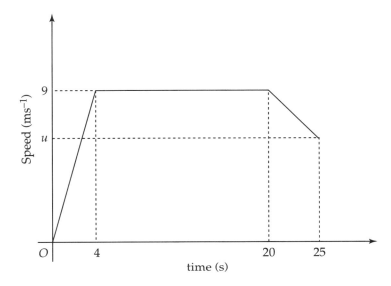

A sprinter runs a race of 200 m. Her total time for running the race is 25 s. A sketch of the speed–time graph for the motion of the sprinter is shown. She starts from rest and accelerates uniformly to a speed of 9 ms^{-1} in 4 s. The speed of 9 ms^{-1} is maintained for 16 s and she then decelerates uniformly to a speed of u ms^{-1} at the end of the race. Calculate

(a) the distance covered by the sprinter in the first 20 s of the race,

(b) the value of u,

(c) the deceleration of the sprinter in the last 5 s of the race. [E]

2.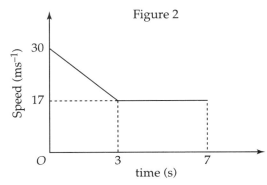

Figure 2

A car moves along a straight horizontal road. In order to obey a speed restriction, the brakes of the car are applied for 3 s, reducing the car's speed from 30 ms^{-1} to 17 ms^{-1}. The brakes are then released and the car continues at a constant speed of 17 ms^{-1} for a further 4 s. Figure 2 shows a sketch of the speed–time graph of the car during this 7 s interval. The graph consists of two straight line segments.

(a) Find the total distance moved by the car during this 7 s interval.

(b) Explain briefly how the speed–time graph shows that, when the brakes are applied, the car experiences a constant retarding force. [E]

3. A train stops at two stations 7.5 km apart. Between the stations it takes 75 s to accelerate uniformly to a speed of 24 ms^{-1}, then travels at this speed for a time T seconds before decelerating uniformly for the final 0.6 km.

(a) Sketch a speed–time graph for this journey.

Hence, or otherwise, find

(b) the deceleration, in ms^{-2}, of the train during the final 0.6 km,

(c) the value of T,

(d) the total time for the journey. [E]

4. A car is travelling along a straight motorway at a constant speed v ms^{-1}. Ten seconds after passing a speed-limit sign, the driver brakes and the car decelerates uniformly for 5 seconds, reducing its speed to 30 ms^{-1}.

(a) Sketch a speed–time graph to illustrate this information.

Given that the car covers a distance of 600 m in the 15 second period, find

(b) the value of v,

(c) the deceleration of the car. [E]

5. A racing car emerging from a bend reaches a straight stretch of road. The start of the straight stretch is the point O and there are two marker points, A and B, further down the road. The distance $\overrightarrow{OA} = 64$ m and the distance $\overrightarrow{OB} = 250$ m. The car passes O at time 0 s and, moving with constant acceleration, passes A and B at times 2 s and 5 s respectively. Find

(a) the acceleration of the car,

(b) the speed of the car at B. [E]

6. An electric train starts from rest at a station A and moves along a straight level track. The train accelerates uniformly at 0.4 ms^{-2} to a speed of 16 ms^{-1}. This speed is then maintained for a distance of 2000 m. Finally the train retards uniformly for 20 s before coming to rest at a station B. For this journey from A to B,

(a) find the total time taken,

(b) find the distance from A to B,

(c) sketch the distance–time graph, showing clearly the shape of the graph for each stage of the journey. [E]

7. A train starts from rest at a station A and moves with uniform accelera[tion] along a straight horizontal track. The train passes a signal box B with s[peed] 15.5 ms^{-1}. From B, the train then covers a 900 m stretch of level track i[n ...] with the same uniform acceleration. By considering a speed–time sket[ch, or] otherwise, find

   (a) the acceleration, in ms^{-2}, of the train,

   (b) the time, in s, taken by the train to move from A to B. [E]

8. A straight stretch of railway line passes over a viaduct which is 600 m long. An express train on this stretch of line normally travels at a speed of 50 ms^{-1}. Some structural weakness in the viaduct is detected and engineers specify that all trains passing over the viaduct must do so at a constant speed of no more than 10 ms^{-1}. Approaching the viaduct, the train therefore reduces its speed from 50 ms^{-1} with constant deceleration 0.5 ms^{-2}, reaching a speed of precisely 10 ms^{-1} just as it reaches the viaduct. It then passes over the viaduct at a constant speed of 10 ms^{-1}. As soon as it reaches the other end of the viaduct, it accelerates to its normal speed of 50 ms^{-1} with constant acceleration 0.5 ms^{-2}.

   (a) Sketch a speed–time graph to show the motion of the train during the period from the time when it starts to reduce speed to the time when it is running at full speed again.

   (b) Find the total distance travelled by the train while its speed is less than 50 ms^{-1}.

   (c) Find the extra time taken by the train for the journey due to the speed restriction on the viaduct. [E]

9. A car starts from rest at a point S on a straight racetrack. The car moves with constant acceleration for 20 s, reaching a speed of 25 ms^{-1}. The car then travels at a constant speed of 25 ms^{-1} for 120 s. Finally it moves with constant deceleration, coming to rest at a point F.

   (a) Sketch a speed–time graph to illustrate the motion of the car.

   The distance between S and F is 4 km.

   (b) Calculate the total time the car takes to travel from S to F.

   A motorcycle starts at S, 10 s after the car has left S. The motorcycle moves with constant acceleration from rest and passes the car at a point P which is 1.5 km from S. When the motorcycle passes the car, the motorcycle is still accelerating and the car is moving at a constant speed. Calculate

   (c) the time the motorcycle takes to travel from S to P,

   (d) the speed of the motorcycle at P. [E]

Part 2

Basic vectors

2.1 Vectors and Scalars

A vector has both size and direction.

A scalar has size only.

Examples of vector quantities are displacement, velocity, acceleration, force, weight, momentum and impulse. These quantities will be defined throughout this book, but force is a well known quantity that depends on its strength and the direction it is acting. The direction can be stated in many ways including left or right, up or down, on a bearing, at an angle to a particular direction or by writing the quantity in vector form.

Examples of scalars are distance, speed, mass and time. Time, for example, does not depend on direction.

2.2 Representing vectors

(a) using a directed line segment

Any vector can be represented by a directed line segment.

The direction of the vector is given by the direction of the arrow on the line and the size (or magnitude) of the vector is represented by the length of the line.

The vector above is written as $\overrightarrow{OA}$.

The magnitude of the vector is written as $|\overrightarrow{OA}|$.

The vector $\overrightarrow{OA}$ can also be written as **a**.

The letter is printed in bold type (**a**) but is written with a line underneath (a̲).

(b) using i and j vectors

Vector **i** represents a vector of magnitude one unit in the positive direction along the *x*-axis.

Vector **j** represents a vector of magnitude one unit in the positive direction along the *y*-axis.

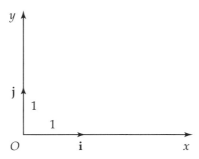

Example 1

$$\mathbf{r} = 4\mathbf{i} + 3\mathbf{j}$$

This vector represents 4 units along the positive *x* direction and 3 units in the positive *y* direction.

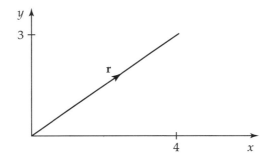

The magnitude of this vector is found using Pythagoras.

$$\text{magnitude of } \mathbf{r} = \sqrt{4^2 + 3^2}$$
$$= 5$$

The direction is found using trigonometry.

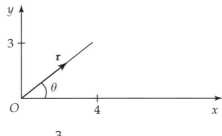

$$\tan \theta = \frac{3}{4}$$
$$\theta = 36.9°$$

this angle together with the diagram defines the direction of **r**.

Example 2
$$r = -4i + 3j$$

This vector represents 4 units along the negative x direction and 3 units in the positive y direction.

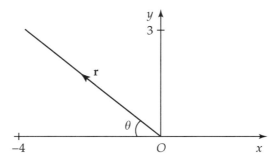

As before,
$$\text{magnitude of } \mathbf{r} = \sqrt{(-4)^2 + 3^2}$$
$$= 5$$
$$\theta = 36.9° \quad \text{(in the above diagram)}$$

2.3 Multiplying a vector by a constant

Example 3

Given that $\mathbf{r} = 4\mathbf{i} + 3\mathbf{j}$ find $2\mathbf{r}$.

Just multiply the **i** component by 2 and the **j** component by 2 so:
$$2\mathbf{r} = 8\mathbf{i} + 6\mathbf{j}$$

In graphical form:

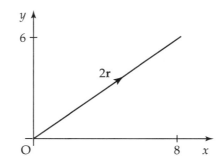

$$\text{magnitude of } \mathbf{r} = \sqrt{8^2 + 6^2}$$
$$= 10 \quad \text{(ie. doubled)}$$

The direction is given by $\tan\theta = \dfrac{6}{8}$

$$\theta = 36.9° \quad \text{(ie. the same)}$$

2.4 Adding vectors in i–j notation

Add the **i** and the **j** components separately.

Example 4

Given that $\mathbf{a} = 3\mathbf{i} + 4\mathbf{j}$ and $\mathbf{b} = 2\mathbf{i} - \mathbf{j}$ find $\mathbf{a} + \mathbf{b}$.

$$\mathbf{a} + \mathbf{b} = (3+2)\mathbf{i} + (4-1)\mathbf{j}$$
$$= 5\mathbf{i} + 3\mathbf{j}$$

This can be represented by line segments in a vector diagram

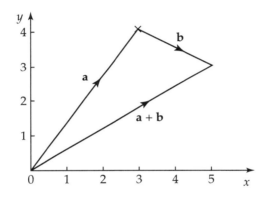

We can see that going along vector **a** + **b** is equivalent to going along vector **a** and then along vector **b**.

2.5 Subtracting vectors in i–j notation

Subtract the **i** and **j** components separately.

Example 5

Given that $\mathbf{a} = 5\mathbf{i} + 3\mathbf{j}$ and $\mathbf{b} = 2\mathbf{i} - 4\mathbf{j}$, find $\mathbf{a} - \mathbf{b}$.

$$\mathbf{a} - \mathbf{b} = (5-2)\mathbf{i} + (3-(-)4)\mathbf{j}$$
$$= 3\mathbf{i} + 7\mathbf{j}$$

2.6 Equal vectors

Two vectors are equal if their **i** components and their **j** components are separately equal.

Example 6

Find the values of the scalars p and q if:

$$p\mathbf{i} + q\mathbf{j} = 3(2\mathbf{i} - \mathbf{j}) + 4\mathbf{i} + \mathbf{j}$$
$$p\mathbf{i} + q\mathbf{j} = 6\mathbf{i} - 3\mathbf{j} + 4\mathbf{i} + \mathbf{j}$$
$$= 10\mathbf{i} - 2\mathbf{j}$$

Equating the **i** and **j** components:

$$p = 10$$
$$q = -2$$

2.7 Parallel vectors

Vectors **a** and **b** are parallel if:

$k\mathbf{a} = \mathbf{b}$ where k is a constant.

In other words, if you can multiply one vector by a constant to get the other vector, then those vectors are parallel.

Example 7

Vectors

$$\mathbf{a} = 2\mathbf{i} + \mathbf{j}$$
$$\mathbf{b} = 4\mathbf{i} + 2\mathbf{j}$$
$$\mathbf{c} = 6\mathbf{i} + 3\mathbf{j} \quad \text{are all parallel.}$$

2.8 Finding a unit vector parallel to a given vector

Example 8

Find the unit vector which is parallel to the vector $5\mathbf{i} + 12\mathbf{j}$.

The vector $5\mathbf{i} + 12\mathbf{j}$ has magnitude $\sqrt{5^2 + 12^2} = 13$ units.

So the vector $\dfrac{5\mathbf{j} + 12\mathbf{j}}{13}$ will be parallel to $5\mathbf{i} + 12\mathbf{j}$ and will be of unit length.

(A 'unit vector' is a vector of length 1 unit.)

2.9 Obtaining a vector given its magnitude and direction

Example 9

The vector **v** has magnitude 20 and is in the direction of the vector $3\mathbf{i} + 4\mathbf{j}$. Find **v** in the form $p\mathbf{i} + q\mathbf{j}$.

The vector $3\mathbf{i} + 4\mathbf{j}$ has magnitude $\sqrt{3^2 + 4^2} = 5$ units.

So the vector $\dfrac{3\mathbf{i} + 4\mathbf{j}}{5}$ is a *unit* vector parallel to $3\mathbf{i} + 4\mathbf{j}$.

The required vector **v** has magnitude 20 units

$$\therefore \quad \mathbf{v} = 20\left(\frac{3\mathbf{i}+4\mathbf{j}}{5}\right)$$
$$\mathbf{v} = 4(3\mathbf{i}+4\mathbf{j})$$
$$\mathbf{v} = 12\mathbf{i}+16\mathbf{j}.$$

2.10 Vector representation

Example 10

Given that $\overrightarrow{OA} = 2\mathbf{i}+\mathbf{j}$ and $\overrightarrow{OB} = 5\mathbf{i}+7\mathbf{j}$. Find the vector $\overrightarrow{AB}$.

Sketch a diagram showing *any* triangle OAB. Make no attempt to show $\overrightarrow{OA}$ and $\overrightarrow{OB}$ to scale or in the actual directions of $\overrightarrow{OA}$ and $\overrightarrow{OB}$. We simply want a triangle so that we can put arrows on it!

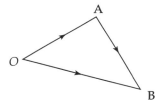

Now $\quad \overrightarrow{AB} = \overrightarrow{AO} + \overrightarrow{OB}$
$$= -\overrightarrow{OA} + \overrightarrow{OB}$$
$$= -(2\mathbf{i}+\mathbf{j}) + (5\mathbf{i}+7\mathbf{j})$$
$$\overrightarrow{AB} = 3\mathbf{i}+6\mathbf{j}$$

Example 11

Four points have the following co-ordinates:

$A(3,4), B(0,2), C(-1,5), D(-3,-2)$.

Write down in the form $a\mathbf{i}+b\mathbf{j}$ the vectors:

(a) $\overrightarrow{OA}$ (b) $\overrightarrow{OB}$, (c) $\overrightarrow{AB}$, (d) $\overrightarrow{OC}$, (e) $\overrightarrow{AC}$, (f) $\overrightarrow{BD}$, (g) $\overrightarrow{DB}$

(a) $\overrightarrow{OA} = 3\mathbf{i}+4\mathbf{j}$

(b) $\overrightarrow{OB} = 2\mathbf{j}$

(c)
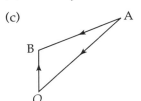

Going from A to B is equivalent to going from A to O and then from O to B.
$$\vec{AB} = -\vec{OA} + \vec{OB}$$
$$= -(3\mathbf{i} + 4\mathbf{j}) + 2\mathbf{j}$$
$$= -3\mathbf{i} - 2\mathbf{j}$$

(d) $\vec{OC} = -\mathbf{i} + 5\mathbf{j}$

(e) Going from A to C is equivalent to going from A to O and then from O to C.
$$\vec{AC} = -\vec{OA} + \vec{OC}$$
$$= -(3\mathbf{i} + 4\mathbf{j}) + (-\mathbf{i} + 5\mathbf{j})$$
$$= -4\mathbf{i} + \mathbf{j}$$

(f)
$$\vec{BD} = -\vec{OB} + \vec{OD}$$
$$= -2\mathbf{j} + (-3\mathbf{i} - 2\mathbf{j})$$
$$= -3\mathbf{i} - 4\mathbf{j}$$

(g)
$$\vec{DB} = -\vec{BD}$$
$$= 3\mathbf{i} + 4\mathbf{j}$$

Example 12

ABCDEFGH is a regular octagon, with $\vec{AB} = \mathbf{a}$, $\vec{BC} = \mathbf{b}$, and $\vec{CD} = \mathbf{c}$.

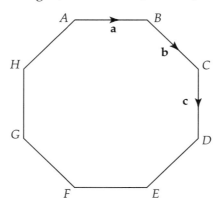

Find in terms of **a**, **b**, and **c**:

(a) $\vec{FE}$, (b) $\vec{GH}$, (c) $\vec{AC}$, (d) $\vec{AD}$, (e) $\vec{HE}$.

(a) $\vec{FE} = \mathbf{a}$

(b) $\vec{GH} = -\mathbf{c}$

(c) $\vec{AC} = \vec{AB} + \vec{BC}$
$\quad\quad = \mathbf{a} + \mathbf{b}$

(d) $\overrightarrow{AD} = \overrightarrow{AB} + \overrightarrow{BC} + \overrightarrow{CD}$
$= \mathbf{a} + \mathbf{b} + \mathbf{c}$

(e) $\overrightarrow{HE} = \overrightarrow{AD}$
$= \mathbf{a} + \mathbf{b} + \mathbf{c}$

Exercise 2A

In these questions **i** and **j** are unit vectors in the direction of the positive x and y axes respectively.

1. Given that $\mathbf{a} = 2\mathbf{i} + 3\mathbf{j}$ and $\mathbf{b} = 4\mathbf{i} - \mathbf{j}$, find in terms of **i** and **j**:
   (a) $2\mathbf{a}$
   (b) $-3\mathbf{b}$
   (c) $2\mathbf{a} - 3\mathbf{b}$
   (d) $\mathbf{a} + \mathbf{b}$
   (e) $\mathbf{a} - \mathbf{b}$
   (f) $2\mathbf{a} + \mathbf{b}$
   (g) $\mathbf{a} + 2\mathbf{b}$
   (h) $-3\mathbf{a} + \mathbf{b}$
   (i) $\mathbf{a} - 3\mathbf{b}$

2. Find the magnitude of the following vectors:
   (a) $3\mathbf{i} + 4\mathbf{j}$
   (b) $-5\mathbf{i} + 12\mathbf{j}$
   (c) $7\mathbf{i} - 24\mathbf{j}$
   (d) $\mathbf{i} + \mathbf{j}$
   (e) $5\mathbf{i} - 2\mathbf{j}$
   (f) $-3\mathbf{i} + 2\mathbf{j}$

3. Find the acute angle that each of the following vectors makes with the vector **i**:
   (a) $\mathbf{i} + \mathbf{j}$
   (b) $2\mathbf{i} + \mathbf{j}$
   (c) $\mathbf{i} + 3\mathbf{j}$
   (d) $2\mathbf{i} - 3\mathbf{j}$
   (e) $-\mathbf{i} + 2\mathbf{j}$
   (f) $-4\mathbf{i} - 5\mathbf{j}$

4. Find a unit vector in the direction of each of the following vectors:
   (a) $\mathbf{i} + \mathbf{j}$
   (b) $2\mathbf{i} + 3\mathbf{j}$
   (c) $3\mathbf{i} + 4\mathbf{j}$
   (d) $-2\mathbf{i} + 5\mathbf{j}$
   (e) $12\mathbf{i} + 16\mathbf{j}$
   (f) $-6\mathbf{i} - 8\mathbf{j}$

5. Find λ if:
   (a) $2\mathbf{i} + 3\mathbf{j}$ is parallel to $\lambda\mathbf{i} + 9\mathbf{j}$
   (b) $3\mathbf{i} - 4\mathbf{j}$ is parallel to $12\mathbf{i} - \lambda\mathbf{j}$
   (c) $-5\mathbf{i} + 2\mathbf{j}$ is parallel to $-15\mathbf{i} + \lambda\mathbf{j}$

6. Find in the form $a\mathbf{i} + b\mathbf{j}$:
   (a) a vector of magnitude 30 in the direction of $3\mathbf{i} + 4\mathbf{j}$
   (b) a vector of magnitude 26 in the direction of $-5\mathbf{i} + 12\mathbf{j}$
   (c) a vector of magnitude 10 in the direction of $7\mathbf{i} - 24\mathbf{j}$

7. Four points have the following coordinates: $A(1, 2)$, $B(4, -3)$, $C(-2, -2)$ and $D(0, 4)$.

   Write down in the form $\mathbf{r} = a\mathbf{i} + b\mathbf{j}$ the following vectors

   (a) A relative to the origin, $\overrightarrow{OA}$
   (b) B relative to the origin, $\overrightarrow{OB}$
   (c) D relative to the origin, $\overrightarrow{OD}$
   (d) A relative to D, $\overrightarrow{DA}$
   (e) A relative to B, $\overrightarrow{BA}$
   (f) B relative to C, $\overrightarrow{CB}$
   (g) D relative to C, $\overrightarrow{CD}$

8. Find the distance of each of the following points from the origin:
   $A(3, 4)$, $B(-5, 12)$, $C(1, -2)$, $D(-1, -3)$

9. The points A and B have position vectors $(5\mathbf{i} + 7\mathbf{j})m$ and $(17\mathbf{i} + 2\mathbf{j})m$ respectively.

   (a) How far is A from the origin?
   (b) Find $\overrightarrow{AB}$ in vector form.
   (c) Find the distance from A to B.

10. In the following questions find the values of the scalars a and b.

    (a) $a\mathbf{i} + b\mathbf{j} = 3(4\mathbf{i} - 5\mathbf{j})$
    (b) $a\mathbf{i} + b\mathbf{j} = (3\mathbf{i} - 2\mathbf{j}) + (-5\mathbf{i} + \mathbf{j}) + (\mathbf{i} + 3\mathbf{j})$
    (c) $10\mathbf{i} - 6\mathbf{j} = 2(a\mathbf{i} + b\mathbf{j})$
    (d) $a\mathbf{i} + b\mathbf{j} = 2\mathbf{i} - 3\mathbf{j} + 4(\mathbf{i} + 2\mathbf{j})$

11. Given the following position vectors of points A and B, find the vector $\overrightarrow{AB}$.

    (a) $\overrightarrow{OA} = 2\mathbf{i} + 5\mathbf{j}$ $\overrightarrow{OB} = 6\mathbf{i} + 10\mathbf{j}$
    (b) $\overrightarrow{OA} = -3\mathbf{i} + 4\mathbf{j}$ $\overrightarrow{OB} = 7\mathbf{i} - 2\mathbf{j}$
    (c) $\overrightarrow{OA} = 5\mathbf{i} - \mathbf{j}$ $\overrightarrow{OB} = 3\mathbf{i} + 3\mathbf{j}$
    (d) $\overrightarrow{OA} = -8\mathbf{i} + 10\mathbf{j}$ $\overrightarrow{OB} = -5\mathbf{i} - 4\mathbf{j}$

12. Given the following position vectors of points A and B, find the vector $\overrightarrow{BA}$.

    (a) $\overrightarrow{OA} = 9\mathbf{i} + 5\mathbf{j}$ $\overrightarrow{OB} = 6\mathbf{i} + 3\mathbf{j}$
    (b) $\overrightarrow{OA} = -4\mathbf{i} + 7\mathbf{j}$ $\overrightarrow{OB} = 8\mathbf{i} - 2\mathbf{j}$
    (c) $\overrightarrow{OA} = 12\mathbf{i} - 10\mathbf{j}$ $\overrightarrow{OB} = -5\mathbf{i} + 6\mathbf{j}$
    (d) $\overrightarrow{OA} = -5\mathbf{i} - 4\mathbf{j}$ $\overrightarrow{OB} = -8\mathbf{i} - 9\mathbf{j}$

Exercise 2B

In these questions **i** and **j** are unit vectors in the direction of the positive x and y axes respectively.

1. Given that $\mathbf{a} = 5\mathbf{i} - \mathbf{j}$ and $\mathbf{b} = 6\mathbf{i} + 3\mathbf{j}$ find in terms of **i** and **j**:

   (a) $3\mathbf{b}$
   (b) $\frac{1}{3}\mathbf{b}$
   (c) $2\mathbf{a}$
   (d) $3\mathbf{b} + 2\mathbf{a}$
   (e) $\mathbf{a} + \mathbf{b}$
   (f) $-\mathbf{a} + \mathbf{b}$
   (g) $2(\mathbf{b} + \mathbf{a})$
   (h) $-4\mathbf{a}$
   (i) $\mathbf{b} + \mathbf{b}$

2. Find the magnitude of the following vectors:

   (a) $15\mathbf{j} + 20\mathbf{i}$
   (b) $\mathbf{i} + 2\mathbf{j}$
   (c) $24\mathbf{i} - 7\mathbf{j}$
   (d) $\mathbf{i} + \mathbf{i} + \mathbf{i}$
   (e) $\sqrt{2}\mathbf{i} - \sqrt{2}\mathbf{j}$
   (f) $\mathbf{i} + \sqrt{15}\mathbf{j}$

3. Find the acute angle between vectors **a** and **b**, where
   $\mathbf{a} = \mathbf{i} + \mathbf{j}$ and $\mathbf{b} = 2\mathbf{i}$.

4. (a) Find a unit vector in the direction of the vector $-3\mathbf{i} - 4\mathbf{j}$.

   (b) Find λ if $3\mathbf{i} - \mathbf{j}$ is parallel to $\lambda\mathbf{i} - 4\mathbf{j}$.

5. Find in the form $a\mathbf{i} + b\mathbf{j}$:

   (a) a vector of magnitude 15 in the direction of $4\mathbf{i} + 3\mathbf{j}$
   (b) a vector of magnitude 26 in the direction of $12\mathbf{i} - 5\mathbf{j}$
   (c) a vector of magnitude 50 in the direction of $7\mathbf{i} + 24\mathbf{j}$
   (d) a vector of magnitude 1 (a unit vector) in the direction of $4\mathbf{i} + 3\mathbf{j}$
   (e) a vector of magnitude 82 in the direction of $-9\mathbf{i} - 40\mathbf{j}$

6. Four points have the following co-ordinates: $A(4, 1)$, $B(2, 5)$, $C(1, -3)$ and $D(0, 5)$. Find in the form $\mathbf{r} = a\mathbf{i} + b\mathbf{j}$ the following vectors:

   (a) $\overrightarrow{OA}$,
   (b) $\overrightarrow{OB}$,
   (c) $\overrightarrow{AB}$,
   (d) $\overrightarrow{OC}$
   (e) $\overrightarrow{AC}$,
   (f) $\overrightarrow{OD}$,
   (g) $\overrightarrow{DA}$,
   (h) $\overrightarrow{BC}$

7. Find the distance of each of the following points from the origin:

   (a) $A(8, 6)$
   (b) $B(12, -5)$
   (c) $C(1, -1)$
   (d) $D(-3, -4)$
   (e) $E(-6, 0)$
   (f) $C(15, 12)$

8. Points P and Q are given by $\overrightarrow{OP} = (-3\mathbf{i} + \mathbf{j})$ and $\overrightarrow{OQ} = 6\mathbf{i} + 3\mathbf{j}$.
   Find:

   (a) the distance OP
   (b) $\overrightarrow{PQ}$ in vector form
   (c) the distance PQ.

9. Points A and B are given by $\overrightarrow{OA} = (-3\mathbf{i} + 5\mathbf{j})$ and $\overrightarrow{OB} = (\mathbf{i} + 9\mathbf{j})$.

   Find:

   (a) the distance $\overrightarrow{OA}$

   (b) $\overrightarrow{BA}$ in vector form

   (c) the distance $\overrightarrow{BA}$.

10. The diagram shows a regular hexagon $ABCDEF$ with centre O. Vectors $\overrightarrow{OA} = \mathbf{a}$ and $\overrightarrow{OB} = \mathbf{b}$.

    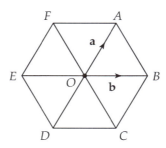

    Find the following in terms of **a** and **b**:

    (a) $\overrightarrow{AO}$,   (b) $\overrightarrow{AB}$,   (c) $\overrightarrow{FO}$

    (d) $\overrightarrow{DE}$ (e) $\overrightarrow{DA}$,   (f) $\overrightarrow{DB}$

    (g) $\overrightarrow{EA}$,   (h) $\overrightarrow{CE}$,   (i) $\overrightarrow{FB}$.

11. The diagram shows a triangle ABC where M is the mid-point of BC. If $\overrightarrow{AB} = \mathbf{s}$ and $\overrightarrow{CA} = \mathbf{t}$, find $\overrightarrow{AM}$ in terms of **s** and **t**.

    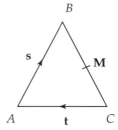

12. The diagram shows a regular hexagon $ABCDEF$.

    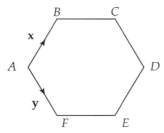

    Vectors $\overrightarrow{AB} = \mathbf{x}$ and $\overrightarrow{AF} = \mathbf{y}$.

    Find the vector $\overrightarrow{AD}$ in terms of **x** and **y**.

Forces – Types of force

Part 3

3.1 Force

The definition of force will be given in part 5 of this book.

People can exert forces, such as pushing, pulling, twisting and squeezing. Force is a vector quantity, which is stated in terms of magnitude and direction. The magnitude of force is measured in units called newtons, which are given the symbol N.

Types of force which you will meet in mechanics are described here.

3.2 Weight

Weight, which acts on all bodies on the earth, is the gravitational attraction between a body and the earth. Weight always acts vertically downwards.

The weight W newtons of a mass m kilograms is often written as

$$W = mg$$

where g is the acceleration due to gravity and is taken to be approximately $9.8 \, \text{ms}^{-2}$ in this book.

3.3 Normal Reaction

If an object touches a surface the surface exerts a reaction force on the object. Since the reaction is perpendicular to the surface, it is called the normal reaction.

For example, if a book lies on a horizontal desk, the desk exerts a force on the book, otherwise the book would fall.

The forces acting on the book are weight (W) and normal reaction (R).

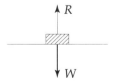

3.4 Tension

If a body is attached to a taut string, there is a force on the body due to the tension in the string.

For example, if a body hangs at the end of a string, the tension in the string exerts a force on the body otherwise the body would fall freely. The forces acting on the body are weight (W) and tension (T).

3.5 Thrust

Thrust is the force acting in a spring or rod to oppose compression.

For example, if a body rests on the top of a spring as shown in the diagram, the forces acting on the body are weight (W) and thrust (T) due to the spring.

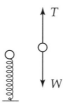

3.6 Friction

Friction is a force which opposes the motion of a body on a rough surface.

For example, if a horizontal force P is applied to push a book along a rough desk, then a friction force will oppose motion. In this case four forces will act on the book.

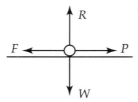

If a surface is smooth then there is no friction so $F = 0$.

3.7 Driving force

A vehicle has a driving force (D) due to its engine. If a car moves on a horizontal road the driving force acts forward and resistance forces (F) act backwards.

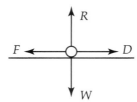

3.8 Force diagrams

In any problem involving the action of forces on a body, Edexcel encourages candidates to draw clearly labelled diagrams which are not too small.

Remember:

(1) Weight acts vertically downwards on all bodies unless they are described as *light*.

(2) If a body is in contact with a surface, there will be a normal reaction force acting on the body perpendicular to the surface.

(3) If a body is in contact with a rough surface, a friction force will act on the body in such a direction as to oppose motion.

(4) If a body is connected to a string, there will be a force on the body due to the tension in the string. If it is connected to a compressed spring there will be a thrust.

(5) Vehicles have driving forces.

(6) We usually show the force on a body as an arrow acting *away from* the body. The arrow is drawn from the body.

3.9 Drawing force diagrams

In mechanics objects such as books, crates, stones and cars etc. can be modelled as particles. These objects can then be represented in the force diagram by a small circle.

This is a realistic assumption provided the forces acting cause or tend to cause linear movement and not rotation. Only in the chapter on moments will rotation be considered.

Examples

Draw a diagram showing the forces acting in the following situations:

(1) A book is pushed along a rough horizontal desk by a horizontal force P.

Note: (i) the book can be modelled as a particle

(ii) the book will have weight

(iii) the desk will exert a normal reaction force

(iv) the desk is rough so there will be a friction force opposing motion.

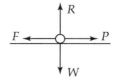

(2) A block is sliding down a smooth plane inclined at an angle θ to the horizontal.

Note: (i) the block can be modelled as a particle
(ii) the block has weight which acts vertically downwards
(iii) the plane exerts a normal reaction force on the block in a direction perpendicular to the plane
(iv) the plane is smooth so there is no friction

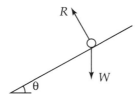

(3) An object is held by two strings; one horizontal and the other inclined at 30° above the horizontal.

Note: (i) the object has weight
(ii) the object is not touching anything so there are no normal reaction or friction forces
(iv) the strings exert two different forces due to their tensions T_1 and T_2.

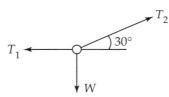

(4) A particle is pushed up a rough inclined plane by a horizontal force P.

Note: (i) weight acts vertically downwards
(ii) the normal reaction is perpendicular to the plane
(iii) the plane is rough so there is a friction force which acts down the plane to oppose motion up the plane
(iv) the horizontal force is drawn so all forces act away from the particle

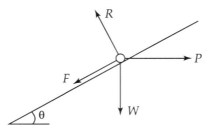

(5) A particle of weight W is placed on a rough slope inclined at 35° to the horizontal. A light string attached to the particle, lies along the line of greatest slope of the plane and passes over a smooth pulley fixed at the top of the plane. Another particle of weight $2W$ hangs vertically from the other end of the string.

Show the forces acting on each particle and the pulley.

Note: (i) the expression 'line of greatest slope' means the string is straight up the slope and not angled across it
(ii) the $2W$ particle will tend to move the other particle up the plane so the friction force will act down the plane to oppose motion
(iii) the strings are light so they have no weight
(iv) the pulley is smooth so there is no friction in the pulley this means that the tension will be uniform throughout the string
(v) the string exerts a force on the pulley vertically downwards and down the plane

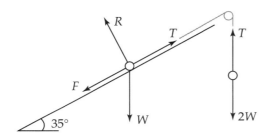
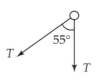

Forces on pulley

Exercise 3A

1. Draw diagrams showing all the forces acting on the block (of weight W) in the following situations. (Always let the frictional force be F and the reaction force be R)

    (a) A block is placed on a smooth horizontal table.
    (b) A block is placed on a rough horizontal table and is pushed with a horizontal force which is insufficient to cause it to move.
    (c) A block is placed on a rough horizontal table and a string is attached to the block. The string, with tension T, passes over a smooth pulley at the end of the table so that it is horizontal. Its other end is attached to a block of weight $\frac{W}{2}$. Both blocks remain at rest.
    (d) A block is placed on a rough horizontal table and a string is attached to the block. The string passes over a smooth pulley at the end of the table so that it is horizontal. Its other end is attached to a block of weight $2W$. Both blocks remain at rest.
    (e) A block is placed on a smooth table inclined at 30° to the horizontal and slides down.
    (f) A block is placed on a rough table inclined at 45° to the horizontal and is stationary.
    (g) A block is placed on a rough table inclined at 60° to the horizontal and a string is attached, pulling the block down the slope (parallel to it). The tension in the string is T.

(h) A block is placed on a smooth table inclined at 40° to the horizontal and a string is attached, pulling the block up the slope (parallel to it). The tension in the string is T.

(i) A block is placed on a rough table inclined at 50° to the horizontal and a string is attached, pulling the block up the slope (parallel to it). The tension in the string is T.

(j) A block is placed on a rough slope inclined at 45° to the horizontal and a string, making an angle of 60° to the horizontal is attached, pulling the block up the slope. The tension in the string is T.

(k) A block is placed on a rough slope inclined at 35° to the horizontal and a string is attached running parallel to the slope. The string, with tension T, passes over a smooth pulley at the top of the slope and its other end is attached to a block of weight $2W$ which hangs vertically. The $2W$ block begins to move downwards.

(l) A block is placed on a rough slope inclined at 45° to the horizontal and a string is attached running parallel to the slope. The string, with tension T, passes over a smooth pulley at the top of the slope and its other end is attached to a block of weight $\frac{W}{2}$ which hangs vertically. The $\frac{W}{2}$ block begins to move upwards.

2. Draw diagrams showing all the forces acting on the block (of weight W) in the following situations:

(a) A block is held by a vertical string with tension T.

(b) A block is held at rest by two strings with tension T both inclined at an angle of 30° to the horizontal.

(c) A block is held by a vertical string which passes over a smooth pulley and then hangs vertically on the other side and is attached to a block of weight $2W$. The tension in the string is T.

(d) A block is held at rest by a string with tension T_1 pulling at an angle of 30° above the horizontal and by a second string with tension T_2 pulling horizontally.

Exercise 3B

Draw diagrams to show the forces acting in the following situations:

1. A book is placed on a smooth horizontal table.

2. A book is placed on a rough horizontal table and pushed with a horizontal force P.

3. An object is placed on a rough horizontal table and is pulled by a string inclined at 30° above the horizontal.

4. A stone is dropped from the top of a cliff.

5. A block is held by a vertical string.

6. A ball is thrown upwards. Show the forces after it is released

7. An object sliding down a smooth surface inclined at 20° to the horizontal.

8. A crate is sliding down a rough slope inclined at 30° to the horizontal.

9. A block is pulled up a rough plane surface inclined at 15° to the horizontal, by a string parallel to the plane.

10. A block rests on a rough plane inclined at 30° to the horizontal. A horizontal force P moves the block up the plane.

11. A car, which is accelerating, is pulling a caravan. Friction forces F_1 and F_2 act on the car and caravan respectively.

    Draw diagrams showing all the forces acting on

    (a) the car
    (b) the caravan

12. Two particles of weight W and $2W$ are connected by a vertical string which passes over a smooth pulley.

    Draw diagrams showing the forces acting on

    (a) each particle
    (b) the pulley

13. A block is placed on a rough plane inclined at 20° to the horizontal. A string, attached to the block, pulls it directly down the plane.

14. Two books are put one on top of the others on a horizontal surface. Draw diagrams showing

    (a) forces acting on the top book
    (b) forces acting on the bottom book.

15. A van, which is braking, is pulling a trailer. Draw diagrams showing all the forces acting on

    (a) the van
    (b) the trailer.

Part 4

Statics

4.1 Resolving forces into components

It is particularly useful in mechanics to express a single force in terms of two components acting at right angles.

A force **F** can be replaced by two forces $\mathbf{F}_x$ and $\mathbf{F}_y$ acting along directions O_x and O_y.

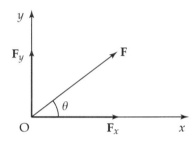

Using simple trigonometry: $\mathbf{F}_x = \mathbf{F}\cos\theta$

$\mathbf{F}_y = \mathbf{F}\sin\theta$

These two components acting along O_x and O_y have the same effect as the single force **F** acting at angle θ to O_x.

4.2 Which component uses $\cos\theta$?

Remember from GCSE: $\cos\theta = \dfrac{\text{adjacent}}{\text{hypoteneuse}}$

Adjacent means next to.

> The component next to the angle uses $\cos\theta$
> The component away from the angle uses $\sin\theta$.

Example 1

A force of 40 N acts at an angle of 30° to the x-axis. Find its two components along the x-axis and the y-axis.

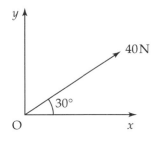
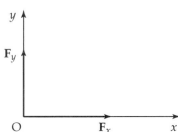

Along O_x: $\quad\quad\quad\quad\quad\quad \mathbf{F}_x = 40\cos 30°$ (next to the angle)

$\quad\quad\quad\quad\quad\quad\quad\quad\quad\quad\quad = 34.6\,\text{N}$

Along O_y: $\quad\quad\quad\quad\quad\quad \mathbf{F}_y = 40\sin 30°$

$\quad\quad\quad\quad\quad\quad\quad\quad\quad\quad\quad = 20\,\text{N}$

Example 2

Find the components of the given forces in the directions of O_x and O_y.

(a)

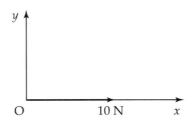

$$\mathbf{F}_x = 10\cos 0°$$
$$= 10\,\text{N}$$
$$\mathbf{F}_y = 10\sin 0°$$
$$= 0\,\text{N}$$

This force was already in direction O_x!

(b)

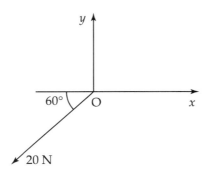

$$\mathbf{F}_x = -20\cos 60° \text{ (this acts in the negative direction)}$$
$$= -10\,\text{N}$$
$$\mathbf{F}_y = -20\sin 60°$$
$$= -17.3\,\text{N}$$

(c)

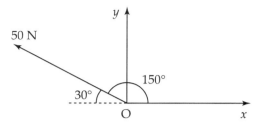

Use the acute angle:
$$F_x = -50\cos 30°$$
$$= -43.3\,\text{N}$$
$$F_y = 50\sin 30°$$
$$= 25\,\text{N}$$

(d) Resolve the following force into two components along O_x and O_y. Given that unit vector **i** is along O_x and **j** is along O_y, express your answer in the form $p\mathbf{i} + q\mathbf{j}$.

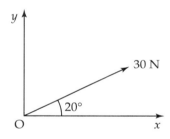

$$F_x = 30\cos 20° = 28.2$$
$$F_y = 30\sin 20° = 10.3$$
$$\mathbf{F} = (28.2\mathbf{i} + 10.3\mathbf{j})\,\text{N}$$

4.3 Resultant of two or more forces

A resultant force is one which will have the same effect as two or more forces.

Example 3

Find the magnitude of the resultant of the following forces and the angle it makes with the x-axis.

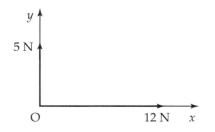
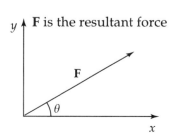

F is the resultant force

44

Using Pythagoras: $|\mathbf{F}| = \sqrt{5^2 + 12^2} = 13$

Using trigonometry: $\tan\theta = \frac{5}{13}$ $\frac{5}{12}$

$\theta = 21.0°$ $\theta = 22.6°$

The magnitude of the resultant is 13 N and the angle with the x-axis is 21.0°.

Example 4

Find the resultant of the following forces.

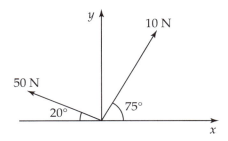

Step 1: Resolve the forces into components along O_x and O_y.

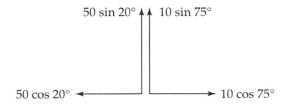

Step 2: Work out the values.

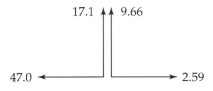

Step 3: Add forces in the same direction and subtract forces in opposite directions.

F is the resultant force

45

Step 4: Use Pythagoras and trigonometry.

$$|\mathbf{F}| = \sqrt{44.4^2 + 26.8^2} = 51.9$$

$$\tan \theta = \frac{26.8}{44.4} = 31.1°$$

The magnitude of the force is 51.9 N at an angle 31.1° as shown in the diagram.

Example 5

Find the resultant of the following system of forces.

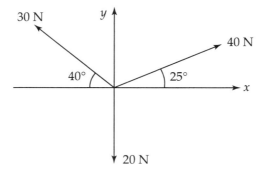

Step 1: Resolve the forces into components along O_x and O_y.

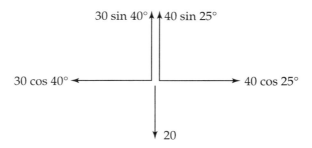

Step 2: Work out the values.

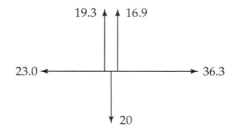

Step 3: Add forces in the same direction and subtract forces in the opposite direction.

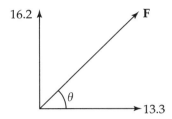

Step 4: Use Pythagoras and trigonometry.
$$|\mathbf{F}| = \sqrt{13.3^2 + 16.2^2}$$
$$= 21.0\,\text{N}$$
$$\tan\theta = \frac{16.2}{13.3}$$
$$\theta = 50.6°$$

The magnitude of the force is 21.0 N at an angle 50.6° as shown in the diagram.

Example 6

A particle is acted on by three forces:
$$\mathbf{F}_1 = (3\mathbf{i} - 4\mathbf{j})\text{N}$$
$$\mathbf{F}_2 = (5\mathbf{i} + 2\mathbf{j})\text{N}$$
$$\mathbf{F}_3 = (-4\mathbf{i} + 5\mathbf{j})\text{N}$$

Find the resultant force **F** in vector form. Also find the magnitude of the resultant force and the angle it makes with the vector **i**.

$$\mathbf{F} = \mathbf{F}_1 + \mathbf{F}_2 + \mathbf{F}_3$$
$$= (3\mathbf{i} - 4\mathbf{j}) + (5\mathbf{i} + 2\mathbf{j}) + (-4\mathbf{i} + 5\mathbf{j})$$
$$\mathbf{F} = (4\mathbf{i} + 3\mathbf{j})\text{N}$$

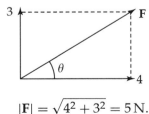

$$|\mathbf{F}| = \sqrt{4^2 + 3^2} = 5\,\text{N}.$$
$$\tan\theta = \frac{3}{4} \Rightarrow \theta = 36.9°$$

The magnitude of the resultant force is 5 N and acts at an angle 36.9° as shown.

Exercise 4A

1. Resolve each force in the direction of
   (i) the positive x-axis
   (ii) the positive y-axis.

(a)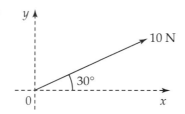

(b)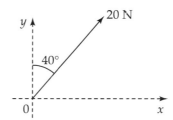

(c)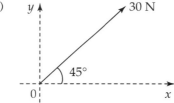

(d)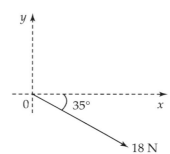

(e)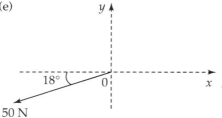

(f)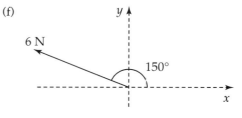

2. Find the horizontal and vertical components of the following forces:
   (a) a force of 40 N acting at 20° to the horizontal
   (b) a force of 7 N acting at 50° to the horizontal
   (c) a force of 35 N acting at 80° to the horizontal

3. Find in terms of P and θ, the components of the following forces in the direction of the positive x and y axes.

(a)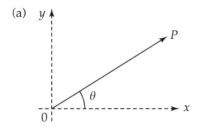

(b)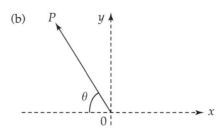

4. Resolve the following forces (i) parallel and (ii) perpendicular to the inclined plane.

(a)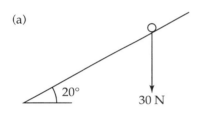

(b)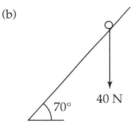

(c)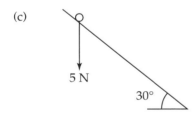

(d)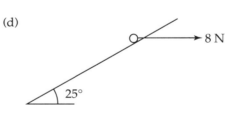

(e)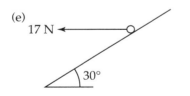

(f)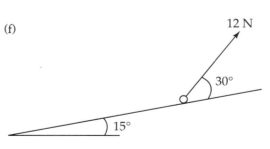

(g)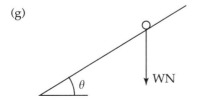

(h)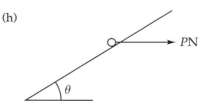

5. Find the sum of the components of the following forces in:

   (i) the positive x direction

   (ii) the positive y direction

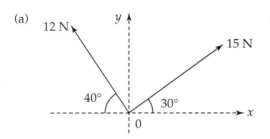
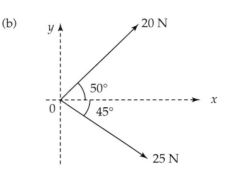
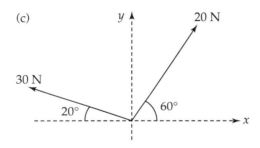
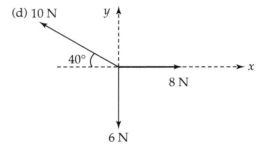
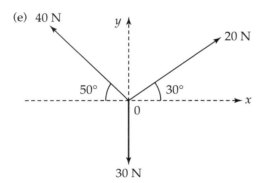
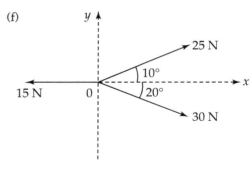

6. Express each of the following forces in the form $a\mathbf{i} + b\mathbf{j}$, where $\mathbf{i}$ and $\mathbf{j}$ are unit vectors in the directions of the positive x-axis and y-axis respectively.

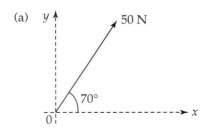
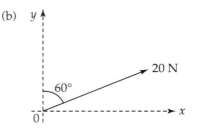

7. Find the magnitude of the resultant force and the angle it makes with the largest force.

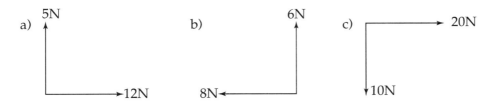

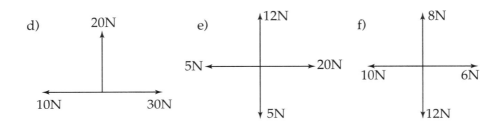

8.

The diagram shows three forces acting on a particle at O.

Find the magnitude of the resultant force and the angle its line of action makes with the line Ox when:

(a) $A = 3\,N$, $B = 5\,N$, $C = 2\,N$, $b = 60°$, $c = 30°$

(b) $A = 8\,N$, $B = 10\,N$, $C = 12\,N$, $b = 50°$, $c = 40°$

(c) $A = 10\,N$, $B = 6\,N$, $C = 4\,N$, $b = 30°$, $c = 45°$

(d) $A = 20\,N$, $B = 8\,N$, $C = 14\,N$, $b = 20°$, $c = 10°$

9. The diagram shows three forces acting on a particle at P.

Find the magnitude of the resultant force and the angle its line of action makes with the line of action of force C.

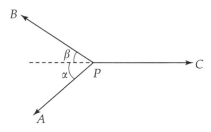

(a) $A = 4\,\text{N}$, $B = 5\,\text{N}$, $C = 10\,\text{N}$, $\alpha = 40°$, $\beta = 30°$

(b) $A = 15\,\text{N}$, $B = 20\,\text{N}$, $C = 12\,\text{N}$, $\alpha = 50°$, $\beta = 60°$

(c) $A = 40\,\text{N}$, $B = 30\,\text{N}$, $C = 20\,\text{N}$, $\alpha = 55°$, $\beta = 75°$

10. The resultant R, of the three forces shown in the diagram, acts along the line Oy.

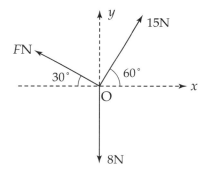

(a) Show that $F = 8.66$ (b) Find the magnitude of R.

11. Find the magnitude of the force $(3\mathbf{i} + 4\mathbf{j})$ N and the angle it makes with the direction of $\mathbf{i}$.

12. Find the magnitude of the force $(-5\mathbf{i} + 8\mathbf{j})$N and the angle it makes with the direction of $\mathbf{j}$.

13. For each of the following sets of forces find,

the resultant in the form $a\mathbf{i} + b\mathbf{j}$

the magnitude of the resultant

the angle the resultant makes with the direction of $\mathbf{i}$.

(a) $(4\mathbf{i} + 2\mathbf{j})$ N, $(6\mathbf{i} + 3\mathbf{j})$ N, $(2\mathbf{i} + 5\mathbf{j})$ N

(b) $(7\mathbf{i} - 4\mathbf{j})$ N, $(-3\mathbf{i} + 5\mathbf{j})$ N, $(2\mathbf{i} - 3\mathbf{j})$ N

(c) $(3\mathbf{i} - \mathbf{j})$ N, $(-8\mathbf{i} - 2\mathbf{j})$ N, $(4\mathbf{i} + 5\mathbf{j})$ N.

14. If the resultant of the forces $(4\mathbf{i} + 5\mathbf{j})$ N, $(a\mathbf{i} + b\mathbf{j})$ N and $(-2\mathbf{i} + \mathbf{j})$ N is $(7\mathbf{i} - 6\mathbf{j})$ N, find a and b.

4.4 Equilibrium of forces

A system of forces is in equilibrium when the resultant force is zero. A body is in equilibrium when it is at rest or is moving with constant velocity.

In this book we are dealing with forces acting in the same plane. When a system of such forces is resolved into two perpendicular directions, the algebraic sum of the components in each direction will be zero.

Example 1

Find T_1 and T_2 if the following system of forces is in equilibrium.

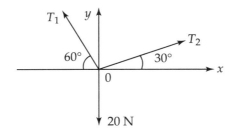

Resolve the forces along O_x and O_y:

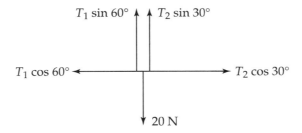

Along O_x, subtract the forces in the opposite direction:

$$T_1 \cos 60 - T_2 \cos 30° = 0$$

$$0.5\, T_1 - 0.866\, T_2 = 0$$

$$T_1 = 1.73\, T_2 \qquad [A]$$

Along O_y, add the forces in the same direction and subtract forces in the opposite direction:

$$T_1 \sin 60° + T_2 \sin 30° - 20 = 0$$

$$0.866\, T_1 + 0.5\, T_2 - 20 = 0 \qquad [B]$$

Substitute for T_1 from [A]: $(0.866 \times 1.73\, T_2) + 0.5\, T_2 = 20$

$$1.5\, T_2 + 0.5\, T_2 = 20$$
$$2\, T_2 = 20$$
$$T_2 = 10\,\text{N}$$
$$T_1 = 1.73 \times 10$$
$$T_1 = 17.3\,\text{N}$$

Example 2

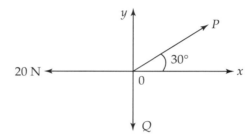

The diagram shows a particle in equilibrium under the action of the forces shown. Find the forces P and Q.

Resolve the forces along O_x and O_y:

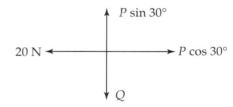

Along the direction O_x there is only one unknown value:
$$P \cos 30 - 20 = 0$$

$$P = \frac{20}{\cos 30°}$$

$$P = 23.1\,\text{N}$$

Along O_y:
$$Q - P \sin 30° = 0$$

$$Q - 23.1 \sin 30° = 0$$

$$Q = 11.6\,\text{N}$$

Example 3

A particle is in equilibrium under the action of the forces shown in the diagram. Find the magnitude of P and the angle θ.

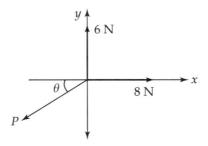

Resolve the forces along O_x and O_y:

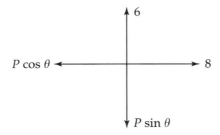

Along O_y: $P \sin \theta = 6$

Along O_x: $P \cos \theta = 8$

Using the identity $\dfrac{\sin \theta}{\cos \theta} = \tan \theta$ and dividing the equations:

$$\tan \theta = \frac{6}{8}$$

$$\theta = 36.9°$$

Substituting, $P \sin 36.9° = 6$

$$P = 10\,\text{N}$$

Example 4

A particle is in equilibrium under the action of the forces shown in the diagram. Find the unknown forces P and Q.

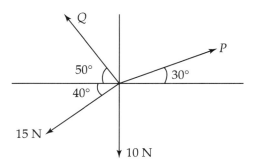

Resolve along O_x and O_y:

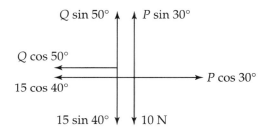

Along O_y: $\qquad Q \sin 50° + P \sin 30° = 15 \sin 40 + 10$

$$0.766Q + 0.5P = 19.6$$

$$0.5P = 19.6 - 0.766\,Q$$

$$P = 39.2 - 1.53\,Q \qquad \text{[A]}$$

Along O_x: $\qquad Q \cos 50° + 15 \cos 40° = P \cos 30°$

$$0.643Q + 11.5 = 0.866\,P \qquad \text{[B]}$$

Substitute for P from [A]: $\qquad 0.643Q + 11.5 = 0.866\,(39.2 - 1.53Q)$

$$= 33.9 - 1.32Q$$

$$1.96Q = 22.4$$

$$Q = 11.4\,\text{N}$$

Substitute for Q: $\qquad P = 39.2 - 1.53 \times 11.4$

$$P = 21.7\,\text{N}$$

Example 5

In any questions where smooth beads or rings are threaded onto a string, the tensions in the string either side of the bead are the same.

A smooth ring is threaded onto a light inextensible string. The bead is held in equilibrium by a 4 N force acting horizontally, as shown in the diagram. Find:

(a) The tension in the string (b) The weight of the bead.

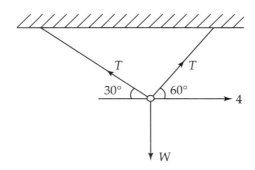

Resolving horizontally:
$$T \cos 30 = T \cos 60 + 4$$
$$T(\cos 30 - \cos 60) = 4$$
$$T = 10.9$$
$$\text{Tension} = 10.9 \, \text{N}$$

Resolving vertically:
$$10.9 \sin 30 + 10.9 \sin 60 = W$$
$$W = 14.9$$
$$\text{Weight} = 14.9 \, \text{N}$$

Example 6

The following set of forces is in equilibrium. Find a and b.

$$\mathbf{F}_1 = (5\mathbf{i} - 4\mathbf{j})\text{N}, \quad \mathbf{F}_2 = (-2\mathbf{i} + 3\mathbf{j})\text{N}, \quad \mathbf{F}_3 = (a\mathbf{i} + b\mathbf{j})\text{N}.$$

In equilibrium the vector sum of the forces equals zero. In column vector form:

$$\begin{pmatrix} 5 \\ -4 \end{pmatrix} + \begin{pmatrix} -2 \\ 3 \end{pmatrix} + \begin{pmatrix} a \\ b \end{pmatrix} = \begin{pmatrix} 0 \\ 0 \end{pmatrix}$$

Equating **i** components:
$$5 - 2 + a = 0$$
$$a = -3$$

Equating **j** components:
$$-4 + 3 + b = 0$$
$$b = 1$$

Exercise 4B

1. The following systems of forces are in equilibrium. Find the magnitude of forces P and Q

(a)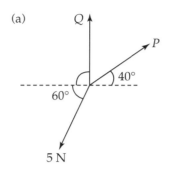

(b)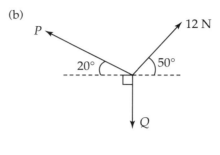

(c)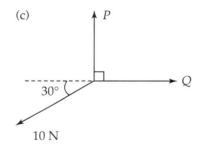

(d)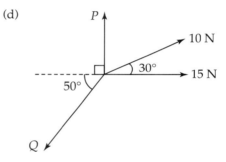

2. The diagram shows a particle in equilibrium.

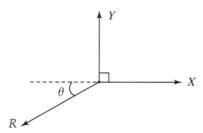

Find the magnitude of R and the angle θ when

(a) $X = 8\,\text{N}$, $Y = 6\,\text{N}$

(b) $X = 7\,\text{N}$, $Y = 24\,\text{N}$

(c) $X = 5\,\text{N}$, $Y = 9\,\text{N}$

3. The diagrams show forces acting on a particle which is in equilibrium at P. Find the magnitude of forces X and Y.

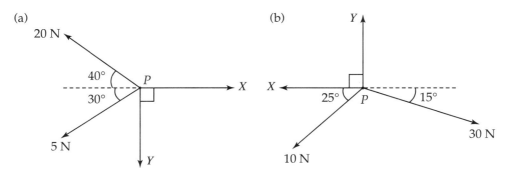

4. A particle is in equilibrium under the action of the forces P, Q and R. Find the values of a and b.

   (a) $P = 3\mathbf{i} - 4\mathbf{j}$, $Q = -5\mathbf{i} + 8\mathbf{j}$, $R = a\mathbf{i} + b\mathbf{j}$
   (b) $P = a\mathbf{i} + 2\mathbf{j}$, $Q = 3\mathbf{i} - 6\mathbf{j}$, $R = 5\mathbf{i} + b\mathbf{j}$
   (c) $P = 4\mathbf{i} - b\mathbf{j}$, $Q = a\mathbf{i} - \mathbf{j}$, $R = -2\mathbf{i} + 3\mathbf{j}$

5. The diagram shows a particle of weight W supported in equilibrium by two light inextensible strings inclined at 30° and 50° to the horizontal.

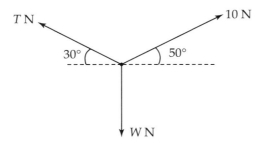

   Calculate the magnitude of the tension T and the weight W.

6. A body B of weight 100 N is held in equilibrium by two light inextensible ropes, one of which is horizontal.

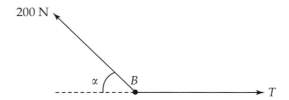

   Find:

   (a) the angle α

   (b) the tension T in the horizontal rope

7.

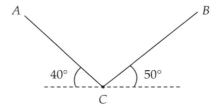

A Christmas decoration of weight W N is attached at C to the ends of two light inextensible strings AC and BC. The decoration hangs in equilibrium with AC and BC inclined at $40°$ and $50°$ to the horizontal respectively.

Given that the tension in BC is 3 N, calculate the magnitude of:

(a) the tension in AC

(b) the weight W N.

8. A mass of 5 kg is suspended from a string, which makes an angle of $30°$ with the vertical. The mass is in equilibrium when it is acted on by a horizontal force P N as shown in the diagram.

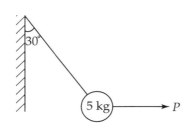

(a) Draw a diagram showing all the forces acting on the mass.

(b) Find the tension in the string.

(c) Find P.

(d) Write a modelling assumption about the string.

9. Three forces $\mathbf{F}_1$, $\mathbf{F}_2$ and $\mathbf{F}_3$ act on a particle where

$$\mathbf{F}_1 = (6\mathbf{i} - 3\mathbf{j})\text{N}$$
$$\mathbf{F}_2 = (-2\mathbf{i} + \mathbf{j})\text{N}$$
$$\mathbf{F}_3 = (p\mathbf{i} + q\mathbf{j})\text{N}$$

(a) Given that the particle is in equilibrium, find the values of p and q.

(b) The resultant of forces $\mathbf{F}_1$ and $\mathbf{F}_2$ is $\mathbf{F}$. Calculate the magnitude of $\mathbf{F}$.

(c) Calculate the angle between the line of action of $\mathbf{F}$ and the vector $\mathbf{i}$.

10. A crate of weight W is held at rest by two ropes. One rope has a tension of 5000 N and makes an angle of 25° with the horizontal. The other has tension T and makes an angle of 50° to the horizontal.

    (a) Draw a diagram showing the three forces acting on the crate

    (b) Find T

    (c) Find W

11. A crate is held at rest by two ropes. One rope has a tension of 50 N and makes an angle of 25° with the horizontal. The other has a tension of 80 N and makes an angle α with the horizontal.

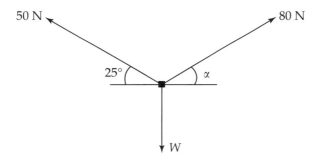

    Find (a) the angle α

    (b) the weight of the crate

12. A block of weight W N is suspended by two chains. One chain makes an angle of 20° with the upward vertical and has a tension of 50 N. The other rope makes an angle of 40° with the upward vertical and has a tension T N. Find T and W.

13. One end of a rope is attached to a point A. The other end is attached to a block B of weight 60 N. The block is then pulled horizontally by another rope so the angle between AB and the vertical is 40° and finishes in equilibrium.

    (a) Draw a diagram showing the forces acting on the block and the distances involved.

    (b) Find the tension in rope AB.

    (c) Find the tension in the horizontal rope.

14. A body of mass 3 kg is suspended by two light strings and hangs in equilibrium.

    Resolve in the direction of O_x and O_y and obtain two equations.

    Solve these equations to find the tension in each string.

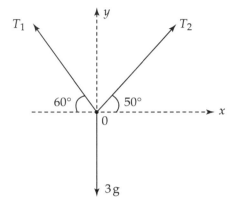

15. A block of weight 100 N is suspended by two chains. One chain makes an angle of 50° with the horizontal and has a tension T_1. The other chain makes an angle of 30° with the horizontal and has a tension T_2.

    (a) Draw a diagram showing the three forces acting on the block.
    (b) Find the tensions T_1 and T_2.

4.5 Friction and the coefficient of friction

There are two types of surface: rough and smooth.

If a surface is rough there will be a friction force opposing the motion of any object placed upon it.

If a surface is smooth there is no friction.

Suppose you are trying to pull a heavy bag across a rough desk. The forces acting are:

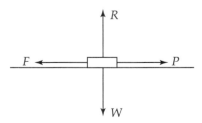

As you increase the pulling force P, the bag will first of all remain at rest, but eventually the bag will move.

There is a maximum friction force $\mathbf{F}_{max}$ which can exist between two surfaces. $\mathbf{F}_{max}$ is called the *limiting friction force*.

If $P < \mathbf{F}_{max}$, the friction will take a value just sufficient to oppose P.

If $P = \mathbf{F}_{max}$, the bag will be 'on the point of moving' and is said to be in *limiting equilibrium*.

If $P > \mathbf{F}_{max}$, the bag will move and the friction force will remain at its maximum value, $\mathbf{F}_{max}$.

It can be shown experimentally that the maximum frictional force between two surfaces is directly proportional to the normal reaction.

The maximum frictional force, called the limiting frictional force between two surfaces, is given by:

$$\mathbf{F}_{max} = \mu \mathbf{R}$$

The symbol μ is called the **coefficient of friction**. Its value depends on the materials of the surfaces concerned.

Example 1

A crate of mass 10 kg lies on a rough horizontal surface. The coefficient of friction between the crate and the surface is 0.5. Calculate the frictional force acting on the crate when the magnitude of a horizontal force P applied to the block is:

(a) 30 N

(b) 49 N

(c) 60 N.

State in each case whether the crate will move.

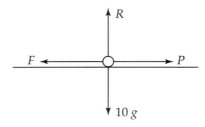

Resolving vertically: $\quad R = 10\,g$

Maximum frictional force: $\quad \mathbf{F} = \mu R$

$\qquad\qquad\qquad\qquad\qquad = 0.5 \times 10\,g$

$\qquad\qquad\qquad\qquad\qquad = 49\,\text{N}$

(a) If $P = 30\,\text{N}$ then P is less than $49\,\text{N}$, so there is no motion.

   Resolving horizontally: $\quad\mathbf{F} = \mathbf{P}$

   $\quad\quad\quad\quad\quad\quad\quad\quad\quad\quad\quad = 30$

   The frictional force $= 30\,\text{N}$

(b) If $P = 49\,\text{N}$ then P equals the maximum frictional force and the crate is on the point of moving.

   The frictional force $= 49\,\text{N}$

(c) If $P = 60\,\text{N}$ then P is greater than the maximum frictional force and motion takes place.

   The frictional force $= 49\,\text{N}$.

Example 2

A block of mass 5 kg rests on a rough horizontal plane. The coefficient of friction between the block and the plane is 0.4. A horizontal force P is applied to the particle. If the block is about to slide, find the magnitude of P.

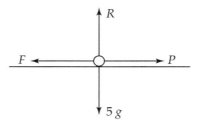

Resolving vertically: $\quad\quad\quad\quad R = 5g$

Resolving horizontally: $\quad\quad\quad P = F$

Limiting friction: $\quad\quad\quad\quad\quad F = \mu R$

$\quad\quad\quad\quad\quad\quad\quad\quad\quad\quad\quad = 0.4 \times 5g$

$\quad\quad\quad\quad\quad\quad\quad\quad\quad\quad\quad = 19.6$

$\quad\quad\quad\quad\quad\quad\quad\quad\quad P = 19.6\,\text{N}$

Example 3

A box of mass 4 kg lies on a rough horizontal surface. A rope, inclined at 40° above the horizontal, is attached to the box.

The box is on the point of moving when the tension in the rope is 20 N. Find the coefficient of friction between the box and the surface.

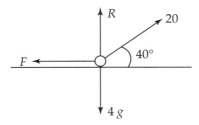

Resolve the 20 N force horizontally and vertically:

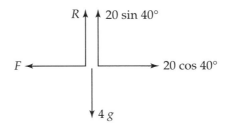

Resolving vertically: $\quad R + 20\sin 40° = 4g$

$$R = 26.3\,\text{N}$$

Resolving horizontally: $\quad F = 20\cos 40°$

$$= 15.3\,\text{N}$$

Limiting equilibrium: $\quad F = \mu R$

$$15.3 = \mu 26.3$$

$$\mu = 0.582$$

Coefficient of friction $= 0.582$

Example 4

A box is being pulled at a steady speed, along a rough horizontal surface, by a rope inclined at 20° above the horizontal. The tension in the rope is 60 N. If the coefficient of friction between the box and the surface is 0.3, find the weight of the box.

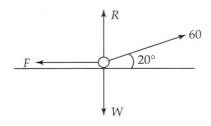

Resolve the 60 N force horizontally and vertically:

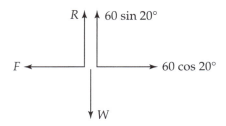

At a steady speed the force forward = the force backward and the friction will be limiting.

Resolving horizontally: $\quad F = 60 \cos 20° = 56.4\,\text{N}$

Limiting friction: $\quad F = \mu R$

$$R = \frac{56.4}{0.3} = 188\,\text{N}$$

Resolving vertically: $\quad W = 188 + 60 \sin 20° = \cancel{244}\ 208$

Weight of the box = $\cancel{244}\text{N}\ 208\,\text{N}$

Exercise 4C

1. The diagrams show a particle of mass 5 kg initially at rest on a rough horizontal plane. The coefficient of friction between the body and the plane is 0.4. The particle is subject to the horizontal force shown. In each case find the magnitude of the friction force and state whether the particle will remain at rest or will accelerate along the plane.

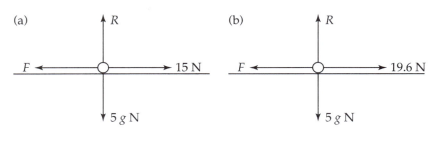

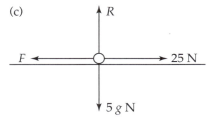

2.

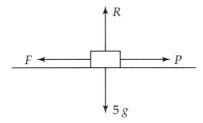

A body of mass 5 kg is at rest on a rough horizontal plane. A horizontal force P acts on the body. The coefficient of friction between the body and the plane is μ. Given that the body is on the point of moving, find the magnitude of P in each case.

(a) $\mu = \dfrac{1}{7}$ (b) $\mu = \dfrac{1}{2}$ (c) $\mu = 0.3$

3. A box of mass 20 kg is at rest on a rough horizontal plane. When a horizontal force of 49 N is applied, the box is on the point of moving. Find the coefficient of friction between the plane and the box.

4. A particle of weight W N is in limiting equilibrium on a rough horizontal plane when a horizontal force P N is applied. The coefficient of friction between the particle and the plane is μ.

Find (a) μ, given that $W = 10$ N and $P = 4$ N

(b) P, given that $W = 20$ N and $\mu = 0.3$

(c) W, given that $P = 8$ N and $\mu = 0.4$

5. A sledge is modelled as a particle mass 20 kg. The diagram shows the forces that act on the sledge as it is pulled across a rough horizontal surface.

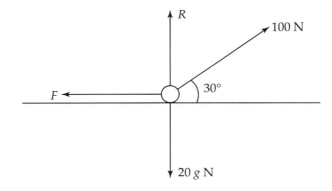

If the sledge is on the point of sliding, find:

(a) the normal reaction R

(b) the friction force **F**

(c) the coefficient of friction between the ground and the sledge.

6. A block of mass 10 kg is in limiting equilibrium on a rough horizontal plane, when a force P acts as shown.

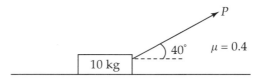

   (a) Draw a diagram showing all the forces acting on the block
   (b) Resolve the forces horizontally and vertically
   (c) Find the force P.

7. A crate of mass 5 kg lies on a rough horizontal floor. The coefficient of friction between the floor and the crate is 0.45. A rope is attached to the box to pull the crate along the floor.

   Find the magnitude that the tension must exceed in order to move the box if the rope is

   (a) horizontal
   (b) 50° above the horizontal.

8. A ring of mass 5 kg slides on a fixed, rough horizontal pole. The coefficient of friction between the ring and the pole is 0.3. A light string is attached to pull the ring along the pole. If the ring is on the point of moving, find the magnitude of the tension in the string if the string is

   (a) horizontal
   (b) at 30° above the horizontal
   (c) at 30° below the horizontal

9.

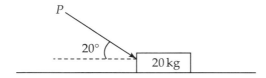

A case of mass 20 kg lies on a rough horizontal floor under the action of a force P N as shown in the diagram. The coefficient of friction between the case and the floor is 0.3.

If the case is being moved at constant velocity, find the value of P.

4.6 Forces on an inclined plane

In M1 it simplifies calculations if we resolve forces parallel and perpendicular to the plane.

4.6.1 Resolving weight

Consider a mass m kg resting on a plane inclined at an angle θ to the horizontal:

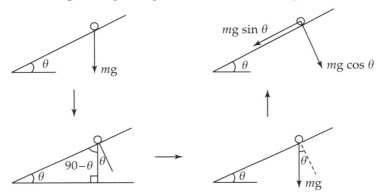

The angle between the normal or perpendicular to the plane and the vertical is θ. Remember the component next to the angle uses $\cos\theta$, so the component perpendicular to the plane is $mg\cos\theta$ and the component parallel to the plane is $mg\sin\theta$.

This is so important that it is worth repeating:

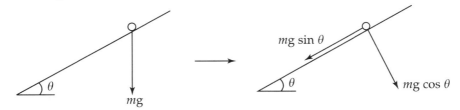

Example 1

A particle of mass 3 kg rests in limiting equilibrium on a rough plane inclined at 30° to the horizontal. Find the normal reaction force, the frictional force and the coefficient of friction.

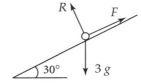

The particle will tend to slide down the plane so the frictional force acts up the plane.
Resolve the forces parallel and perpendicular to the plane.

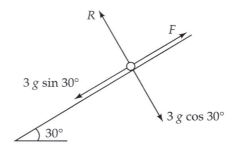

$$R = 3 \times 9.8 \cos 30° = 25.5 \, \text{N}$$
$$F = 3 \times 9.8 \sin 30° = 14.7 \, \text{N}$$
$$\text{coefficient of friction, } \mu = \frac{F}{R} = \frac{14.7}{25.5} = 0.576$$

4.6.2 Greatest and least forces and the direction of the friction force

Suppose a horizontal force P is applied to a particle on a rough inclined plane. Equilibrium can be broken by the particle tending to move up the plane or down the plane.

a) particle tending to move up the plane

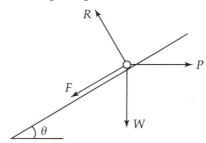

The friction force **F** acts down the plane opposing motion up the plane. The magnitude of P is greatest.

b) particle tending to move down the plane

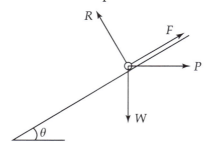

The friction force acts up the plane opposing motion down the plane.

The magnitude of P is least.

> All forces are considered to act along the line of greatest slope. In other words they are acting directly up the plane, not at any angle across the plane.

4.6.3 Forces acting along the plane

Example 2

A body of mass 6 kg lies on a rough plane inclined at 30° to the horizontal. When a force of 20 N is applied to the body in a direction directly up the plane, the body is on the point of moving down the plane.

Find the coefficient of friction between the body and the plane.

Draw a diagram showing all the forces acting. Note that the friction force acts up the plane to oppose motion down the plane.

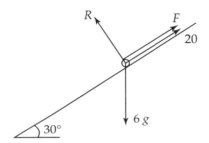

Resolve all forces parallel and perpendicular to the plane:

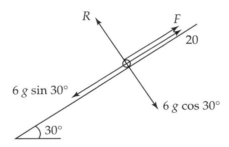

Perpendicular to the plane there is no motion:
$$R = 6g \cos 30° = 50.9 \, \text{N}$$

Parallel to the plane, the body is on the point of moving down the plane, but the forces are still balanced.
$$F + 20 = 6g \sin 30° = 29.4$$
$$F = 9.4 \, \text{N}$$

The coefficient of friction:
$$\mu = \frac{F}{R}$$
$$= \frac{9.4}{50.9}$$
$$= 0.185$$

4.6.4 Horizontal forces

If a horizontal force P acts on a particle on a plane inclined at an angle θ to the horizontal:

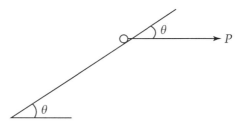

The angle between the plane and force P is also θ (corresponding or **F** angles)

The component next to the angle uses $\cos \theta$ so resolving P results in:

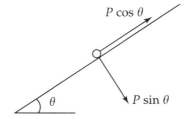

Example 3

A particle at rest on a smooth plane inclined at an angle 36.9° to the horizontal, is kept in equilibrium by a horizontal force of 6 N acting in a vertical plane containing the line of greatest slope of the inclined plane through the particle. Find:

(a) the weight of the particle

(b) the magnitude of the force exerted by the plane on the particle.

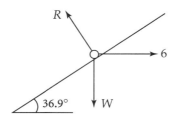

Notice there is no friction since the plane is smooth.

Resolve the forces parallel and perpendicular to the plane:

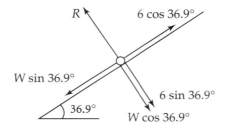

a) Parallel to the plane: $\quad W \sin 36.9° = 6 \cos 36.9°$

$$W \times 0.6 = 6 \times 0.8$$

$$W = 8\,\text{N}$$

$$\text{Weight} = 8\,\text{N}$$

b) Perpendicular to the plane: $\quad R = W \cos 36.9° + 6 \sin 36.9°$

Substituting W: $\quad R = 8 \cos 36.9° + 6 \sin 36.9°$

$$R = 10\,\text{N}$$

Normal reaction $= 10\,\text{N}$

Example 4

A body of mass 4 kg lies on a rough plane which is inclined at 25° to the horizontal. A horizontal force of 40 N is applied to the body so that it is on the point of moving up the plane.

Find the coefficient of friction between the plane and the body.

Draw a diagram to show all the forces acting. Note that the friction force acts down the plane to oppose motion up the plane.

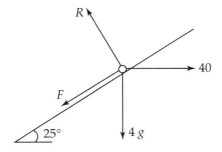

Resolve all forces parallel and perpendicular to the plane.

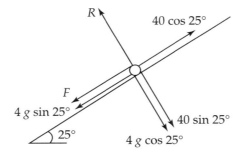

Perpendicular to the plane there is no motion.
$$R = 40 \sin 25° + 4g \cos 25° = 52.4 \, \text{N}$$

Parallel to the plane the body is on the point of moving up the plane but the forces are still balanced.
$$F + 4g \sin 25° = 40 \cos 25°$$
$$F = 19.7 \, \text{N}$$

Coefficient of friction,
$$\mu = \frac{F}{R}$$
$$= \frac{19.7}{52.4} = 0.38$$

Example 5

A body of mass 5 kg rests on a rough plane inclined at 30° to the horizontal. The coefficient of friction between the plane and the body is 0.35. A horizontal force P is applied to the body such that it is about to move up the plane. Find the magnitude of P.

Draw a diagram showing all the forces acting. Notice that the friction force acts down the plane to oppose potential motion.

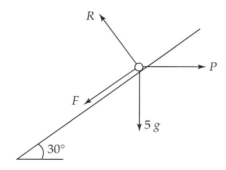

Resolve all the forces parallel and perpendicular to the plane:

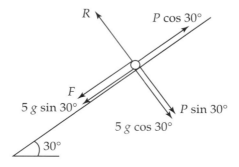

Perpendicular to the plane:
$$R = P\sin 30° + 5g\cos 30°$$
$$R = 0.5P + 42.4 \quad \ldots (1)$$

Parallel to the plane:
$$F + 5g\sin 30° = P\cos 30° \quad \ldots (2)$$

Coefficient of friction:
$$F = \mu R = 0.35 R \quad \ldots (3)$$

Combining equations (1), (2) and (3):
$$0.866P - 24.5 = 0.35(0.5P + 42.4)$$
$$= 0.175P + 14.8$$
$$P = 56.9\,\text{N}$$

4.6.5 Force at an angle to the plane

Example 6

A body of mass 3 kg rests on a rough plane inclined at 40° to the horizontal. The coefficient of friction between the body and the plane is 0.2. A force P, acting at 50° to the horizontal, keeps the body in limiting equilibrium, when it is about to slip down the plane. Find the magnitude of P.

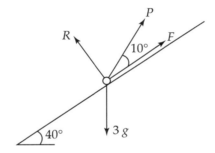

Notice the force P acts at 50° to the horizontal, so it acts at $50° - 40° = 10°$ to the plane. The body is about to slip down the plane so the friction force acts up the plane.

Resolve all forces parallel and perpendicular to the plane:

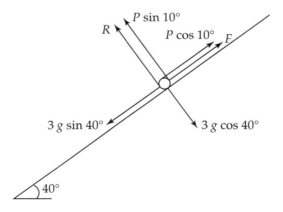

Perpendicular to the plane: $\quad R + P \sin 10° = 3g \cos 40°$

$$R = 22.5 - 0.174\, P \qquad \ldots (1)$$

Parallel to the plane: $\quad F + P \cos 10° = 3g \sin 40° \qquad \ldots (2)$

Coefficient of friction: $\quad F = \mu R = 0.2\, R \qquad \ldots (3)$

Substitute (1) and (2) in (3): $\quad 18.9 - 0.985\, P = 0.2\,(22.5 - 0.174 P)$

$$= 4.5 - 0.0348\, P$$

$$P = 15.2 \,\text{N}$$

Do bear in mind that in this type of question there are a lot of marks for resolving forces and obtaining the three equations, not just for solving them.

Exercise 4D

1. A particle of mass 3 kg is held in equilibrium on a smooth inclined plane by a force P as shown. Find P in each case.

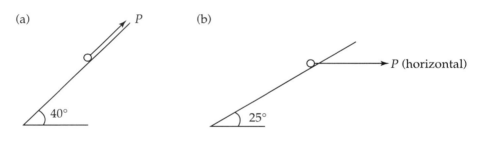

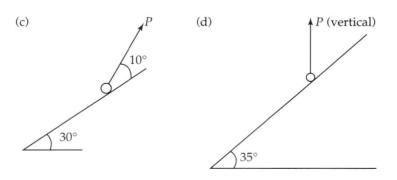

2. A particle rests on a smooth plane inclined at 30° to the horizontal. The particle is kept in equilibrium by a horizontal force of 10 N. Find:

   (a) the weight of the particle

   (b) the force the plane exerts on the particle.

3. A particle of mass 5 kg rests on a smooth plane inclined at an angle of 25° to the horizontal. The particle is held in equilibrium by the pull of a string inclined at 35° to the horizontal. Find the tension T in the string.

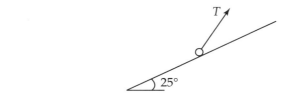

4.

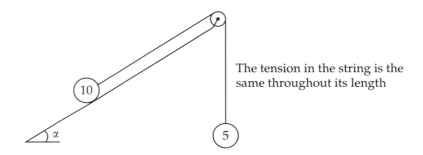

The tension in the string is the same throughout its length

The diagram shows two blocks, of mass 10 kg and 5 kg, connected by a string over a smooth pulley. The 10 kg mass rests on a smooth inclined plane and the 5 kg mass hangs freely. The system is in equilibrium.

Find: (a) the tension in the string

(b) the angle of inclination α

(c) the force the plane exerts on the 10 kg mass.

5. A particle of mass 3 kg rests in limiting equilibrium on a rough plane inclined at 25° to the horizontal.

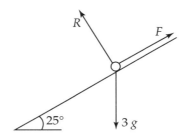

Find: (a) the normal reaction R

(b) the frictional force F

(c) the coefficient of friction between the particle and the plane.

6. A particle of mass 4 kg is at rest on a rough plane inclined at 40° to the horizontal. A force of 20 N acting parallel to and up the plane just prevents the particle moving down the plane.

   Find the coefficient of friction between the particle and the plane.

7.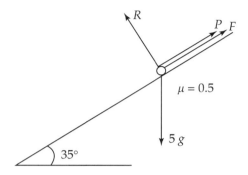

   The diagram shows a particle of 5 kg which is on the point of sliding down an inclined plane. It is held by a force P N. If the coefficient of friction between the particle and the plane is 0.5 find the magnitude of P.

8. Repeat question 7 if the particle is about to move up the plane. Remember the friction force will act to oppose motion.

9. For each of the following, resolve the force

   (i) parallel and

   (ii) perpendicular to the plane.

   (a)

   (b)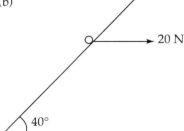

   (c)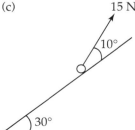

   (d)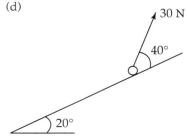

10. Each of the following diagrams shows a bag of mass 4 kg on a rough inclined plane. The coefficient of friction between the plane and the particle is 0.2. R is the normal reaction and F the friction force. Find the magnitude of force P if the bag is on the point of moving down the plane.

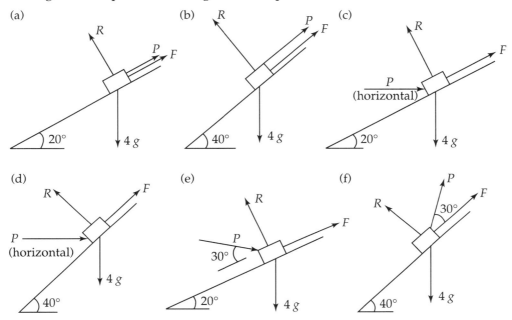

11. Each of the following diagrams shows a particle of mass 3 kg on a rough inclined plane. The coefficient of friction between the plane and the particle is 0.3. R is the normal reaction and F the friction force.

Find the magnitude of force P if the body is on the point of moving up the plane.

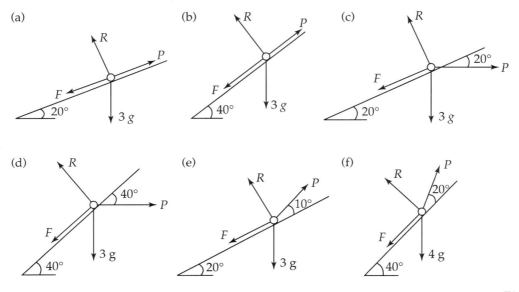

12.

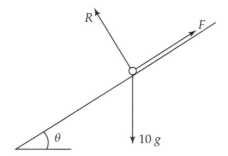

A particle of mass 10 kg lies in limiting equilibrium on a rough plane which is inclined at an angle θ to the horizontal. The coefficient of friction between the particle and the plane is 0.7. Find

(a) the angle θ

(b) the frictional force acting.

13. A book of weight 5 N rests in equilibrium on a surface inclined at 23° to the horizontal.

(a) Find the frictional force acting on the book.

(b) The coefficient of friction between the book and the surface is 0.45. Find if the equilibrium is limiting.

14. A body of mass 3 kg is put on a rough plane inclined at 40° to the horizontal. If the coefficient of friction between the body and the plane is 0.4, find the force which must be applied to the body in a direction parallel to the plane so that

(a) the body is just stopped from sliding down the plane

(b) the body is just about to move up the plane.

15. A body of mass 20 kg lies on a rough plane inclined at 35° to the horizontal. A vertical string holds the body at rest on the point of moving down the slope.

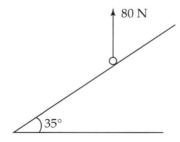

The tension in the string is 80 N.

Draw a diagram showing all the forces acting on the body. Find

(a) the frictional force

(b) the normal reaction

(c) the coefficient of friction between the body and the plane.

16. A block of weight 150 N rests on a rough slope which is inclined at 60° to the horizontal. A horizontal force X is applied to the block in order to stop it slipping down the slope. The frictional force is 50 N when the block is just about to slip.

    (a) Draw a diagram showing all the forces acting on the block

    (b) Find the horizontal force X

    (c) Find the normal reaction force of the slope on the block.

17. A mass of 5 kg is at rest on a plane inclined at 30° to the horizontal. A force P newtons acts on the mass in a direction up the plane. The coefficient of friction between the mass and the plane is 0.4.

    Find the range of values of P.

18. A box of mass 10 kg rests in limiting equilibrium on a rough plane inclined at 25° to the horizontal. The coefficient of friction between the box and the plane is 0.25. A horizontal force X is applied to the box so the box is on the point of moving upwards. Find the magnitude of X.

19. A body of mass 4 kg is held in limiting equilibrium on a rough plane inclined at 35° to the horizontal by a horizontal force X. The coefficient of friction between the body and the plane is 0.25. Find X when the body is on the point of

    (a) slipping up the plane.

    (b) slipping down the plane.

20. A body of mass 400 g is placed on a rough plane which is inclined at 30° to the horizontal. If the coefficient of friction between the body and the plane is 0.5, find

    (a) the frictional force acting

    (b) the component of weight down the plane. State whether motion will occur.

Examination Exercise 4

1.

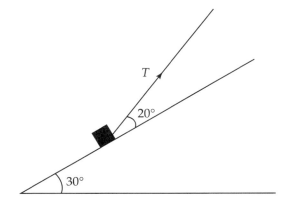

A box of mass 1.5 kg is placed on a plane which is inclined at an angle of 30° to the horizontal. The coefficient of friction between the box and the plane is $\frac{1}{3}$. The box is kept in equilibrium by a light string which lies in a vertical plane containing a line of greatest slope of the plane. The string makes an angle of 20° with the plane, as shown in the diagram. The box is in limiting equilibrium and is about to move up the plane. The tension in the string is T newtons. The box is modelled as a particle.

Find the value of T. [E]

2. Two forces $\mathbf{F}_1 = (2\mathbf{i} + 3\mathbf{j})$ N and $\mathbf{F}_2 = (\lambda\mathbf{i} + \mu\mathbf{j})$ N, where λ and μ are scalars, act on a particle. The resultant of the two forces is $\mathbf{R}$, where $\mathbf{R}$ is parallel to the vector $\mathbf{i} + 2\mathbf{j}$.

   (a) Find, to the nearest degree, the acute angle between the line of action of $\mathbf{R}$ and the vector $\mathbf{i}$.

   (b) Show that $2\lambda - \mu + 1 = 0$.

   Given that the direction of $\mathbf{F}_2$ is parallel to $\mathbf{j}$,

   (c) find, to 3 significant figures, the magnitude of $\mathbf{R}$. [E]

3. Three forces $\mathbf{F}_1$, $\mathbf{F}_2$ and $\mathbf{F}_3$ act on a particle and

   $\mathbf{F}_1 = (-3\mathbf{i} + 7\mathbf{j})$ newtons, $\mathbf{F}_2 = (\mathbf{i} - \mathbf{j})$ newtons, $\mathbf{F}_3 = (p\mathbf{i} + q\mathbf{j})$ newtons.

   (a) Given that this particle is in equilibrium, determine the value of p and the value of q.

   The resultant of the forces $\mathbf{F}_1$ and $\mathbf{F}_2$ is $\mathbf{R}$.

   (b) Calculate, in N, the magnitude of $\mathbf{R}$.

   (c) Calculate, to the nearest degree, the angle between the line of action of $\mathbf{R}$ and the vector $\mathbf{j}$. [E]

4.

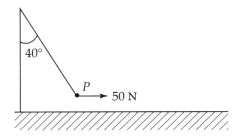

A tennis ball P is attached to one end of a light inextensible string, the other end of the string being attached to the top of a fixed vertical pole. A girl applies a horizontal force of magnitude 50 N to P, and P is in equilibrium under gravity with the string making an angle of 40° with the pole, as shown in the diagram.

By modelling the ball as a particle find, to 3 significant figures,

(a) the tension in the string,

(b) the weight of P. [E]

5.

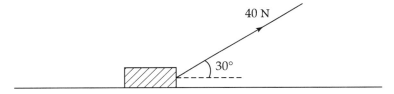

A box of mass 10 kg lies on a rough horizontal floor and is attached to one end of a rope. The rope is at an angle of 30° to the horizontal and the tension in it is 40 N, as shown in Fig. 3. The box is in limiting equilibrium. By modelling the box as a particle and the rope as light and inextensible, find, to 2 significant figures, the coefficient of friction between the box and the ground.

6.

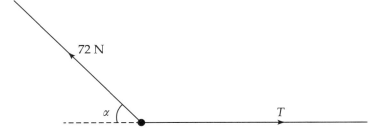

A body of mass 5 kg is held in equilibrium under gravity by two inextensible light ropes. One rope is horizontal, the other is at an angle α to the horizontal, as shown in the diagram. The tension in the rope inclined at α to the horizontal is 72 N. Find

(a) the angle α, giving your answer to the nearest degree,

(b) the tension T in the horizontal rope, giving your answer to the nearest N. [E]

7.

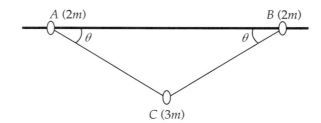

Two small rings, A and B, each of mass $2m$, are threaded on a rough horizontal pole. The coefficient of friction between each ring and the pole is μ. The rings are attached to the ends of a light inextensible string. A smooth ring C, of mass $3m$, is threaded on the string and hangs in equilibrium below the pole. The rings A and B are in limiting equilibrium on the pole, with $\angle BAC = \angle ABC = \theta$, where $\tan\theta = \frac{3}{4}$ as shown in the diagram.

(a) Show that the tension in the string is $\frac{5}{2}mg$.

(b) Find the value of μ.

8.

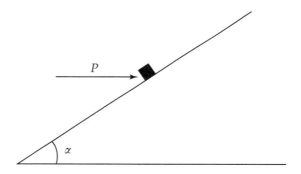

A box of mass m is placed on a plane, which is inclined at an angle α to the horizontal, where $\tan\alpha = \frac{3}{4}$. The plane is rough and the coefficient of friction between the box and the plane is $\frac{1}{2}$. The box is kept in equilibrium on the plane by applying a horizontal force of magnitude P to it, acting in a vertical plane containing a line of greatest slope of the plane, as shown in the diagram. Given that P has the smallest possible value which will enable the box to remain in equilibrium,

(a) draw a diagram, showing all the forces acting on the box, and indicating clearly the direction in which they act,

(b) find P in terms of m and g.

If instead P were to have the largest value which would enable the box to stay in equilibrium,

(c) state how the diagram of forces acting on the box should, if at all, be changed. [E]

9.

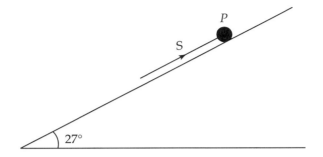

A small parcel P, of mass 1.5 kg, is placed on a rough plane inclined at an angle of 27° to the horizontal. The coefficient of friction between the parcel and the plane is 0.3. A force S, of variable magnitude, is applied to the parcel as shown in Fig. 1. The line of action of S is parallel to a line of greatest slope of the inclined plane.

Determine, in N to 1 decimal place, the magnitude of S when the parcel P is in limiting equilibrium and on the point of moving

(a) down the plane,

(b) up the plane. [E]

10.

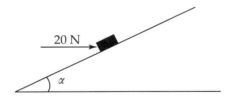

A parcel of mass 5 kg lies on a rough plane inclined at an angle α to the horizontal, where $\tan \alpha = \frac{3}{4}$. The parcel is held in equilibrium by the action of a horizontal force of magnitude 20 N, as shown. The force acts in a vertical plane through a line of greatest slope of the plane. The parcel is on the point of sliding down the plane. Find the coefficient of friction between the parcel and the plane. [E]

11.

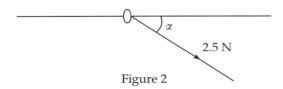

Figure 2

A ring of mass 0.3 kg is threaded on a fixed, rough horizontal curtain pole. A light inextensible string is attached to the ring. The string and the pole lie in the same vertical plane. The ring is pulled downwards by the string which makes an angle α to the horizontal, where $\tan \alpha = \frac{3}{4}$, as shown in Fig. 2. The tension in the string is 2.5 N. Given that, in this position, the ring is in limiting equilibrium,

(a) find the coefficient of friction between the ring and the pole.

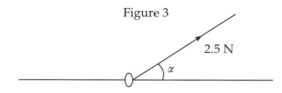

Figure 3

The direction of the string is now altered so that the ring is pulled upwards. The string lies in the same vertical plane as before and again makes an angle α with the horizontal, as shown in Fig. 3. The tension in the string is again 2.5 N.

(b) Find the normal reaction exerted by the pole on the ring.

(c) State whether the ring is in equilibrium in the position shown in Fig. 3, giving a brief justification for your answer. You need make no further detailed calculation of the forces acting.

12.

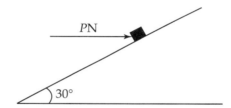

A box of mass 6 kg lies on a rough plane inclined at an angle of 30° to the horizontal. The box is held in equilibrium by means of a horizontal force of magnitude P newtons, as shown in the diagram. The line of action of the force is in the same vertical plane as a line of greatest slope of the plane. The coefficient of friction between the box and the plane is 0.4. The box is modelled as a particle.

Given that the box is in limiting equilibrium and on the point of moving up the plane, find,

(a) the normal reaction exerted on the box by the plane,

(b) the value of P.

The horizontal force is removed.

(c) Show that the box will now start to move down the plane. [E]

Part 5
Dynamics of a particle moving in a straight line

In this part all bodies can be modelled as particles.

5.1 Force and Newton's laws of motion

Newton's first law

A body will remain at rest or will continue to move with constant speed in a straight line unless acted on by a resultant force.

Consider a book lying on a horizontal desk. The forces acting are:

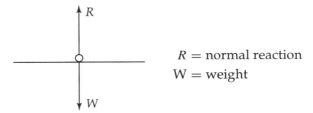

R = normal reaction
W = weight

In the absence of a resultant force $R = W$ and the book will remain at rest.

Consider a car moving at constant speed along a straight horizontal road. The forces acting are:

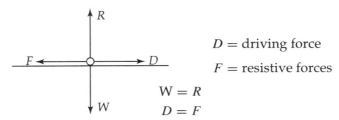

D = driving force
F = resistive forces
$W = R$
$D = F$

In the absence of a resultant force, the car will continue to move at constant velocity.

Newton's second law

Consider the book lying on a smooth horizontal desk.

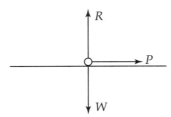

87

If you want to move the book you would give it a push with force P and the book would accelerate in the direction of this force.

Consider the car moving at constant speed along a straight horizontal road.

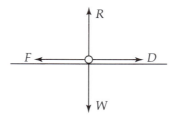

If you want the car to go faster you would "put your foot down" to make the driving force greater than the resistive forces, so the car would accelerate forward. If you want the car to slow down you would make the force backward greater than the force forward by applying the brakes. The car would then decelerate.

- In simplified form, Newton's second law states that if a resultant force F newtons (N) acts on a body of mass m kg, then the acceleration a ms^{-2} produced is given by:

$$F = ma$$

Definition of force

The unit of force is the Newton (N). The Newton is defined so that a force of 1 newton produces an acceleration of 1 ms^{-2} when applied to a particle of mass 1 kg.

Weight

All objects falling freely near the surface of the earth have approximately the same acceleration of 9.8 ms^{-2}. This acceleration is given the symbol g.
The force producing this acceleration is the force of gravity which the earth exerts on any object. This force is commonly called weight.

By Newton's second law: $W = mg$ (Or $W = 9.8\,m$)

Newton's third law

This states that if a body A exerts a force on a body B, then B exerts a force on A of the same magnitude but in the opposite direction.

Consider a car pulling a trailer at constant velocity along a horizontal road.

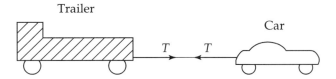

The trailer is pulled forwards by a tension T in the tow-bar. The trailer will exert an equal and opposite force T on the car.

Consider two particles A and B connected by a light inextensible string passing over a friction free pulley.

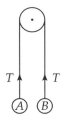

Particle A exerts a force on the rope so the rope exerts an equal and opposite force T on A. Likewise with particle B.

These forces are the forces exerted on the particles by the rope, whether the system is moving or not.

Consider a book on a desk.

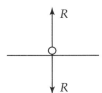

the desk exerts a force R on the book

the book exerts an equal and opposite force R on the desk

We would generally be concerned with the book and so would draw a diagram showing forces acting on the book only, not the desk.

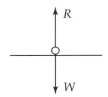

W is not the force exerted by the book on the desk.

W is the force exerted by the earth on the book.

Consider a man in a lift.

The lift exerts a force R on the man and the man exerts a force R on the lift. If we are concerned with the motion of the man, we would draw a diagram showing the forces acting on the man.

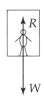

If the lift is accelerating upwards, then $R > W$.

These forces are only equal when the lift is moving with constant velocity or is at rest.

5.2 Applications of Newton's second law

5.2.1 Horizontal and vertical motion

Example 1

Find the acceleration produced when a body of mass 2 kg experiences a resultant force of 10 N.

Using $F = ma$, the equation of motion is:
$$10 = 2a$$
$$a = 5$$

The acceleration $= 5\,\text{ms}^{-2}$

Example 2

A car of mass 600 kg moves along a level road against resistances of 800 N. If its engine is exerting a driving force of 1100 N, find the acceleration produced.

Using $F = ma$, the equation of motion is:
$$1100 - 800 = 600a$$
$$300 = 600a$$
$$a = 300 \div 600 = 0.5$$

The acceleration $= 0.5\,\text{ms}^{-2}$.

Example 3

A particle of mass 3 kg is pulled along a smooth horizontal surface by a horizontal string. If the particle travels a distance of 3 m while uniformly accelerating from rest to a speed of $2\,\text{ms}^{-1}$, find the tension in the string.

First find the acceleration: $\quad u = 0, \quad v = 2, \quad a = ?, \quad s = 3$

$$v^2 = u^2 + 2as$$
$$2^2 = 0 + (2 \times a \times 3)$$
$$a = \frac{2}{3}\,\text{ms}^{-2}$$

The equation of motion is: $\quad T = 3 \times \dfrac{2}{3} = 2 \quad$ [i.e., '$F = ma$']

Tension $= 2\,\text{N}$

Example 4

A stone of mass 0.05 kg falls vertically through some liquid with an acceleration of 4 ms^{-2}. Find the resistive force acting on the stone.

Using $F = ma$ the equation of motion is:
$$0.05 \times 9.8 - R = 0.05 \times 4$$
$$R = 0.29$$

The resistive force $= 0.29$ N

Example 5

A lift of mass 400 kg contains a load of mass 200 kg. If the lift accelerates upwards from rest to a speed of 4 ms^{-1} over a distance of 2 m, find:

(a) the acceleration of the lift

(b) the tension in the lift cable

(c) the force the floor of the lift exerts on the load.

(a) $u = 0, \quad v = 4, \quad a = ?, \quad s = 2$
$$v^2 = u^2 + 2as$$
$$4^2 = 0 + (2 \times a \times 2)$$
$$a = 4$$

The acceleration of the lift $= 4$ ms^{-2}.

(b) Forces on the lift:

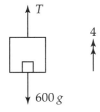

Note that the total mass is 600 kg

Using $F = ma$, the equation of motion is:
$$T - 600g = 600 \times 4$$
$$T = 8280 \text{ N}$$

Tension in the lift cable $= 8280$ N

(c) Consider forces acting on the load only:

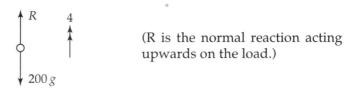

(R is the normal reaction acting upwards on the load.)

Using $F = ma$, the equation of motion is:
$$R - 200 \times 9.8 = 200 \times 4$$
$$R = 2760$$

The force the floor of the lift exerts on load $= 2760$ N

5.2.2 Horizontal motion with friction

Example 6

A block of mass 5 kg rests on a rough horizontal plane. The coefficient of friction between the block and the plane is 0.3. When a horizontal force of 40 N acts on the block, find its acceleration.

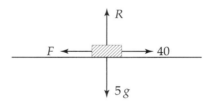

| Resolving vertically: | $R = 5g$ N | (no acceleration vertically) |

Friction force:
$$F = \mu R$$
$$= 0.3 \times 5 \times 9.8$$
$$= 14.7 \text{ N}$$

Resolving horizontally: $40 - 14.7 = 5a$ (using $F = ma$)
$$a = 5.06$$
Acceleration $= 5.06 \text{ ms}^{-2}$

Example 7

A boy sits on a sledge such that their combined mass is 75 kg. A friend then pulls the rope attached to the sledge so that it makes an angle of 30° to the horizontal. When the friend is pulling with a force 200 N the sledge is accelerating at 1.25 ms^{-2}.

(a) Draw a diagram showing all the forces acting on the sledge.

(b) Find the coefficient of friction between the sledge and the floor.

(a)
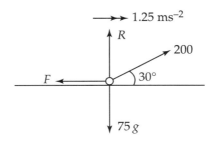

(b) Resolve the force of 200 N horizontally and vertically:

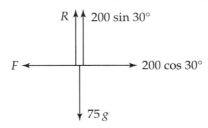

Resolving vertically: $\quad R + 200 \sin 30 = 75 \times 9.8$

$$R = 635 \, \text{N}$$

Resolving horizontally: $\quad 200 \cos 30 - F = 75 \times 1.25 \quad$ (using '$F = ma$')

$$F = 79.5 \, \text{N}$$

Using $F = \mu R$: $\quad \mu = \dfrac{79.5}{635} = 0.125$

Coefficient of friction $= 0.125$

Exercise 5A

1. Each of the following diagrams shows all the forces acting on a body causing it to accelerate as shown.

   Find the magnitude of the unknown force P.

   (a) 10 kg ⟶ P
   ⟶ 2 ms^{-2}

   (b) 15 N ⟵ 10 kg ⟶ P
   ⟶ 3 ms^{-2}

   (c) 5 kg, ↑ P, ↑ 2 ms^{-2}, ↓ $5g$ N

   (d) 5 kg, ↑ P, ↓ 2 ms^{-2}, ↓ $5g$ N

   (e) 15 N ⟵ 4 kg ⟶ P, ⟶ 10 N
   ⟶ 2.5 ms^{-2}

   (f) 10 N ⟵ 4 kg ⟶ P, ⟶ 5 N
   ⟶ 3 ms^{-2}

2. Each of the following diagrams shows all the forces acting on a body causing it to accelerate in the direction shown.

   Find the magnitude of the acceleration.

   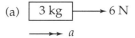

   (a) 3 kg ⟶ 6 N ⟶ a

   (b) 5 N ⟵ 2 kg ⟶ 8 N ⟶ a

   (c) 4 N ⟵ 5 kg ⟶ 10 N, ⟶ 6 N ⟶ a

   (d) 6 N ⟵, 4 N ⟵ 5 kg ⟶ 20 N ⟶ a

3. The engine of a car of mass 1000 kg which is travelling along a straight horizontal road, is producing a driving force of 1500 N. Assuming there are no forces resisting the motion, calculate the acceleration of the car.

4. A resultant force of 12 N causes a body to accelerate at $4\,\text{ms}^{-2}$. Find the mass of the body.

5. A car of mass 500 kg accelerates uniformly from rest to $10\,\text{ms}^{-1}$ in a distance of 25 m.

   Find (a) the acceleration of the car

   (b) the magnitude of the accelerating force.

6. A bullet of mass 0.01 kg is fired into a block of wood with a velocity of $400\,\text{ms}^{-1}$. It penetrates a distance of 0.2 m.

   Find (a) the deceleration of the bullet

   (b) the resistance of the wood, assuming it to be uniform.

7. A van of mass 1000 kg is moving along a horizontal road with a constant velocity of $20\,\text{ms}^{-1}$. If the truck experiences resistances of 800 N, what is the driving force of the van?

8. A car of mass 600 kg is accelerated uniformly from $10\,\text{ms}^{-1}$ to $30\,\text{ms}^{-1}$ in 12 s. If the total resistances to motion are 500 N, find the driving force of the car.

9. A case of mass 20 kg, which is initially at rest on a smooth horizontal surface, is pulled by a horizontal force of 30 N. Find the time taken for the case to attain a speed of $3\,\text{ms}^{-1}$.

10. A trunk of mass 40 kg is being dragged along a horizontal floor by a horizontal force of 150 N. If the acceleration of the case is $0.2\,\text{ms}^{-2}$, calculate the frictional force between the floor and the trunk.

11. A sledge of mass 25 kg is pulled along a smooth frozen lake by a rope which is pulled at an angle of 30° to the horizontal. If the sledge accelerates at 1.5 ms⁻², find the tension in the rope and the normal reaction force.

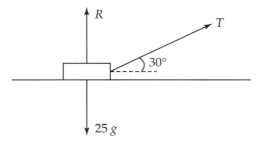

12. A string is attached to a block of mass 30 kg and is pulled with a tension of 120 N at an angle of 60° to the horizontal, so that the block accelerates at 0.8 ms⁻² along a rough horizontal surface.

    Draw a diagram showing all forces acting on the block. Find the coefficient of friction between the block and the surface.

13. A stone of mass m kg, slides in a straight line across a frozen pond. The initial speed of the stone is 6 ms⁻¹ and it slides 24 m before coming to rest.

    Draw a diagram showing all the forces acting on the stone.

    Calculate the coefficient of friction between the stone and the surface of the pond.

14. A van of mass 750 kg is travelling along a straight horizontal road with an acceleration of 2 ms⁻². The driving force exerted by the engine is 2000 N. Find the magnitude of the resistance to motion.

15. A crate of mass 5 kg is placed on the floor of a van. The coefficient of friction is 0.35. Find the greatest possible acceleration of the van if the crate is not to slip.

16.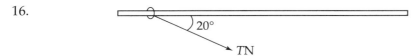

    A ring of mass 4 kg is threaded on a fixed rough horizontal rod. A light string, attached to the ring, is pulled with a force acting at 20° to the horizontal. If the coefficient of friction between the ring and the rod is 0.4, find the value of the force that is just sufficient to move the ring.

17. A box B of mass 50 kg is to be moved along a rough horizontal floor. The diagram shows two different ways a force can be applied to move the box.

    If the coefficient of friction between the box and the ground is 0.5, find the least values of forces X and Y to just move the box.

18. The combined mass of a boy and a sledge is 80 kg. A friend pulls a rope attached to the sledge, so it makes an angle of 25° with the horizontal. The coefficient of friction between the sledge and the ground is $\frac{2}{3}$. The sledge accelerates at $2\,\text{ms}^{-2}$. Find the force with which the friend is pulling the rope.

19. A horizontal force of 100 N is exerted on a crate of mass 20 kg lying on a rough horizontal surface. The coefficient of friction is 0.4.

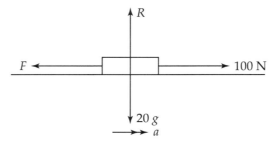

Find the acceleration of the block.

20.

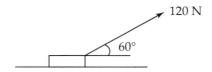

A rope is attached to a box of mass 30 kg and is pulled with a tension of 120 N at an angle of 60° to the horizontal, so the box accelerates at $0.8\,\text{ms}^{-2}$ along a rough horizontal surface. Complete the diagram showing all the forces and show that the coefficient of friction between the box and the surface is just less than $\frac{1}{5}$.

21. A body of mass 0.3 kg is suspended by a string from the roof of a van. The string makes an angle of 10° with the vertical. The van is moving horizontally with constant acceleration.

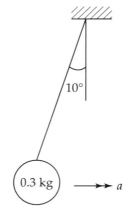

Draw a diagram showing all the forces acting on the body.

Find (a) the tension in the string.

(b) the acceleration of the body.

22. A crate of mass 10 kg is at rest on a rough horizontal surface. The coefficient of friction between the crate and the surface is 0.25. A horizontal force of magnitude P N is applied to the crate causing it to accelerate at $1.2\,\mathrm{ms}^{-2}$.

   (a) Find the value of P

   (b) When the crate reaches a speed of $5\,\mathrm{ms}^{-1}$, the force P is removed. Find the distance the crate then travels before coming to rest.

23. A stone of mass 0.6 kg is dropped into some water and falls vertically with an acceleration of $7\,\mathrm{ms}^{-2}$. Find the resistive force R acting on the stone.

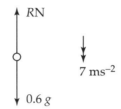

24. A load of mass 1000 kg is being lowered by a vertical cable. If the acceleration of the load is $2\,\mathrm{ms}^{-2}$ downwards, find the tension in the lift cable.

25. An empty lift of mass 500 kg is moving vertically upwards with an acceleration of $0.2\,\mathrm{ms}^{-2}$. Find the tension in the lift cable.

26.

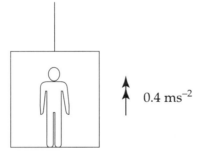

   A man of mass 90 kg travels in a lift. The acceleration of the lift is $0.4\,\mathrm{ms}^{-2}$ upwards.

   (a) Draw a diagram showing the forces exerted on the man.

   (b) Find the force exerted on the man by the floor of the lift.

   (c) What force does the man exert on the floor of the lift?

27. A lift of mass 450 kg contains a crate of mass 200 kg. When the lift is accelerating upwards at $2\,\mathrm{ms}^{-2}$, find

   (a) the force exerted on the crate by the floor of the lift.

   (b) the tension in the lift cable.

28. Repeat question **28** with the lift moving upwards with a deceleration of $2\,\mathrm{ms}^{-2}$.

5.2.3 Motion on an inclined plane

Example 1

A block of mass 50 kg lies on a rough slope inclined at 30° to the horizontal. The coefficient of friction between the block and the slope is $\frac{1}{3}$. A cable attached to the block is pulled with a force of 600 N in a direction parallel to the slope, so the block is accelerating up the slope. Find the acceleration of the block.

Assume the weight of the cable is negligible compared with the weight of the block.

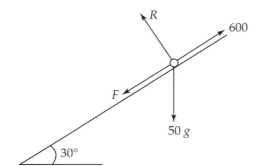

Note: the block is accelerating up the slope so the friction force acts down the slope to oppose motion.

Resolve forces parallel and perpendicular to the plane:

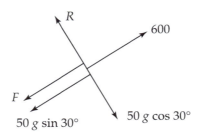

Perpendicular to the slope: $\qquad R = 50\,g \cos 30°$
$$= 424\,\text{N}$$

Friction: $\qquad F = \mu R$
$$= \tfrac{1}{3} \times 424$$
$$= 141\,\text{N}$$

Parallel to the slope, using $F = ma$:
$$600 - (141 + 50 \times 9.8 \times \sin 30) = 50a$$
$$214 = 50a$$
$$a = 4.28$$
Acceleration $= 4.28\,\text{ms}^{-2}$.

Example 2

A body of mass 2 kg is released from rest on a rough surface inclined at an angle θ to the horizontal, where $\tan \theta = \frac{3}{4}$. If after 3 seconds the body is moving with a speed of 6 ms^{-1}, find the coefficient of friction between the body and the surface.

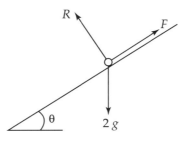

Find the angle: $\tan \theta = \dfrac{3}{4}$

$\theta = 36.9°$

or, using Pythagoras: $\sin \theta = \dfrac{3}{5}$ and $\cos \theta = \dfrac{4}{5}$

(3, 4, 5 △)

Find the acceleration: $u = 0, \quad v = 6, \quad a = ?, \quad t = 3$

$$v = u + at$$

$$6 = 0 + a \times 3$$

$$a = 2 \,\text{ms}^{-2}$$

Resolve forces into components parallel and perpendicular to the plane.

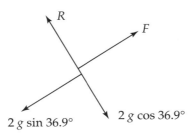

Perpendicular to the slope: $R = 2 \times 9.8 \cos 36.9$

$= 15.7 \,\text{N}$

Parallel to the slope using $F = ma$:

$$2 \times 9.8 \sin 36.9 - F = 2 \times 2$$

$$11.8 - F = 4$$

$$F = 7.8 \,\text{N}$$

(note that F in the question stands for friction, while in $F = ma$, F stands for resultant force).

Coefficient of friction: $\mu = \dfrac{7.8}{15.7}$

$= 0.497$

Example 3

A block of mass 45 kg lies on a rough slope inclined at 10° to the horizontal. A string is attached to the block and is pulled with a force of 500 N at 25° to the horizontal in order to pull the block directly up the slope with an acceleration $3\,\text{ms}^{-2}$. Find the coefficient of friction between the block and the slope.

Note: In questions like this, which look complicated, always draw a clear diagram. Then there are plenty of marks available for clear working out such as resolving forces parallel and perpendicular to the plane, writing an equation for each direction and using $F = \mu R$.

The angle the 500 N force makes with the plane is $25° - 10° = 15°$.
Resolve all forces into components parallel and perpendicular to the plane. Remember that the component next to the angle uses $\cos\theta$.

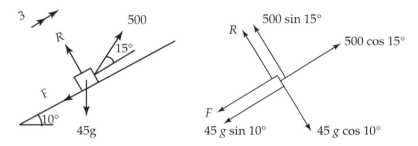

Perpendicular to the slope:

$$R + 500 \sin 15° = 45 \times 9.8 \cos 10°$$

$$R = 305\,\text{N}$$

Parallel to the plane, using $F = ma$:

$$500 \cos 15° - F - 45 \times 9.8 \sin 10° = 45 \times 3$$

$$483 - F - 76.6 = 135$$

$$F = 271\,\text{N}$$

$$\text{Coefficient of friction} = \dfrac{271}{305} \quad \left(= \dfrac{F}{R}\right)$$

$$= 0.89$$

Exercise 5B

1. A particle of mass 5 kg, initially at rest, slides down a smooth slope inclined at 25° to the horizontal.

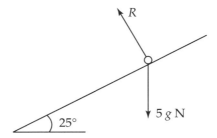

Find (a) the force the slope exerts on the particle
(b) the acceleration of the particle
(c) the velocity of the particle after 3 seconds.

2. A particle of mass 8 kg is released from rest on a smooth plane inclined at 35° to the horizontal.

Find (a) the acceleration of the particle
(b) the velocity of the particle when it has travelled 4 m down the plane.

3. A particle of mass 10 kg is sliding down a smooth inclined plane with an acceleration 4.9 ms^{-2}. Find the angle of inclination of the plane.

4. Each of the following diagrams shows a particle of mass 5 kg accelerating along a smooth inclined plane in the direction shown. All forces acting are shown.

Find the unknown forces, accelerations and angles.

In parts (a), (b), (c) find P. In part (d) find θ and a.

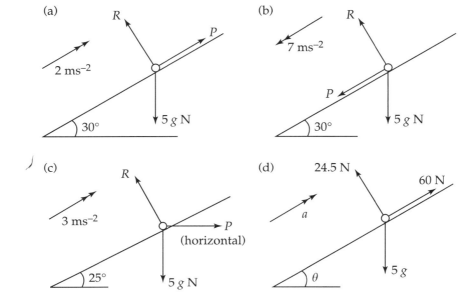

5. Each of the following diagrams shows a particle of mass 5 kg accelerating along a rough inclined plane in the direction shown.

   Find (i) the normal reaction between the plane and the particle

   (ii) the friction force

   (iii) the coefficient of friction.

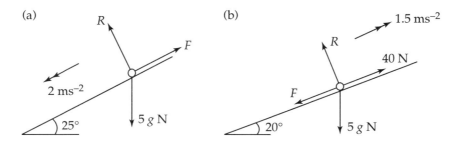

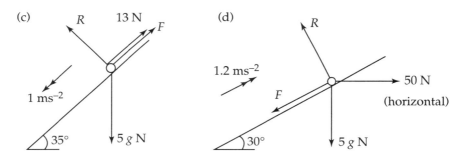

6. A particle of mass 3 kg rests on a rough plane inclined at 20° to the horizontal. The coefficient of friction between the particle and the plane is 0.5. Find the acceleration of the particle when it experiences a force of 30 N applied along the line of greatest slope up the plane.

7. A particle of mass 3 kg is released from rest on a rough plane inclined at an angle θ to the horizontal, where $\sin \theta = 0.6$. After a time of 4 seconds the particle has a speed of 6 ms^{-1}.

   (a) Find the acceleration of the particle.

   (b) Draw a diagram showing all the forces acting on the particle.

   (c) Find the coefficient of friction between the particle and the plane.

8. A body of mass 5 kg rests on a rough plane which is inclined at 40° to the horizontal. The coefficient of friction between the body and the plane is 0.45.

   Find the horizontal force PN which must be applied to the box so:

   (a) the body is on the point of moving up the plane

(b) the body is on the point of moving down the plane
(c) the body moves up the plane with an acceleration of $2\,\text{ms}^{-2}$.

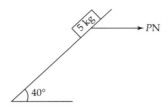

9. The diagram shows the forces acting on a particle on a rough inclined plane, with coefficient of friction between the particle and the plane of 0.4.

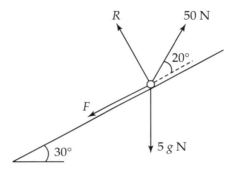

If the particle is accelerating up the plane

(a) draw a diagram showing all the components of the forces parallel and perpendicular to the plane
(b) find the normal reaction R
(c) find the friction force F
(d) find the acceleration of the particle.

10. A body of mass 5 kg is released from rest on a rough plane inclined at an angle θ to the horizontal, where $\sin\theta = 0.6$. After travelling a distance of 2 m the velocity of the body is $3\,\text{ms}^{-1}$. Find:

(a) the acceleration of the body
(b) the coefficient of friction between the body and the plane.

11.

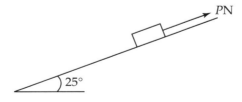

The diagram shows a crate of mass 6 kg at rest on a plane inclined at 25° to the horizontal, under the action of a force of magnitude P N acting up the plane. The coefficient of friction between the crate and the plane is 0.3.

(a) If the crate is on the point of sliding down the plane find the value of P.
(b) If the force P is removed, find the acceleration of the crate.

103

12. A rough plane is inclined at 10° to the horizontal. A coin of mass m kg, is projected with a speed of $3\,\text{ms}^{-1}$ directly up the plane. The coefficient of friction between the coin and the plane is 0.15.

    (a) Find the distance moved by the coin moving up the plane.

    (b) Will the coin stop completely or will it move back down the plane? Justify your answer.

13. A particle of mass 2 kg is released from rest at the top of a rough plane inclined at 30° to the horizontal. If the particle moves a distance of 1.5 m in a time of 1.2 seconds find:

    (a) the acceleration of the particle

    (b) the coefficient of friction between the plane and the particle.

14. A boy of mass 35 kg starts from rest and slides down a straight slide. The slide is inclined at an angle of 30° to the horizontal and its length is 5 m.

    The coefficient of friction between the boy and the slide is 0.2. Find

    (a) the acceleration of the boy

    (b) his speed at the bottom of the slide.

5.2.4 Connected particles

Example 1

Two particles of mass 5 kg and 3 kg are on a smooth horizontal plane and are connected by a light inextensible string, which is taut. The 5 kg particle is pulled by a horizontal force P and the particles move with an acceleration of $0.6\,\text{ms}^{-2}$. Find:

(a) the tension in the string

(b) the magnitude of P.

Only the horizontal forces will be shown in the diagrams.

We can consider forces on each particle or on the whole system. Each particle has the same velocity and acceleration.

When applying Newton's second law to an individual particle, the tension is included in the equation, because in this situation it acts as an external force.

However, when dealing with the whole system the tension forces are internal forces and are not included in the equation.

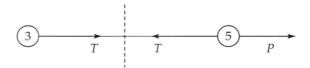

(a) Applying $F = ma$ to the 3 kg particle:
$$T = 3 \times 0.6 = 1.8$$
$$\text{Tension} = 1.8\,\text{N}$$

(b) Applying $F = ma$ to the whole system:
$$P = (5+3) \times 0.6 = 4.8\,\text{N}$$

Example 2

Two particles of mass 10 kg and 5 kg are connected by a taut string and rest on a rough horizontal surface. The 10 kg particle is pulled by a horizontal force of 90 N. If the coefficient of friction between each particle and the surface is 0.3, find the acceleration of the system and the tension in the string.

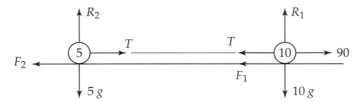

First find the friction forces by resolving vertically and using $F = \mu R$

10 kg: $\quad R_1 = 10g$

$\quad\quad\quad F_1 = 0.3 \times R_1$

$\quad\quad\quad F_1 = 0.3 \times 10 \times 9.8 = 29.4\,\text{N}$

5 kg: $\quad R_2 = 5g$

$\quad\quad\quad F_2 = 0.3 R_2$

$\quad\quad\quad F_2 = 0.3 \times 5 \times 9.8 = 14.7\,\text{N}$

Apply $F = ma$ to the whole system:
$$90 - 29.4 - 14.7 = (10 + 5)a$$
$$a = 3.06$$

The acceleration of the whole system $= 3.06\,\text{ms}^{-2}$

Apply $F = ma$ to the 5 kg mass:
$$T - 14.7 = 5 \times 3.06$$
$$T = 30$$

The tension in the string $= 30\,\text{N}$

Example 3

A car of mass 1000 kg is towing a caravan of mass 800 kg along a straight horizontal road at a constant speed. The resistance force on the car is 200 N and on the caravan 500 N. Calculate:

(a) the force on the caravan from the tow-bar.

(b) the driving force on the car.

(c) The car then brakes causing a deceleration of $1.5\,\text{ms}^{-2}$. Assuming the driving force is now zero, calculate the force exerted on the car by the tow-bar. Is this force a thrust or a tension?

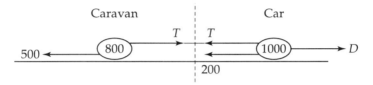

(a) At constant speed there is no resultant force on the caravan so (Newton's third law), so:
$$T = 500$$
Force on the caravan $= 500\,\text{N}$

(b) At constant speed the resultant force on the system is zero (Newton's third law) so:
$$D = 200 + 500 = 700$$
Driving force $= 700\,\text{N}$

(c) Draw a new diagram for the new situation and if T is in the wrong direction it will come out negative.

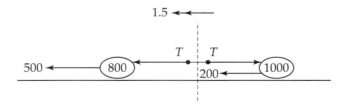

Applying $F = ma$ to the caravan:
$$500 + T = 800 \times 1.5$$
$$T = 700$$

Force exerted on the car by the tow bar $= 700\,\text{N}$

This force is a thrust as T is positive in the direction shown on our diagram.

Example 4

A car of mass 1000 kg is towing a caravan of mass 500 kg along a straight level road. When the car and caravan are accelerating at $2\,\text{ms}^{-2}$, they experience resistances to motion of 600 N and 400 N respectively. Find:

(a) the driving force exerted by the car's engine

(b) the tension in the tow-bar joining the car to the caravan.

(c) The car and caravan then come to a hill inclined at angle α to the horizontal, where $\sin\alpha = \frac{1}{15}$. Assuming the driving force and resistances to motion remain the same, find the acceleration of the car and caravan up the hill.

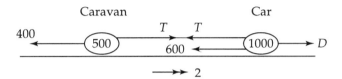

(a) Applying $F = ma$ to the whole system:

$$D - 600 - 400 = (1000 + 500) \times 2$$

$$D = 4000$$

Driving force $= 4000\,\text{N}$

(b) Applying $F = ma$ to the caravan:

$$T - 400 = 500 \times 2$$

$$T = 1400$$

Tension in the tow bar $= 1400\,\text{N}$

(c) A new diagram is needed for going up the hill.

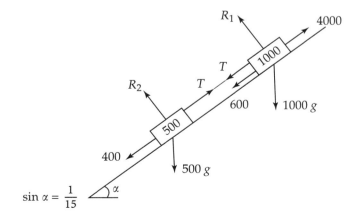

The components of the weight down the hill have now got to be taken into account. If we consider the whole system, the forces acting along the hill are:

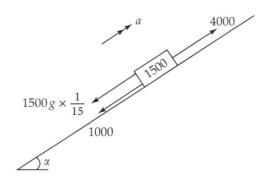

Applying $F = ma$: $\quad 4000 - 1000 - 1500g \times \dfrac{1}{15} = 1500a$

$$a = 1.35$$

$$\text{Acceleration} = 1.35\,\text{ms}^{-2}$$

Example 5

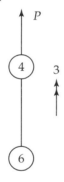

The diagram shows particles of mass 4 kg and 6 kg suspended by strings. A force P is applied to the upper string causing the particles to accelerate upwards at $3\,\text{ms}^{-2}$.

(a) Find the tension in the string joining the two particles.

(b) Find the magnitude of the force P.

Draw a diagram showing all the forces acting on the particles.

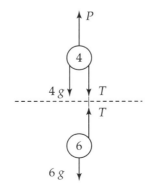

(a) Applying $F = ma$ to the 6 kg particle:

$$T - 6g = 6 \times 3$$

$$T = 76.8$$

$$\text{Tension} = 76.8\,\text{N}$$

(b) Applying $F = ma$ to the whole system:

$$P - 4g - 6g = (6 + 4) \times 3$$

$$P = 128$$

$$\text{Force } P = 128\,\text{N}$$

Exercise 5C

1. Two particles of masses 3 kg and 2 kg resting on a smooth horizontal surface, are connected by a light inextensible string. A force of 20 N is applied to the 2 kg mass as shown.

   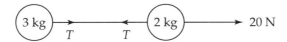

   Find (a) the acceleration

   (b) the tension in the string

2. Repeat question 1 given that the surface is now rough, with the coefficient of friction between the surface and each particle being 0.25.

3. A car of mass 1500 kg tows a trailer of mass 750 kg along a straight horizontal road. The resistance to motion of the car is 800 N and that of the trailer 400 N. If the car and trailer are accelerating at 0.8 ms^{-2} find:

   (a) the driving force produced by the engine

   (b) the tension in the tow bar.

   If the car and trailer now move at a constant speed of 20 ms^{-1}, find:

   (c) the driving force produced by the engine

   (d) the tension in the tow bar.

4. A car of mass 1000 kg tows a trailer of mass 600 kg along a straight horizontal road. The resistance to motion of the car is 300 N and that of the trailer 100 N.

   The driver applies the brakes and the braking force exceeds the driving force by 400 N. Find the deceleration of the car and trailer. Find the magnitude of the force in the tow bar and state whether this force is a tension or a thrust.

5. A car of mass 1200 kg tows a caravan of mass 800 kg along straight horizontal road. If the driving force from the engine is 17.5 KN and the resistances experienced by the car and caravan are 7.5 KN and 2.5 KN respectively, find

   (a) the acceleration of the car and caravan

   (b) the force transmitted through the tow bar.

6. An engine of mass 250 tonnes pushes a coach of mass 40 tonnes with an acceleration of 0.23 ms^{-2}.

   (a) Draw diagrams showing the forces acting on

   (i) the engine

   (ii) the coach

   (b) Neglecting resistances, find the force transmitted through the coupling and the driving force from the engine.

7.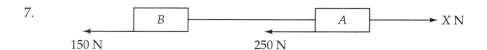

Two trucks A and B, of masses 900 kg and 750 kg respectively, are connected by a horizontal coupling. An engine pulls, the trucks along a straight horizontal truck by exerting a force of magnitude X newtons on truck A. The resistance to motion of truck A, excluding the tension in the coupling, is 250 N and the resistance to motion of truck B is 150 N.

(a) Given the trucks are moving at constant speed, find:

   (i) the tension in the coupling between the trucks,

   (ii) the value of X.

(b) If $X = 750\,\text{N}$ find the acceleration of the trucks and the tension in the coupling.

8. A tug tows three barges in line and has an acceleration of $0.03\,\text{ms}^{-2}$. Each barge has a mass of 90 tonnes. The water offers a resistance of 15 kN to each barge. The towing ropes are horizontal and along the line of the barges.

(a) By considering the three barges as one object, find the tension in the rope between the front barge and the tug.

(b) By considering individual barges, find the tension in each rope connecting the barges.

9. A breakdown van of mass 2500 kg is towing a car of mass 1500 kg along a straight horizontal road. The two vehicles are joined by a tow bar which remains parallel to the road. The van and car experience constant resistances to motion of 1000 N and 300 N respectively. The driving force on the van is 2600 N.

Find: (a) the magnitude of the acceleration of the van and the car

(b) the tension in the tow bar.

10. Two loads, connected by a rope, are suspended from a crane cable as shown. A force of 15 kN is applied by the crane cable and the loads accelerate upwards.

Find the acceleration of the system and the tension in the rope.

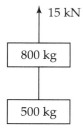

What assumptions have you made about the crane cable and the rope?

11. A particle of mass 3 kg is suspended by a string. A second particle of mass 4 kg is suspended from the first particle by a second string. The particles are raised 20 m in 4 seconds starting from rest. Find the tension in each string.

12. The diagram shows masses of 3 kg and 6 kg hanging at rest on light vertical strings.

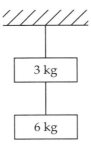

    Find the tension in each string.

13. The diagram shows two boxes of mass 20 kg and 15 kg resting on a horizontal table, with the 15 kg box on top of the 20 kg box.

    Find the reaction between the two boxes and that between the 20 kg box and the table.

14. A car of mass 900 kg is towing a trailer mass 500 kg up a hill inclined at an angle of 10° to the horizontal. The car's engine exerts a driving force of 8000 N and the car and trailer experience resistances to motion of 1500 N and 800 N respectively.

    Find (a) the acceleration of the car and trailer
    (b) the tension in the tow bar.

5.2.5 Connected particles over pulleys

In all examples the following mathematical modelling assumptions will apply:

1. All pulleys are smooth. The tension in the string is the same on each side of the pulley.

2. Strings, ropes and cables are assumed to be light compared with the other masses involved. This means that the weight of the string is not included in the equations of motion.

3. Strings etc. are assumed to be inextensible. This means that the velocities and accelerations of particles either side of the pulley are the same.

4. All objects can be modelled as particles so the weight acts through a point and there is no rotation.

5. All strings on inclined planes are assumed to go up the line of greatest slope. This means the string will go directly up the plane and not at some angle across it.

Example 1

Particles of mass 2 kg and 4 kg are connected by a light, inextensible string, which passes over a smooth, fixed pulley. The particles are released from rest when the 4 kg particle is a distance 1.5 m above the ground. Find:

(a) the acceleration of the system

(b) the tension in the string

(c) the force exerted on the pulley by the string

(d) the speed with which the 4 kg particle hits the ground.

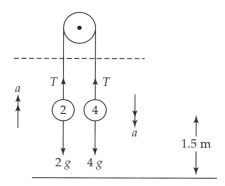

The heavier particle will accelerate downwards and the lighter particle will accelerate upwards.

(a) For each particle separately, define the direction of the acceleration as positive.
Using $F = ma$ for both particles:

4 kg: $\qquad 4g - T = 4a \qquad$ ...(1)

2 kg: $\qquad T - 2g = 2a \qquad$ ...(2)

Adding these two equations to eliminate T gives:

$$4g - 2g = 4a + 2a$$

$$2g = 6a$$

$$a = 3.27$$

Acceleration $= 3.27 \text{ ms}^{-2}$

(b) Using equation (2): $\qquad T = 2 \times 3.27 + 2g$

$$= 26.1 \text{ N}$$

Tension $= 26.1 \text{ N}$

(c)

$$\text{The force exerted on the pulley} = 2T$$
$$= 2 \times 26.1$$
$$= 52.2\,\text{N}$$

(d) The acceleration is constant so we can use a uniform acceleration equation.

$$u = 0,\ v = ?,\ a = 3.27,\ s = 1.5$$
$$v^2 = u^2 + 2as$$
$$v^2 = 2 \times 3.27 \times 1.5$$
$$v = 3.13$$

The 4 kg mass hits the ground at a speed of $3.13\,\text{ms}^{-1}$.

Example 2

Two particles are connected by a string which passes over a smooth pulley. One particle of mass m kg rests on a smooth horizontal surface, while the other, of mass M kg, hangs freely. When the particles are released, find in terms of g:

(a) the acceleration of the system

(b) the tension in the string.

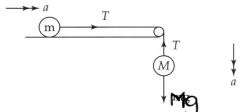

Note that the surface is smooth so there is no friction.

Applying $F = ma$ to both particles:

M kg: $\qquad\qquad Mg - T = Ma \qquad\qquad \ldots (1)$

m kg: $\qquad\qquad T = ma \qquad\qquad \ldots (2)$

113

Adding (1) and (2)
$$Mg = Ma + ma$$
$$= (M+m)a$$
$$\text{Acceleration, } a = \frac{Mg}{M+m}$$

Using (2):
$$\text{Tension } T = \frac{mMg}{M+m}$$

Example 3

Two particles P and Q of mass 2 kg and 3 kg respectively, are connected by a string which passes over a pulley. Particle P lies on a rough horizontal table and particle Q hangs freely 2 m above the ground. The coefficient of friction between P and the table is 0.3. The system is released from rest. Find:

(a) the acceleration of the system

(b) the speed with which Q hits the ground.

(c) the total distance P travels along the table before it comes to rest. Assume P does not hit the pulley.

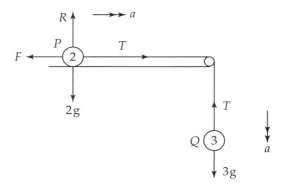

(a) The table is rough so we have to find the friction force.

Resolving vertically for P: $\qquad R = 2g$

Friction: $\qquad F = \mu R$
$$F = 0.3 \times 2g = 5.88 \text{ N}$$

Applying $F = ma$ for P: $\qquad T - 5.88 = 2a \qquad \ldots(1)$

Applying $F = ma$ for Q: $\qquad 3g - T = 3a \qquad \ldots(2)$

Add (1) and (2): $\qquad 3g - 5.88 = 3a + 2a$
$$23.3 = 5a$$
$$a = 4.70$$

Acceleration of the system $= 4.70 \text{ ms}^{-2}$

(b) The acceleration is constant:
$$u = 0, v =?, a = 4.70, s = 2$$
$$v^2 = u^2 + 2as$$
$$v = 4.34$$

Speed Q hits the ground $= 4.34\,\text{ms}^{-1}$

Note: In all these types of question where one particle hits the floor, or the string breaks, it is usually necessary to find this intermediate speed before considering the subsequent motion of the other particle.

(c) We need to draw a new diagram to consider the forces now acting on P. The string is now slack.

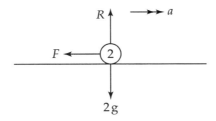

The friction force is unchanged so $F = 5.88$ N.

Taking the positive direction to the right and applying $F = ma$:
$$-5.88 = 2a$$
$$a = -2.94\,\text{ms}^{-2}$$

This is a deceleration as expected.

We know the initial speed of P, because it is the same speed with which Q hit the floor.

$u = 4.34, v = 0$ (comes to rest), $a = -2.94, s =?$
$$v^2 = u^2 + 2as$$
$$0 = (4.34)^2 - 2 \times 2.94\,s$$
$$s = 3.20$$

Q originally fell 2 m so the total distance that P moves $= 3.20 + 2$
$$= 5.20\,\text{m}$$

Exercise 5D

In this section several modelling assumptions are made:

   (i) all strings are light and inextensible
  (ii) all pulleys are smooth, light and fixed
 (iii) all strings are along the line of greatest slope of inclined planes
  (iv) all hanging strings hang vertically
   (v) no particle hits a pulley
  (vi) all bodies are modelled as particles
 (vii) the string is taut
(viii) no air resistance

1. Two particles of masses 5 kg and 3 kg are connected by a string which passes over a pulley.

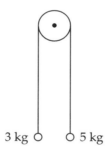

   Find (a) the acceleration of the system

   (b) the tension in the string

   (c) state how you have used the modelling assumption that the string is inextensible.

   (d) state how you have used the modelling assumption that the pulley is smooth.

2. Particles of mass 4 kg and 2 kg are attached to a string which passes over a pulley. The particles are released from rest with the 4 kg particle 3 m above the ground.

   Find (a) the acceleration of the system

   (b) the speed of the 4 kg particle hits the ground

   (c) the force on the pulley.

3. Two particles P and Q, of masses 7 kg and 3 kg respectively are attached to the ends of a string which passes over a pulley. P is 2 m above the ground.

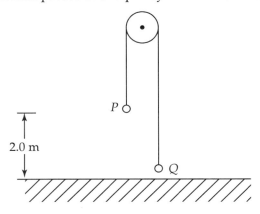

The particles are released from rest. Find

(a) the acceleration of the system
(b) the speed with which P hits the ground
(c) the greatest height of Q above the floor.

4. A string which passes over a smooth peg, has masses of 2 kg and 5 kg tied to its ends. The system starts from rest and after the 5 kg mass has fallen for 2 seconds it lands on a horizontal platform and does not rebound.

(a) What is the acceleration when both are moving?
(b) How far does the 5 kg mass fall?
(c) Find the speed of the 5 kg mass hits the platform?
(d) After what further time will the string again become taut?

5. Particles P and Q are attached to a string which passes over a pulley. The system is released from rest and particle P, of mass 5 kg, drops 3 m in a time of 1.5 seconds.

Find (a) the acceleration of the system
      (b) the tension in the string
      (c) the mass of particle Q

6. A mass of 6 kg lies on a smooth horizontal table. It is connected by a string which passes over a pulley to another mass of 3 kg, which is hanging freely.
Find the acceleration of the system

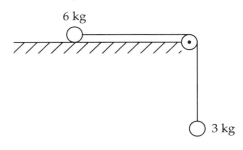

117

7. The table in question 6 is rough, with coefficient of friction between the mass and the table being $\frac{1}{4}$.

    (a) Draw a diagram showing the forces acting on each particle.
    (b) Write down an equation of motion for each mass.
    (c) Find the acceleration of the system.
    (d) Find the tension in the string.
    (e) Find the force exerted on the pulley.

8.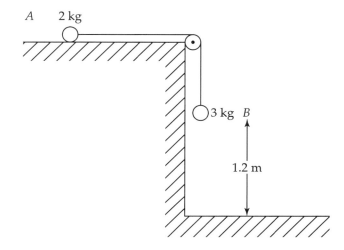

    Two particles A and B of masses 2 kg and 3 kg respectively, are connected by a string which passes over a pulley at the end of a rough horizontal table. The coefficient of friction between A and the table is 0.4. The particles are released from rest with B at a distance 1.2 m above the ground.

    (a) Write down an equation of motion for each particle.
    (b) Find the acceleration of the system before B hits the ground
    (c) Find the speed with which B hits the ground.

    When B hits the ground it does not rebound and A continues moving towards the pulley. Assuming A does not reach the pulley before coming to rest

    (d) Draw a diagram showing the forces acting on A now.
    (e) Find the deceleration of A.
    (f) Find the distance moved by A after the string becomes slack.

9. A mass of 10 kg, resting on a rough table at a distance 3 m from the edge, is connected by a string to a 5 kg mass hanging vertically. The system starts from rest and after 2 seconds the 10 kg mass reaches the edge of the table.

    (a) Show the acceleration of the masses is $1.5\,\mathrm{ms}^{-2}$.
    (b) Find the frictional force acting on the 10 kg mass and show the coefficient of friction is 0.27.

10. The diagram shows two particles P and Q of mass 1.2 kg and 1.5 kg respectively, which are connected by a string which passes over a pulley.

   P is held on a smooth horizontal table a distance of 2 m from the pulley.

   Q hangs freely a distance of 1 m above the floor.

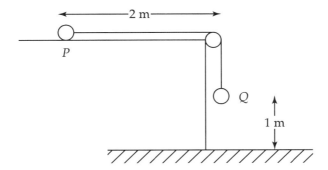

   P is released from rest.

   (a) Find the acceleration of the system before Q hits the floor.

   (b) Find the speed with which Q hits the floor.

   (c) Find the total time taken by P before it hits the pulley.

   (d) Identify three mathematical modelling assumptions used.

5.2.6 Connected particles over a pulley on an inclined plane

Example 4

The diagram shows two particles connected by a light inextensible string passing over a fixed smooth pulley. The particle of mass 5 kg is held at rest on the plane on a plane inclined at 40° to the horizontal. The particle of mass 6 kg hangs freely. The system is released from rest with the string taut.

(a) Write down an equation of motion for each particle.

(b) Find the acceleration of the system.

(c) Find the tension in the string.

(d) Assuming nothing impedes their motion find the speed of the particles after a time of 2 seconds.

(e) At this time the string breaks. Find the further distance the 5 kg mass moves up the plane.

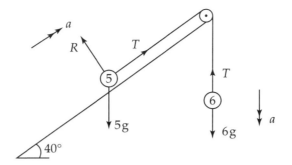

(a) There is no friction on a smooth surface.
The component of weight down the plane is $5\,\text{g} \times \sin 40$.

5 kg: $\qquad T - 5\,\text{g} \times \sin 40 = 5a \qquad \ldots(1)$

6 kg: $\qquad 6\,\text{g} - T = 6a \qquad \ldots(2)$

(b) Add equations (1) and (2):

$$6\,\text{g} - 5\,\text{g} \times \sin 40 = 11a$$

$$a = 2.48$$

$$\text{Acceleration} = 2.48\,\text{ms}^{-2}$$

(c) Substitute for a in (1):

$$T - 5\,\text{g} \times \sin 40 = 5 \times 2.48$$

$$T = 43.9$$

$$\text{Tension} = 43.9\,\text{N}$$

(d) $\qquad u = 0,\, v = ?,\, a = 2.48,\, t = 2$

$$v = u + at$$

$$v = 0 + 2.48 \times 2$$

$$v = 4.96$$

After 2 seconds speed of each particle $= 4.96\,\text{ms}^{-1}$

(e) When the string breaks, we need a new diagram showing the forces on the 5 kg particle.

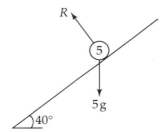

The force is directed down the plane and the acceleration is directed up.

Using $F = ma$:
$$5g \times \sin 40 = 5a$$
$$a = -6.30 \text{ ms}^{-2}$$

Uniform acceleration equation with $v = 0$ because the particle comes to rest:
$$u = 4.96, v = 0, a = -6.30, s = ?$$
$$v^2 = u^2 + 2as$$
$$0 = 4.96^2 - 2 \times 6.30 \, s$$
$$s = 1.95$$

The 5 kg mass moves a further distance of 1.95 m

Example 5

A particle A of mass 3 kg is connected to particle B of mass 5 kg, by a light inextensible string which passes over a smooth pulley. A is held on a rough plane inclined at an angle 30° to the horizontal. B hangs freely a distance 2 m above the floor. The string between A and the pulley is along the line of greatest slope of the plane. Time for B to reach the floor is 2.5 secs. The system is released from rest with the string taut. Find:

(a) the acceleration of the system

(b) the coefficient of friction between A and the plane

(c) the speed with which B hits the floor

(d) the total distance A moves up the plane (assuming it does not reach the pulley).

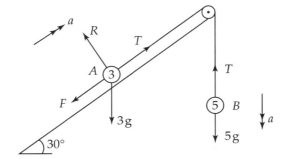

(a) The forces are constant so the acceleration is uniform.
$$u = 0, a = ?, s = 2, t = 2.5$$
$$s = ut + \frac{1}{2}at^2$$
$$2 = \frac{1}{2}a(2.5)^2$$
$$a = 0.64$$
$$\text{Acceleration} = 0.64 \text{ ms}^{-2}$$

(b) Applying $F = ma$ to B:
$$5g - T = 5a \quad \ldots(1)$$

The forces on A resolved parallel and perpendicular to the plane are:

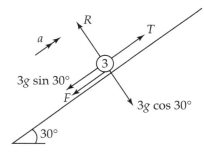

Resolving perpendicular to the plane:
$$R = 3g \cos 30°$$
$$= 25.5\,\text{N} \quad \ldots(2)$$

Applying $F = ma$ parallel to the plane:
$$T - 3g \sin 30° - F = 3a \quad \ldots(3)$$

Add equations (1) and (3):
$$5g - 3g \sin 30° - F = 8a$$
$$= 8 \times 0.64$$
$$= 5.12$$
$$F = 29.2\,\text{N}$$

The coefficient of friction:
$$\mu = \frac{F}{R}$$
$$= \frac{29.2}{25.5}$$
$$= 1.15$$

(c) $u = 0, v = ?, a = 0.64, s = 2$
$$v^2 = u^2 + 2as$$
$$v^2 = 0 + 2 \times 0.64 \times 2$$
$$v = 1.6$$

Speed B hits the floor $= 1.6\,\text{ms}^{-1}$

(d) The string is now slack. A new diagram is needed to consider the forces now acting on A.

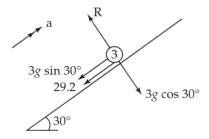

The friction force is unchanged at 29.2 N. Taking the positive direction up the plane and applying $F = ma$ to A:

$$-(3g \sin 30 + 29.2) = 3a$$

$$a = -14.6 \, \text{ms}^{-2}$$

The initial speed of A when B hits the floor is 1.6 ms.

$$u = 1.6, v = 0, a = -14.6, s = ?$$

$$v = u + 2as$$

$$0 = 1.6^2 - 2 \times 14.6 \, \text{ms}$$

$$S = 0.09 \, \text{m}$$

The total distance A moves up the plane $= 2 + 0.09 = 2.09 \, \text{m}$

Example 6

In example 5 the forces exerted on the pulley by the string are shown in the diagram.

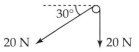

Find the force exerted on the pulley by the string.

Resolve the forces horizontally and vertically and let F be the magnitude of the force and θ the angle it makes with the horizontal.

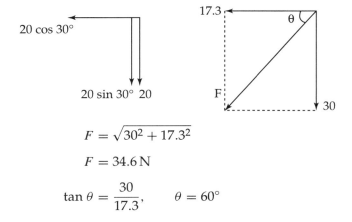

$$F = \sqrt{30^2 + 17.3^2}$$

$$F = 34.6 \, \text{N}$$

$$\tan \theta = \frac{30}{17.3}, \quad \theta = 60°$$

Exercise 5E

1. Each of the following diagrams shows all the forces acting on two particles connected by a string which passes over a smooth pulley. One of the particles is on a *smooth* inclined plane and the other is hanging freely.

   Find the acceleration and the tension in the string in each case.

   (a)   (b)

   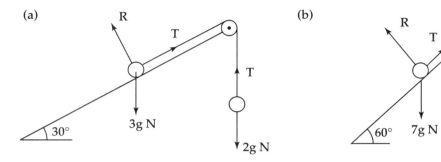

2. Two particles A and B of mass 4 kg and 3 kg respectively, are connected by a string which passes over a smooth peg at the top of a smooth plane inclined at 30° to the horizontal. Particle A lies on the plane at a distance of 1.5 m from the pulley. Particle B hangs vertically.

   The system is released from rest. Find

   (a) the acceleration of the system

   (b) the speed with which A hits the pulley.

3.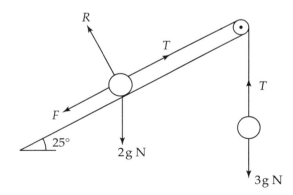

   The diagram shows all the forces acting on 2 particles connected by a string which passes over a pulley. The particle of mass 2 kg rests on a rough inclined plane, coefficient of friction 0.4. The system is released from rest.

   Find (a) the normal reaction R

   (b) the friction force F

   (c) the acceleration of the system

   (d) the tension in the string

4. Two particles P and Q of mass 3 kg and 5 kg respectively, are connected by a light inextensible string, which passes over a smooth pulley. P is held at rest on a smooth plane inclined at an angle of 35° to the horizontal and Q hangs freely.

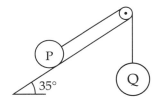

When P is released find:

(a) the acceleration of the system

(b) the tension in the string.

5. Each of the following diagrams shows 2 particles connected by a string which passes over a pulley. One particle is on a rough inclined plane, coefficient of friction 0.35, while the other particle hangs freely.

Find the acceleration of the system in each case.

Find also the force the string exerts on the pulley.

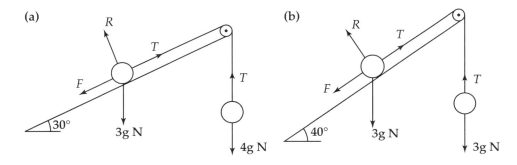

6. A particle P of mass m kg rests on a rough plane inclined at angle θ, where $\sin \theta = \frac{3}{5}$. The coefficient of friction between the particle and the plane is $\frac{1}{4}$. Particle P is connected to a particle Q of mass $2m$ kg by a string which passes over a pulley at the top of the plane. Particle Q hangs freely.

Show the acceleration of the system is $\frac{2}{5} g$ ms^{-2}.

7. A particle of mass 3 kg rests on a rough plane inclined at angle θ, where $\sin \theta = 0.6$. The coefficient of friction between the particle and the plane is 0.2. A string connected to this particle passes over a pulley at the top of the plane. Another particle of mass m kg hangs freely from the other end of the string. If the system accelerates at 2 ms^{-2}, find the unknown mass m kg.

Identify three mathematical modelling assumptions used.

8.

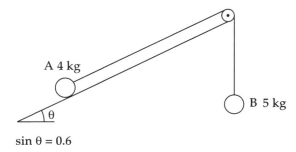

$\sin \theta = 0.6$

Particle A rests on a rough inclined plane, and is connected by a string to particle B, which is hanging freely.

When the system is released from rest. Particle B moves downwards with an acceleration $2\,\text{ms}^{-2}$ and A moves up the plane.

(a) Draw a diagram showing all the forces acting on the particles

(b) By considering particle B, find the tension in the string

(c) Find the force exerted on A by the plane

(d) Write down an equation of motion for A

(e) Find the coefficient of friction between A and the plane.

9. In question 8, explain how you have used the following mathematical models

(a) A and B are particles

(b) The string is light

(c) The string is inextensible

(d) The pulley is smooth.

10.

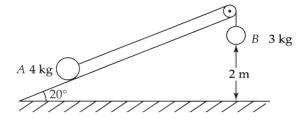

The diagram shows 2 particles, one on a rough inclined plane and the other hanging freely 2 m above a horizontal floor. The coefficient of friction between A and the plane is 0.3.

The system is released from rest.

(a) Find the acceleration of the system.

(b) Find the speed with which B hits the floor.

(c) Draw a diagram showing the forces acting on A after B hits the plane and find the deceleration of A.

(d) Find the total distance A moves up the plane.

11.

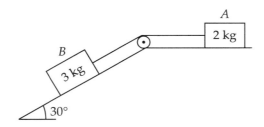

Particles A and B of mass 2 kg and 3 kg respectively, are connected by a string passing over a pulley. Particle A is held on a rough horizontal table with the coefficient of friction between the table and A being 0.3. Particle B rests on a smooth plane inclined at 30° to the horizontal.

The particle A is released from rest and the system accelerates.

(a) Find the acceleration of the system.

(b) When each particle has moved a distance 0.5 m the string breaks. Given that A comes to rest before reaching the pulley, find the total distance moved by A.

12. A block of weight 125 N rests on a rough slope which is inclined at 60° to the horizontal. A string is attached to the block and passes over a smooth pulley at the top of the slope so the string is parallel to the slope. The other end of the string is attached to a weight of 50 N which hangs freely.

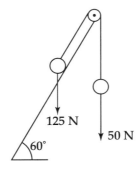

The 125 N weight is on the point of slipping *down* the slope.

(a) Draw a diagram showing all the forces

(b) By resolving vertically for the 50 N weight, find the tension in the string.

(c) By resolving parallel to the slope for the 125 N weight find the frictional force

(d) Find the normal reaction and the coefficient of friction.

13. A block of weight 100 N rests on a smooth slope which is inclined at an angle α to the horizontal. A string is attached to the block and passes over a smooth pulley at the top of the slope so the string is parallel to the slope. The other end of the string is attached to a weight of 50 N which hangs freely.

The system is in equilibrium.

(a) Draw a diagram showing all the forces

(b) Find the tension in the string

(c) Find the angle α.

14.

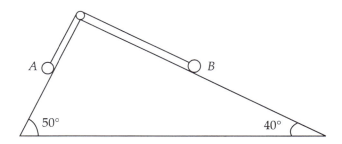

Two particles A and B of mass 5 kg and 3 kg respectively are connected by a string over a pulley. A lies on a rough plane inclined at 50° to the horizontal and B lies on a smooth plane inclined at 40° to the horizontal. The coefficient of friction between A and the plane is 0.2.

Draw a diagram showing all the forces acting on A and B.

Find the acceleration of the system when it is released.

5.2.7 Application of vectors

Example 1

Forces of $(6\mathbf{i} + 7\mathbf{j})$ N, $(5\mathbf{i} - 2\mathbf{j})$ N and $(-2\mathbf{i} + \mathbf{j})$ N act on a particle of mass 3 kg.

(a) Find the acceleration of the particle in vector form.

(b) Find the angle the acceleration makes with the vector **i**.

(c) Find the speed after 3 seconds. *when the initial speed is $(2\mathbf{i} - 3\mathbf{j})$ ms^{-1}*

(a) Using $\mathbf{F} = m\mathbf{a}$ in column vector form:

$$\begin{pmatrix} 6 \\ 7 \end{pmatrix} + \begin{pmatrix} 5 \\ -2 \end{pmatrix} + \begin{pmatrix} -2 \\ 1 \end{pmatrix} = 3\mathbf{a}$$

$$\begin{pmatrix} 9 \\ 6 \end{pmatrix} = 3\mathbf{a}$$

$$\mathbf{a} = \begin{pmatrix} 3 \\ 2 \end{pmatrix}$$

Acceleration $= (3\mathbf{i} + 2\mathbf{j})$ ms^{-2}

(b)

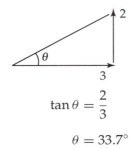

$$\tan \theta = \frac{2}{3}$$

$$\theta = 33.7°$$

(c) The acceleration is constant:

$$\mathbf{u} = \begin{pmatrix} 2 \\ -3 \end{pmatrix}, \mathbf{v} = ?, \mathbf{a} = \begin{pmatrix} 3 \\ 2 \end{pmatrix}, t = 3$$

Using $\mathbf{v} = \mathbf{u} + \mathbf{a}t$, $\quad \mathbf{v} = \begin{pmatrix} 2 \\ -3 \end{pmatrix} + 3 \begin{pmatrix} 3 \\ 2 \end{pmatrix} = \begin{pmatrix} 11 \\ 3 \end{pmatrix}$

Speed after 3 seconds $= \sqrt{11^2 + 3^2} = 11.4 \, \text{ms}^{-1}$

Note: There are further examples on the use of vectors in Part 8.

Exercise 5F

1. A particle of mass 2 kg is accelerating at $(5\mathbf{i} + 2\mathbf{j}) \, \text{ms}^{-2}$. Find in vector form the resultant force acting on the particle.

2. Find in vector form the acceleration produced in a body of mass 5 kg by a resultant force of $(20\mathbf{i} - 15\mathbf{j}) \, \text{N}$.

3. Find in vector form the acceleration produced in a body of mass 2 kg by forces
   $\mathbf{F}_1 = (3\mathbf{i} - 4\mathbf{j}) \, \text{N} \qquad \mathbf{F}_2 = (5\mathbf{i} + 6\mathbf{j}) \, \text{N}$

4. Forces of $(6\mathbf{i} - 2\mathbf{j}) \, \text{N}$, $(-2\mathbf{i} + 7\mathbf{j}) \, \text{N}$ and $(5\mathbf{i} + \mathbf{j}) \, \text{N}$ act on a particle of mass 3 kg.

   (a) Find the magnitude of the acceleration

   (b) Find the angle which the resultant force makes with the vector $\mathbf{i}$.

   (c) If the initial velocity of the particle is $(6\mathbf{i} + \mathbf{j}) \, \text{ms}^{-1}$ find the speed after 2 seconds.

5. A resultant force acts on a particle of mass 3 kg for 2 seconds. During this time the velocity of the particle changes from $(-2\mathbf{i} + 5\mathbf{j})$ to $(4\mathbf{i} + \mathbf{j}) \, \text{ms}^{-1}$.
   Find the resultant force in vector form.

6. A particle of mass 5 kg is initially at rest on a smooth horizontal plane. A force $\mathbf{F} = (-10\mathbf{i} + 15\mathbf{j}) \, \text{N}$ acts on the particle for 12 seconds. Find

   (a) the acceleration of the particle

   (b) the velocity of the particle after 12 seconds

   (c) the displacement of the particle relative to its initial position, after 12 seconds.

7. Two forces $F_1 = (7i + 10j)$ N and $F_2 = (4i - 6j)$ N act on a particle of mass 2 kg. A force F_3 also acts on the particle.

   (a) If the particle moves with constant velocity, find F_3.

   (b) If the particle moves with an acceleration $(3i + 4j)$ ms^{-2}, find F_3.

Examination Exercise 5

1. A small stone moves horizontally in a straight line across the surface of an ice rink. The stone is given an initial speed of 7 ms^{-1}. It comes to rest after moving a distance of 10 m. Find

   (a) the deceleration of the stone while it is moving,

   (b) the coefficient of friction between the stone and the ice. [E]

2. A tile on a roof becomes loose and slides from rest down the roof. The roof is modelled as a plane surface inclined at 30° to the horizontal. The coefficient of friction between the tile and the roof is 0.4. The tile is modelled as a particle of mass m kg.

   (a) Find the acceleration of the tile as it slides down the roof.

   The tile moves a distance 3 m before reaching the edge of the roof.

   (b) Find the speed of the tile as it reaches the edge of the roof.

   (c) Write down the answer to part (a) if the tile had mass $2m$ kg. [E]

3. A car which has run out of petrol is being towed by a breakdown truck along a straight horizontal road. The truck has mass 1200 kg and the car has mass 800 kg. The truck is connected to the car by a horizontal rope which is modelled as light and inextensible. The truck's engine provides a constant driving force of 2400 N. The resistances to motion of the truck and the car are modelled as constant and of magnitude 600 N and 400 N respectively. Find

   (a) the acceleration of the truck and the car,
   (b) the tension in the rope.

   When the truck and car are moving at 20 ms^{-1}, the rope breaks. The engine of the truck provides the same driving force as before. The magnitude of the resistance to the motion of the truck remains 600 N.

   (c) Show that the truck reaches a speed of 28 ms^{-1} approximately 6 s earlier than it would have done if the rope had not broken. [E]

4. A car of mass 1200 kg tows a caravan of mass 600 kg along a level road by means of a light horizontal towbar. The resistances to the motion of the car and the caravan are $2R$ newtons and R newtons respectively, where R is a constant. Given that the car is accelerating at $0.6\,\text{ms}^{-2}$ and that the engine of the car is exerting a driving force of 1500 N,

   Find the tension in the towbar. [E]

5.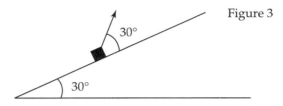

   Figure 3

   A small parcel of mass 2 kg moves on a rough plane inclined at an angle of $30°$ to the horizontal. The parcel is pulled up a line of greatest slope of the plane by means of a light rope which is attached to it. The rope makes an angle of $30°$ with the plane, as shown in Fig. 3. The coefficient of friction between the parcel and the plane is 0.4.

   Given that the tension in the rope is 24 N,

   (a) find, to 2 significant figures, the acceleration of the parcel.

   The rope now breaks. The parcel slows down and comes to rest.

   (b) Show that, when the parcel comes to this position of rest, it immediately starts to move down the plane again.

   (c) Find, to 2 significant figures, the acceleration of the parcel as it moves down the plane after it has come to this position of instantaneous rest. [E]

6.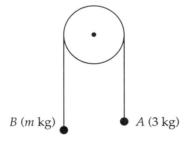

   The diagram shows two particles A and B, connected by a light inextensible string passing over a smooth fixed pulley. The mass of A is 3 kg, and the mass of B is m kg, where $m < 3$. The system is released from rest with the string taut, and the acceleration of each particle is $2.2\,\text{ms}^{-2}$. Find

   (a) the tension in the string.

   (b) the value of m,

   (c) the force exerted on the pulley by the string.

   (d) State how you have used the modelling assumption that the pulley is smooth. [E]

7.

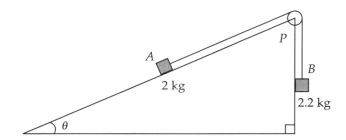

A parcel A of mass 2 kg rests on a rough slope inclined at an angle θ to the horizontal, where $\tan\theta = \frac{3}{4}$. A string is attached to A and passes over a small smooth pulley fixed at P. The other end of the string is attached to a weight B of mass 2.2 kg, which hangs freely, as shown in the diagram. The parcel A is in limiting equilibrium and about to slide up the slope. By modelling A and B as particles and the string as light and inextensible, find

(a) the normal contact force acting on A,

(b) the coefficient of friction between A and the slope [E]

8.

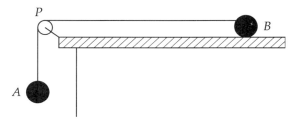

The horizontal surface of a fixed bench is rough. A smooth small pulley P is fixed at an edge of the bench as shown in the diagram. A particle B, of mass 0.5 kg, is placed on the bench at a distance of 1.96 m from P. A light inextensible string is attached to B, passes over P, and has a particle A of mass 0.2 kg hanging freely at the other end. The system is released from rest with the string taut. The particle B moves along the bench with an acceleration of magnitude 0.98 ms^{-2} reaching P after time t seconds.

(a) Find the value of t.

For the motion before B reaches P, find

(b) the tension in the string,

(c) the coefficient of friction between the particle B and the bench,

(d) the magnitude of the resultant force exerted by the string on the pulley P, giving your answer to 2 significant figures. [E]

9.

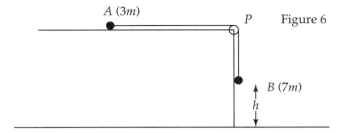

Figure 6

Two particles A and B, of mass $3m$ and $7m$ respectively, are connected by a light inextensible string. Particle A is placed on a rough horizontal table and the coefficient of friction between A and the table is $\frac{1}{3}$. The string passes over a small smooth pulley P fixed at the edge of the table and B hangs freely below P. The particles are released from rest with both sections of the string taut and B at a distance h above the ground, as shown in Fig. 6.

For the period before B hits the ground,

(a) state which information above implies that the magnitudes of the accelerations of the two particles are the same,

(b) write down an equation of motion for each particle and hence find the acceleration of each particle.

When B hits the ground, it does not rebound and A continues moving towards P. Assuming that A does not reach P before coming to rest,

(c) find, in terms of h, the distance moved by A after the string becomes slack.

[E]

10.

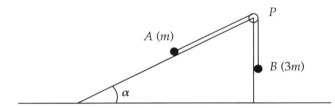

A particle of mass m rests on a rough plane inclined at an angle α to the horizontal, where $\tan \alpha = \frac{3}{4}$. The particle is attached to one end of a light inextensible string which lies in a line of greatest slope of the plane and passes over a small light smooth pulley P fixed at the top of the plane. The other end of the string is attached to a particle B of mass $3m$, and B hangs freely below P, as shown in the diagram. The particles are released from rest with the string taut. The particle B moves down with acceleration of magnitude $\frac{1}{2}g$. Find

(a) the tension in the string,

(b) the coefficient of friction between A and the plane. [E]

11.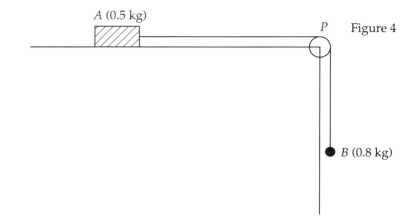

A block of wood A of mass 0.5 kg rests on a rough horizontal table and is attached to one end of a light inextensible string. The string passes over a small smooth pulley P fixed at the edge of the table. The other end of the string is attached to a ball B of mass 0.8 kg which hangs freely below the pulley, as shown in Figure 4. The coefficient of friction between A and the table is μ. The system is released from rest with the string taut. After release, B descends a distance of 0.4 m in 0.5 s. Modelling A and B as particles, calculate

(a) the acceleration of B,

(b) the tension in the string,

(c) the value of μ.

(d) State how in your calculations you have used the information that the string is inextensible. [E]

12. A particle P has mass 3 kg and moves in a horizontal plane under the action of a constant horizontal force. The velocity of P is initially $(2\mathbf{i} + 9\mathbf{j})$ ms^{-1}, and 2 s later is $(5\mathbf{i} + 3\mathbf{j})$ ms^{-1}, where $\mathbf{i}$ and $\mathbf{j}$ are perpendicular horizontal unit vectors.
Find

(a) the magnitude of the horizontal force acting on P, giving your answer in N to 1 decimal place,

(b) the angle this force makes with the vector $\mathbf{j}$, giving your answer in degrees to 1 decimal place. [E]

13. A particle P, of mass 3 kg, moves under the action of two constant forces $(6\mathbf{i} + 2\mathbf{j})$ N and $(3\mathbf{i} - 5\mathbf{j})$ N.

(a) Find, in the form $(a\mathbf{i} + b\mathbf{j})$ N, the resultant force **F** acting on P.

(b) Find, in degrees to one decimal place, the angle between **F** and $\mathbf{j}$.

(c) Find the acceleration of P, giving your answer as a vector.

The initial velocity of P is $(-2\mathbf{i} + \mathbf{j})$ ms^{-1}.

(d) Find, to 3 significant figures, the speed of P after 2 s. [E]

14. A breakdown van of mass 2000 kg is towing a car of mass 1200 kg straight horizontal road. The two vehicles are joined by a towbar remains parallel to the road. The van and the car experience cons resistances to motion of magnitudes 800 N and 240 N respectively constant driving force acting on the van of 2320 N. Find

    (a) the magnitude of the acceleration of the van and the car,

    (b) the tension in the towbar.

    The two vehicles come to a hill inclined at an angle of α to the horizontal, where $\sin \alpha = \frac{1}{20}$. The driving force and the resistances to motion are unchanged.

    (c) Find the magnitude of the acceleration of the van and the car as they move up the hill and state whether their speed increases or decreases. [E]

15. A man travels in a lift to the top of a tall office block. The lift starts from rest on the ground floor and moves vertically. It comes to rest again at the top floor, having moved a vertical distance of 27 m. The lift initially accelerates with a constant acceleration of 2 ms^{-2} until it reaches a speed of 3 ms^{-1}. It then moves with a constant speed of 3 ms^{-1} for T seconds. Finally it decelerates with a constant deceleration for 2.5 s before coming to rest at the top floor.

    (a) Sketch a speed-time graph for the motion of the lift.

    (b) Hence, or otherwise, find the value of T.

    (c) Sketch an acceleration-time graph for the motion of the lift.

    The mass of the man is 80 kg and the mass of the lift is 120 kg. The lift is pulled up by means of a vertical cable attached to the top of the lift. By modelling the cable as light and inextensible, find

    (d) the tension in the cable when the lift is accelerating,

    (e) the magnitude of the force exerted by the lift on the man during the last 2.5 s of the motion. [E]

Part 6

Momentum and impulse

In this part, all bodies can generally be modelled as particles, and all strings are light and inextensible.

6.1 Momentum and impulse

If a constant force F is applied to a particle of mass m then:

$$F = ma \qquad \text{(Newton's second law)}$$

$$a = \frac{v-u}{t} \qquad \text{(uniform acceleration)}$$

Combining these:
$$F = \frac{m(v-u)}{t}$$

$$Ft = mv - mu$$

The quantity mass × velocity is called the momentum of the particle.
The quantity force × time is called the impulse of the force on the particle.

∴ Impulse = final momentum − initial momentum

The unit of both impulse and momentum is newton-second or Ns.
Both impulse and momentum are vector quantities: one depends on force, the other on velocity.

6.2 Change in momentum

Example 1

Find the magnitude of the change in momentum of a particle of mass 5 kg when its speed changes from:

(a) $4\,\text{ms}^{-1}$ to $10\,\text{ms}^{-1}$ in the same direction

(b) $4\,\text{ms}^{-1}$ to $10\,\text{ms}^{-1}$ in the opposite direction.

(a) Diagrams should always be drawn.

Initial motion	Final motion
⑤ ⟶ 4	⑤ ⟶ 10
Initial momentum $= mu$	Final momentum $= mv$
$= 5 \times 4$	$= 5 \times 10$
$= 20\,\text{Ns}$	$= 50\,\text{Ns}$

Change in momentum $= 50 - 20 = 30\,\text{Ns}$

(b) initial motion   Final motion
    ⑤ ⟶ 4   10 ⟵ ⑤

Direction is important here. Take the positive direction of velocity to the left, in the direction of the final motion.

Initial momentum = mu Final momentum = mv
$$= 5 \times (-4)$$ $$= 10 \times 5$$
$$= -20\,\text{Ns}$$ $$= 50\,\text{Ns}$$

Change in momentum = $mv - mu$
$$= 50 - (-20)$$
$$= 70\,\text{Ns}$$

6.3 Impulse

Example 2

A body of mass 4 kg is initially at rest. A force of 8 N acts on the body for 2 seconds. Find:

(a) the magnitude of the impulse given to the body

(b) the final velocity of the body.

(a) Impulse = Ft
$$= 8 \times 2$$
$$= 16\,\text{Ns}$$

(b) Initial motion   Final motion
    ④ ⟶ 0   ④ ⟶ v

Impulse = $mv - mu$
$$16 = 4v - 0$$
$$v = 4$$

The final velocity = $4\,\text{ms}^{-1}$

Example 3

A ball of mass 0.3 kg hits a vertical wall with a speed of $20\,\text{ms}^{-1}$. It rebounds with a speed of $15\,\text{ms}^{-1}$. Find the impulse exerted on the ball by the wall.

Take the positive direction of velocity to the left, in the direction of the final motion.

Initial momentum $= mu$ Final momentum $= mv$

$$= 0.3 \times (-20) \qquad\qquad = 0.3 \times 15$$
$$= -6 \, \text{Ns} \qquad\qquad\qquad = 4.5 \, \text{Ns}$$

$$\text{Impulse} = mv - mu$$
$$= 4.5 - (-6)$$
$$= 10.5 \, \text{Ns}$$

The impulse on the ball is 10.5 Ns to the left.

Example 4

A ball of mass 0.25 kg is travelling horizontally at 20 ms^{-1}, when it is hit straight back at 30 ms^{-1}. If the impact lasts 0.02 seconds, what is the average force on the ball?

Initial motion Final motion

Take the velocity to the left, in the direction of the final motion, as positive.

$$\text{Impulse} = mv - mu$$
$$\mathbf{F} \times 0.02 = 0.25 \times 30 - 0.25 \times (-20)$$
$$= 12.5$$
$$\mathbf{F} = 625$$

The average force = 625 N in the direction of the final motion.

Exercise 6A

1. Find the magnitude of the momentum of the following in kg ms^{-1}.

    (a) A man of mass 80 kg running at 8 ms^{-1}

    (b) A car of mass 1500 kg travelling at 120 kmh^{-1}

    (c) A train of mass 150 tonnes travelling at 25 ms^{-1}

    (d) A particle of mass 2 kg moving at 100 ms^{-1}

2. A van of mass 1200 kg accelerates form rest to 25 ms^{-1}. Find the gain in momentum.

3. A car of mass 1500 kg travelling at 30 ms^{-1} comes to rest. Find the loss in momentum.

4.

                before   after
                → 4 ms⁻¹   → 8 ms⁻¹
  I →   [3 kg]   [3 kg]

A particle of mass 3 kg moving with a speed 4 ms⁻¹ is acted on by an impulse which increases its speed to 8 ms⁻¹. Find the change in momentum of the particle and the magnitude of the impulse I received by the particle.

5. Find the magnitude of the impulse exerted on a ball when a force of 30 N acts on it for 0.15 seconds.

6. A body of mass 2 kg is at rest when it is given an impulse of 10 Ns.

Find the final speed of the body.

7.

                before   after
                → 0 ms⁻¹   → 5 ms⁻¹
    →   [4 kg]   [4 kg]
  15 N for t s

A box rests on a smooth horizontal surface. It has a mass 4 kg and a force of 15 N is applied for t seconds. If the speed of the box after the force is applied is 6 ms⁻¹, find t.

8. A man exerts a horizontal force for 1.5 seconds on a sledge of mass m kg lying at rest on a smooth horizontal surface. The sledge ends up moving with a speed of 6 ms⁻¹. If he applied a force 64 N then find m.

9. A ball of mass 0.4 kg is moving at 30 ms⁻¹. Find the speed of the ball after it receives an impulse of 20 Ns in the opposite direction to its motion.

10. A ball of mass 0.2 kg, travelling at 30 ms⁻¹, hits a vertical wall and rebounds with a speed of 20 ms⁻¹.

Find the impulse exerted by the wall on the ball, given that the ball is always moving at right angles to the wall.

      before   after
        → 30 ms⁻¹   20 ms⁻¹ ←
    (0.2 kg)   (0.2 kg)   I ←

11. A ball of mass 0.2 kg is dropped from a height of 2 m onto a horizontal floor. It then rebounds to a height of 1.5 m.

    Find (a) the speed with which the ball hits the ground

           (b) the speed with which the ball rebounds

           (c) the impulse given to the ball.

12. A gun fires a shot of mass 10 grams at a speed of 300 ms⁻¹. If the shot is in the gun for 0.008 seconds, find the force (assumed constant) acting on the shot.

6.4 Conservation of momentum

If two bodies A and B collide, the force exerted on B by A is equal and opposite to the force exerted on A by B (Newton's third law). A and B are in contact for the same time.

If no external forces are acting, A and B exert equal and opposite impulses on each other.

Therefore the gain in momentum of one body equals the loss in momentum of the other body.

Hence, if no external forces act:

Total momentum before collision = Total momentum after collision

This is known as the principal of conservation of linear momentum. It applies to collisions between bodies and to the separation of bodies.

6.5 Conservation of momentum for bodies colliding

Example 1

A railway truck of mass 2000 kg is travelling along a straight horizontal track with a speed of $5\,\text{ms}^{-1}$, when it collides with a stationary truck of mass 3000 kg. The trucks couple and move off together. Find their common speed after the collision.

before collision   after collision

$\boxed{2000} \longrightarrow 5 \quad \boxed{3000} \longrightarrow 0 \qquad \boxed{2000 + 3000} \longrightarrow v$

Total momentum after the collision = total momentum before the collision

$$5000\,v = 2000 \times 5 + 3000 \times 0$$

$$v = 2$$

The common speed after the collision $= 2\,\text{ms}^{-1}$

Example 2

Two trucks A and B have masses of 1200 kg and 800 kg respectively. They are moving in the same direction on a smooth horizontal track; A is moving at $6\,\text{ms}^{-1}$ and B at $3\,\text{ms}^{-1}$. As a result of the collision, the speed of A is reduced to $5\,\text{ms}^{-1}$. Find:

(a) the speed of B after the collision

(b) the magnitude of the impulse exerted by A on B.

(a) Total momentum after the collision = total momentum before the collision

$$1200 \times 5 + 800\,v = 1200 \times 6 + 800 \times 3$$

$$v = 4.5$$

The speed of B after the collision $= 4.5\,\text{ms}^{-1}$

(b) Impulse on B = final momentum of B − initial momentum of B

$$= 800 \times 4.5 - 800 \times 3$$

$$= 1200\,\text{Ns}$$

Example 3

A block of mass 10 kg travelling at $14\,\text{ms}^{-1}$ collides with another block of mass 8 kg travelling at $12\,\text{ms}^{-1}$ in the opposite direction. If the 10 kg block changes direction and rebounds with a speed of $3\,\text{ms}^{-1}$, find:

(a) the speed of the 8 kg block after the collision

(b) the magnitude of the impulse exerted on the 10 kg block.

before the collision   after the collision

(a) Take velocities to the right as positive.

Total momentum after the collision = total momentum before the collision

$$10 \times (-3) + 8v = 10 \times 14 + 8 \times (-12)$$

$$-30 + 8v = 140 - 96$$

$$v = 9.25$$

The speed of the 8 kg block $= 9.25\,\text{ms}^{-1}$

(b) The velocities of the 10 kg block are:

before the collision   after the collision

Take velocities to the left as positive

Impulse on the 10 kg block = (final momentum − initial momentum) of the 10 kg block

$$= 10 \times 3 - 10 \times (-14)$$

$$= 170\,\text{Ns}$$

Exercise 6B

1. The following diagrams show a collision between 2 particles. Find the unknown mass or velocity.

   before collision   after collision

   (a) $2\,\text{kg} \rightarrow 5\,\text{ms}^{-1}$ $3\,\text{kg} \rightarrow 2\,\text{ms}^{-1}$ $5\,\text{kg} \rightarrow v\,\text{ms}^{-1}$

   (b) $0.5\,\text{kg} \rightarrow 6\,\text{ms}^{-1}$ $1\,\text{kg} \rightarrow 0\,\text{ms}^{-1}$ $1.5\,\text{kg} \rightarrow v\,\text{ms}^{-1}$

   (c) $3\,\text{kg} \rightarrow 6\,\text{ms}^{-1}$ $1\,\text{ms}^{-1} \leftarrow 4\,\text{kg}$ $7\,\text{kg} \rightarrow v\,\text{ms}^{-1}$

   (d) $3\,\text{kg} \rightarrow 6\,\text{ms}^{-1}$ $4\,\text{kg} \rightarrow 1\,\text{ms}^{-1}$ $3\,\text{kg} \rightarrow 2\,\text{ms}^{-1}$ $4\,\text{kg} \rightarrow v\,\text{ms}^{-1}$

   (e) $0.1\,\text{kg} \rightarrow 6\,\text{ms}^{-1}$ $0.2\,\text{kg} \rightarrow 2\,\text{ms}^{-1}$ $0.1\,\text{kg} \rightarrow v\,\text{ms}^{-1}$ $0.2\,\text{kg} \rightarrow 4\,\text{ms}^{-1}$

   (f) $6\,\text{kg} \rightarrow 9\,\text{ms}^{-1}$ $m\,\text{kg} \rightarrow 2\,\text{ms}^{-1}$ $6\,\text{kg} \rightarrow 0\,\text{ms}^{-1}$ $m\,\text{kg} \rightarrow 5\,\text{ms}^{-1}$

   (g) $4\,\text{kg} \rightarrow 3\,\text{ms}^{-1}$ $2\,\text{ms}^{-1} \leftarrow 5\,\text{kg}$ $1\,\text{ms}^{-1} \leftarrow 4\,\text{kg}$ $5\,\text{kg} \rightarrow v\,\text{ms}^{-1}$

   (h) $m\,\text{kg} \rightarrow 7\,\text{ms}^{-1}$ $2\,\text{kg} \rightarrow 3\,\text{ms}^{-1}$ $m\,\text{kg} \rightarrow 2\,\text{ms}^{-1}$ $2\,\text{kg} \rightarrow 4\,\text{ms}^{-1}$

2. A railway truck of mass 2000 kg travelling at 6 ms^{-1} hits another truck of mass 2000 kg which is stationary. The trucks couple and go on together. With what speed do they move after the collision?

3. A particle of mass 4 kg moving at 5 ms^{-1} collides into a particle of mass 6 kg which is initially at rest. If the particles coalesce on impact find their speed after the collision.

4.   before collision   after collision
           $\rightarrow 12\,\text{ms}^{-1}$ $\rightarrow 7\,\text{ms}^{-1}$ $\rightarrow v\,\text{ms}^{-1}$ $\rightarrow 11.5\,\text{ms}^{-1}$
           $3\,\text{kg}$ $2\,\text{kg}$ $3\,\text{kg}$ $2\,\text{kg}$

   A particle of 3 kg moving at 12 ms^{-1} collides with a particle of mass 2 kg which is initially moving with a speed 7 ms^{-1} in the same direction. If the 2 kg particle moves off with speed 11.5 ms^{-1} in the same direction find the speed of the 3 kg particle after the collision.

5. A particle of mass 40 kg travels at 10 ms⁻¹ towards another particle of mass 30 kg travelling in the opposite direction with speed 8 ms⁻¹. If the 30 kg ends up travelling at 4 ms⁻¹ in the opposite direction to its initial speed, what is the speed of the 40 kg particle after impact?

6. A flat truck of mass 300 kg is moving horizontally at 4 ms⁻¹. A man of mass 75 kg drops vertically onto it from above. With what speed does it continue?

7.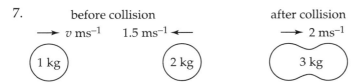

A mass of 1 kg is moving with speed v ms⁻¹. Another mass of 2 kg is moving in the opposite direction with a speed of 1.5 ms⁻¹. The masses collide directly, coalesce and move off with a speed of 2 ms⁻¹ in the original direction of the 1 kg mass. Find v.

8. A particle A of mass m kg moving with a speed 4 ms⁻¹, collides directly with another particle B of mass 5 kg, which is at rest.

   After the collision A moves with a speed 1.0 ms⁻¹ and B moves with a speed 1.5 ms⁻¹.

   Find m if:
   (a) A and B afterwards move in the same direction
   (b) A and B afterwards move in opposite directions.

9. A stone of mass 90 g is skidding across ice with a speed of 5 ms⁻¹. It hits another stone of mass 50 g travelling directly towards it with speed 3 ms⁻¹. On impact the stone of mass 90 g slows down to a speed of 2 ms⁻¹. Find the new speed of the other stone.

10. A body of mass 6 kg moving with speed 15 ms⁻¹ collides directly with another body of mass 4 kg moving with speed 10 ms⁻¹ in the opposite direction.

    Find the speed of the 4 kg body after the collision if the 6 kg body
    (a) comes to rest after the collision.
    (b) changes direction after the collision and moves with speed 2 ms⁻¹.
    (c) continues to move in the same direction with speed 4 ms⁻¹.
    (d) What is the maximum speed with which the 6 kg mass could move in the same direction after the collision?

11.

A and B have masses 3 kg and 2 kg respectively. They are moving in opposite directions, A with a speed of 2 ms⁻¹ and B with a speed of 4 ms⁻¹. They collide directly and after the collision B moves with a speed of $1\,\text{ms}^{-1}$ in the opposite direction. Find the speed of A after the collision and the direction in which it is moving.

12. The diagram shows two masses, $3\,m$ and $2\,m$, moving towards each other with speeds of $3u$ and $4u$ respectively. After they collide the $2\,m$ mass moves in the reverse direction with speed u.

Find the speed of the $3\,m$ mass in terms of u and state its direction of motion.

6.6 Conservation of momentum for bodies separating

Examples of bodies separating are a gun firing a shell and two space vehicles separating. In each case any forces acting are internal forces, not external forces.

In the case of a gun firing a shell, the gun exerts a force on the shell but the shell exerts an equal and opposite force on the gun, causing a recoil.

If a spacecraft separates from a rocket the same principle applies.

Example 1

A gun of mass 2000 kg fires a shell of mass 20 kg.

(a) if the shell has a speed through the air of $500\,\text{ms}^{-1}$, find the speed of recoil of the gun.

(b) find the constant force which would bring the recoiling gun to rest in a time of 2 seconds.

(a) before firing   after firing

Take the velocity to the left as positive.

$$\text{Total momentum after firing} = \text{total momentum before firing}$$
$$2000\,v - 20 \times 500 = 0$$
$$v = 5$$
$$\text{Speed of recoil} = 5\,\text{ms}^{-1}$$

(b) When the gun recoils an impulse is exerted on the gun to bring it to rest.

$$\text{Impulse on the gun} = \text{change in momentum of the gun}$$
$$\mathbf{F} \times 2 = 2000 \times 5$$
$$\mathbf{F} = 5000$$
$$\text{Force on the gun} = 5000\,\text{N}$$

Exercise 6C

1. A bullet of mass 0.03 kg is fired from a gun of mass 2 kg. The bullet leaves the gun with a speed of 400 ms^{-1}.

   Find the speed of recoil of the gun.

2. A gun of mass 3 kg fires a bullet of mass 40 g and recoils with a speed of 2.5 ms^{-1}. Find the speed of the bullet.

3. In an ice-dancing routine, a male dancer, of mass 75 kg, skates with a velocity of 4**i** ms^{-1} towards his female partner, of mass 45 kg, who is stationary. They cling to each other. Assuming resistances to motion are negligible, show that their common speed after they meet is 2.5**i** ms^{-1}.

   While travelling at this velocity, they then separate. Find the velocity of the female skater if:

   (a) the male skater has a velocity of 5.5**i** ms^{-1}.

   (b) they have equal speeds in opposite directions with the male skater travelling in the **i** direction.

4. Three astronauts A, B and C of equal mass are outside a space craft.

   Initially A, B and C are at rest with respect to each other.

   A applies an impulse **I** to B so that B moves with a speed of 4 ms^{-1} towards C. Find the speed of B and C if they move off together.

   B and C then push apart with the same impulse **I**. Find the new speeds of B and C.

6.7 Jerk in a string

If two particles A and B are connected by a light string which is initially slack and one particle is given an impulse so it moves away from the other particle, the string will become taut and there will be a jerk in the string.

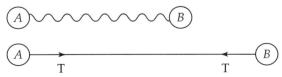

The jerk experienced by A will be equal and opposite to the jerk experienced by B. Hence momentum is conserved.

Example 1

Two particles A and B of mass 6 kg and 12 kg respectively, are connected by a light inextensible string. Initially they are at rest on a smooth horizontal surface with the string slack.
B is projected away from A with a speed of 3 ms^{-1}. Find:

(a) the common speed of A and B when the string jerks taut

(b) the magnitude of the impulse in the string when it jerks taut.

(a)
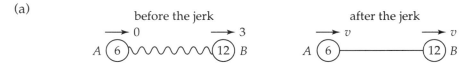

Total momentum after the jerk = total momentum before the jerk

$$6v + 12v = 12 \times 3$$

$$v = 2$$

The common speed $= 2 \text{ ms}^{-1}$

(b) The impulse in the string will be equal to the change in momentum of either A or B.

The impulse on A = final momentum of A − initial momentum of A

$$= 6 \times 2 - 6 \times 0 = 12$$

The impulse in the string $= 12 \text{ Ns}$

Exercise 6D

1. Two particles A and B of mass 2 kg and 5 kg are connected by a light inextensible string which is initially slack. A and B are at rest on a smooth horizontal table. A is projected horizontally directly away from B with a speed of 3.5 ms^{-1}. Find the common speed of the particles when the string becomes taut and the impulse in the string.

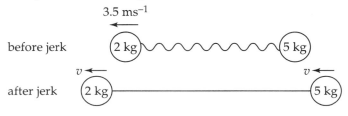

2. Two particles A and B of mass 1 kg and 2 kg respectively are connected by a light inextensible string which is initially slack. B is projected directly away

from A with a speed u ms^{-1}. Find u if the common speed of the two particles after the string becomes taut is 3 ms^{-1}. Find the impulse in the string when it jerks, tight.

3. Two buckets of mass 3 kg are suspended at rest by a string which passes over a fixed smooth horizontal bar. A brick of mass 1 kg is dropped into one of them from a height of 2.5 m.

Find the initial speed of the buckets.

6.8 Momentum and impulse in vector form

Just apply the impulse and momentum equations in vector form.

$$\text{Momentum} = mv$$
$$\text{Impulse } I = Ft = mv - mu$$

Example 1

A particle of mass 5 kg is moving with a velocity $2\mathbf{i}$ ms^{-1}, when it is acted on by a force of $5\mathbf{i}$ N for a time of 2 seconds. Find the new velocity of the particle.

initial motion　　　　　　　final motion

⑤ ⟶ u　　　　　　　⑤ ⟶ v

$$I = mv - mu$$
$$5\mathbf{i} \times 2 = 5v - 5 \times 2\mathbf{i}$$
$$10\mathbf{i} = 5v - 10\mathbf{i}$$
$$20\mathbf{i} = 5v$$

New velocity $v = 4\mathbf{i}$ ms^{-1}

Example 2

A particle of mass 10 kg has a velocity of $(6\mathbf{i} - 2\mathbf{j})$ ms^{-1}. A constant force acts on it for 2 seconds and changes its velocity to $(7\mathbf{i} + 3\mathbf{j})$ ms^{-1}. Find:

(a) the force in vector form

(b) the magnitude of the force.

(a)　　　　　　　　　　　$F = mv - mu$

In column vector form:　$F \times 2 = 10 \begin{pmatrix} 7 \\ 3 \end{pmatrix} - 10 \begin{pmatrix} 6 \\ -2 \end{pmatrix}$

$$F \times 2 = \begin{pmatrix} 70 \\ 30 \end{pmatrix} - \begin{pmatrix} 60 \\ -20 \end{pmatrix} = \begin{pmatrix} 10 \\ 50 \end{pmatrix}$$

The force:　$F = \begin{pmatrix} 5 \\ 25 \end{pmatrix}$ N　or　$F = 5\mathbf{i} + 25\mathbf{j}$

(b) Magnitude of the force:　$F = \sqrt{5^2 + 25^2} = 25.5$ N

Exercise 6E

1. A box of mass 4 kg has a velocity of $7\mathbf{i}$ ms^{-1}. If a force of $5\mathbf{i}$ N acts on the box for 3 seconds find the new speed of the box.

2. A particle of mass 10 kg is moving with a velocity $10\mathbf{i}$ ms^{-1}. A constant force acts on the particle for 5 seconds so that its new velocity is $-10\mathbf{i}$ ms^{-1}. Find the constant force acting on the particle.

3. A particle of mass 10 kg is moving with a velocity $(5\mathbf{i} - 3\mathbf{j})$ ms^{-1}. A constant force acts on the particle for 8 seconds so that afterwards it is moving with a velocity $(9\mathbf{i} + 5\mathbf{j})$ ms^{-1}. Find the constant force acting on the particle in the form $a\mathbf{i} + b\mathbf{j}$.

4. A body of mass 2 kg is moving with a velocity $(2\mathbf{i} - 5\mathbf{j})$ ms^{-1}. A constant force of $(4\mathbf{i} - 3\mathbf{j})$ N acts on the body for 6 seconds. Find the final velocity of the body in vector form and hence obtain its final speed.

5. A particle of mass 5 kg has velocity of $(5\mathbf{i} + 2\mathbf{j})$ ms^{-1}. A constant force acts on it for 4 seconds and changes its velocity to $(8\mathbf{i} - \mathbf{j})$ ms^{-1}. Find the force that was acting.

6.9 Further momentum and impulse questions

Example 1

A vertical post of mass 5 kg is to be driven into the ground. A pile-driver of mass 100 kg is released from rest from a height of 4 m above the top of the post.

(a) Find the speed with which the pile-driver hits the post.

(b) Assuming the pile-driver does not bounce off the post, find the speed with which the post enters the ground.

(c) If the combined mass comes to rest when the post has been driven into the ground to a depth 0.2 m, find the deceleration of the combined mass.

(d) Find the constant force with which the ground resists the post.

(a)
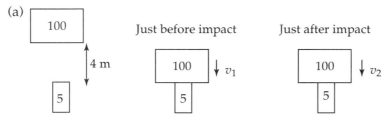

The 100 kg mass falls a distance of 4 m.

$+\downarrow \quad u = 0, v = v_1, a = 9.8$ ms^{-2}, $s = 4$ m

$$v^2 = u^2 + 2as$$
$$v_1^2 = 0 + 2 \times 9.8 \times 4$$
$$v_1 = \sqrt{78.4} \text{ ms}^{-1}$$

(b) In the impact momentum is conserved.

$$100\, v_1 = 105\, v_2$$
$$100 \times \sqrt{78.4} = 105\, v_2$$
$$v_2 = 8.433 \text{ ms}^{-1}$$

(c) Consider the motion of the pile-driver and post over a distance of 0.2 m until it comes to rest.

$+\downarrow \qquad u = 8.433, v = 0, s = 0.2, a = a_1$

$$v^2 = u^2 + 2as$$
$$0 = 8.433^2 + (2 \times a_1 \times 0.2)$$
$$a_1 = -177.8 \text{ ms}^{-2}$$

(d) The diagram shows the forces acting on the pile-driver and post.

Using $F = ma$,

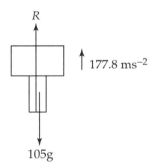

$$R - (105 \times 9.8) = 105 \times 177.8$$
$$R = 19698 \text{ N}$$

The ground resists the post with a force of 19700 N (3 sf).

Exercise 6F

1. A man exerts a horizontal force of 64 N for 1.5 seconds on a sledge of mass m kg lying at rest on a smooth horizontal surface. If the sledge ends up moving with a speed 6 ms^{-1}, then find m.

2.

Particles A and B of mass 5 kg and 3 kg are moving towards each other with speeds of 4 ms^{-1} and 6 ms^{-1} respectively.

After the collision the direction of motion of B is reversed and it is moving with speed 2 ms^{-1}.

Find the speed and direction of motion of A after the collision.

Find the magnitude of the impulse exerted on A by B.

3. Two small beads A and B of masses 0.06 kg and 0.04 kg respectively are moving towards each other on a smooth horizontal rail, A is moving with a speed of 0.8 ms^{-1} and B with a speed of 1.2 ms^{-1}. Bead A is brought to rest by the collision.

   (a) Find the speed of B immediately after the collision
   (b) Find the magnitude of the impulse exerted on A in the collision.

4. A particle of mass 40 kg travels at a speed 10 ms^{-1} towards another particle of mass 30 kg travelling in the opposite direction with speed 8 ms^{-1}. If the 30 kg mass ends up travelling at 3 ms^{-1} in the opposite direction, find the speed of the 40 kg mass after impact.

5. A particle of mass 3 kg moving at 12 ms^{-1} collides into a particle of mass 2 kg which is initially moving with speed 7 ms^{-1} in the same direction. If the 2 kg particle moves off with speed 10 ms^{-1}, find the speed of the 3 kg particle after the collision. Comment on the situation.

6.

   Particles of mass 5 m kg and 2 m kg are moving directly towards each other with speeds of u ms^{-1} and 2u ms^{-1} respectively.

   After the collision the particle of mass 2 m kg has speed u ms^{-1} in the opposite direction to which it was initially travelling. In terms of u, find the speed of the 5 m kg mass and the direction in which it is travelling.

   In terms of m and u find the magnitude of the impulse exerted on each particle.

7. Two particles P and Q of masses 5 kg and 2 kg respectively are moving towards each other. P is moving with a speed of 2 ms^{-1} and Q with a speed of 6 ms^{-1}.

   After the collision the speed of P is 0.5 ms^{-1} in the reverse direction.

   (a) Calculate the speed of Q after the collision.
   (b) State in which direction Q then moves.
   (c) Find the impulse exerted on particle P.

8. Particles of mass 6m and m are moving directly towards each other with speeds of u and 3u respectively. Immediately after they collide, the particle of mass m has a speed of u in the opposite direction. Find the speed of the particle of mass 6m in terms of u, immediately after the collision.

   Find also the impulse exerted on the smaller mass in terms of m and u.

9.

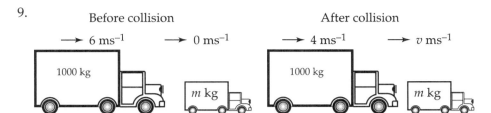

A truck A, of mass 1000 kg is moving with a speed of 6 ms^{-1} along a straight horizontal track. It collides with a stationary truck B. After the collision A continues in the same direction with a speed 4 ms^{-1}.

(a) Find the momentum of B after the collision.

(b) Show that the mass of B cannot exceed 500 kg.

10. Two particles A and B have masses of 1.2 kg and 0.8 kg respectively. They are initially at rest on a smooth horizontal table. Particle A is given an impulse of magnitude 6 Ns, so that it moves directly towards B.

(a) Find the speed of A.

Particles A and B then collide. The speed of A immediately after the collision is 2 ms^{-1}; its direction of motion being unchanged.

(b) Find the speed of B immediately after the collision.

(c) Find the magnitude of the impulse exerted on B in the collision. State clearly the units of impulse.

11. Two particles of mass $3m$ kg and $2m$ kg move towards each other with speeds of 5 ms^{-1} and 4 ms^{-1} respectively. After the collision the $2m$ kg mass has its direction of motion reversed and it is travelling with speed 2 ms^{-1}.

Find the speed and direction of motion of the $3m$ kg mass after the collision.

Find in terms of m the magnitude of the impulse exerted by the heavier particle on the lighter particle.

12. A vertical post of mass 6 kg is to be driven into the ground. A pile-driver of mass 84 kg is released from rest at a height 0.9 m above the top of the post.

(a) Show that the speed with which the pile-driver hits the post is 4.2 ms^{-1}.

(b) Assuming the pile-driver does not bounce off the post, find the speed with which the post enters the ground.

(c) If the combined mass comes to rest after 0.05 seconds, find the resistive force from the ground.

13.

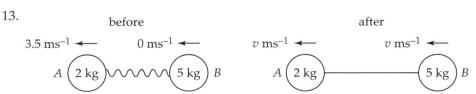

Two particles A and B of masses 2 kg and 5 kg respectively are connected by a light inextensible string which is initially slack. They are resting on a smooth horizontal surface. A is projected away from B with a speed of 3.5 ms^{-1}. Find the common speed of the particles when the string jerks and find the impulse in the string.

14. A truck of mass 2000 kg and travelling with a speed of 10 ms^{-1} along a straight horizontal track, collides with a stationary truck of mass 3000 kg. After the collision the trucks move on together and come to rest after 16 seconds.

    (a) Find the speed of the trucks immediately after collision

    (b) Find the magnitude of the impulse exerted on the stationary truck in the collision.

    (c) Find the constant force resisting the motion of the trucks after the collision.

15. A vertical post of mass 5 kg is to be driven into the ground. A pile-driver of mass 80 kg is released from rest from a height of 2 m above the top of the post.

    (a) Find the speed with which the pile-driver hits the post.

    (b) Assuming the pile-driver does not bounce off the post, find the speed with which the post enters the ground.

    (c) If the combined mass comes to rest when the post has been driven into the ground to a depth 0.3 m, find the deceleration of the combined mass.

    (d) Find the constant force with which the ground resists the post.

16.

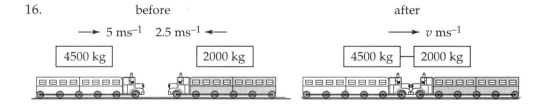

Two trucks of masses 4500 kg and 2000 kg moving with speeds 5 ms^{-1} and 2.5 ms^{-1} respectively, are moving towards each other on a smooth horizontal track.

In the collision the trucks couple together and move off together.

(a) Find the speed of the combined trucks immediately after the collision.

(b) Find the magnitude of the impulse exerted on the heavier truck in the collision.

(c) A constant braking force R newtons, brings the combined trucks to rest in a distance of 20 m. Find R.

Examination Exercise 6

1. Two small balls A and B have masses 0.5 kg and 0.2 kg respectively. They are moving towards each other in opposite directions on a smooth horizontal table when they collide directly. Immediately before the collision, the speed of A is $3\,\text{ms}^{-1}$ and the speed of B is $2\,\text{ms}^{-1}$. The speed of A immediately after the collision is $1.5\,\text{ms}^{-1}$. The direction of motion of A is unchanged as a result of the collision. By modelling the balls as particles, find

   (a) the speed of B immediately after the collision,

   (b) the magnitude of the impulse exerted on B in the collision. [E]

2. Particle A has mass 0.2 kg and particle B has mass 0.5 kg. The particles are travelling towards each other in the same line and they collide. Immediately before the collision the speed of A is $6\,\text{ms}^{-1}$ and the speed of B is $4\,\text{ms}^{-1}$. Particle B is brought to rest by the collision. Find the speed of A immediately after the collision. [E]

3. Two beads, A and B, of mass 0.05 kg and 0.06 kg respectively, are threaded onto a smooth straight fixed horizontal wire on which each bead is free to move. Initially the beads are placed on the wire at a distance 3.8 m apart. Instantaneously, A is given a speed of $1.2\,\text{ms}^{-1}$ towards B, and B is given a speed of $0.7\,\text{ms}^{-1}$ towards A.

   The beads subsequently collide and A is brought to rest by the collision. Calculate

   (a) the time for which A is in motion,

   (b) the distance A moves,

   (c) the speed of B after the collision,

   (d) the magnitude of the impulse exerted by B on A in the collision, and state the units in which your answer is measured. [E]

4. A truck A of mass 900 kg moving on a straight horizontal railway line with speed $7\,\text{ms}^{-1}$ collides with a second truck B of mass 500 kg which is stationary. At the collision the trucks are automatically coupled and move off together. By modelling the trucks as particles,

   (a) Show that the speed of the trucks immediately after the collision is $4.5\,\text{ms}^{-1}$.

   (b) Find the magnitude of the impulse exerted on B by A in the collision.

   After the collision, the trucks continue to move with a constant speed of $4.5\,\text{ms}^{-1}$. They crash into some buffers which bring the trucks to rest. The buffers provide a total constant force of 95 000 N as they are compressed.

   (c) Find the total distance by which the buffers are compressed in bringing the trucks to rest. [E]

5. A post is driven into the ground by means of a blow from a pile-driver. The pile-driver falls from rest from a height of 1.6 m above the top of the post.

   (a) Show that the speed of the pile-driver just before it hits the post is $5.6\,\text{ms}^{-1}$.

   The post has mass 6 kg and the pile-driver has mass 78 kg. When the pile-driver hits the top of the post, it is assumed that there is no rebound and that both then move together with the same speed.

   (b) Find the speed of the pile-driver and the post immediately after the pile-driver has hit the post.

   The post is brought to rest by the action of a resistive force from the ground acting for 0.06 s.

   By modelling this force as constant throughout this time,

   (c) find the magnitude of the resistive force,
   (d) find, to 2 significant figures, the distance travelled by the post and the pile-driver before they come to rest. [E]

6. A particle A of mass m is moving along a straight line with constant speed $4u$. It collides with a particle B of mass $2m$ moving with constant speed u along the same line and in the same direction as A. Immediately after the collision the particles continue to move in the same direction, and the speed of B is twice the speed of A. Find

   (a) the speed of A immediately after the collision,
   (b) the impulse exerted by B on A, stating clearly its magnitude and direction. [E]

7. Two particles A and B, of masses 0.5 kg and 0.6 kg respectively, are moving directly towards each other with speeds of $1.2\,\text{ms}^{-1}$ and $0.7\,\text{ms}^{-1}$ respectively and they collide. After the collision B has speed $0.8\,\text{ms}^{-1}$ and its direction of motion is reversed. Find the speed of A after the collision and the direction in which A is moving. [E]

8. A truck A of mass 6000 kg is moving with a speed of $12\,\text{ms}^{-1}$ along a straight horizontal railway line when it collides with another truck B of mass 9000 kg which is stationary. After the collision the two trucks move on together.

   (a) Find the speed of the trucks immediately after the collision.
   (b) Find the magnitude of the impulse exerted on B when the trucks collide, stating the units in which your answer is given.

   After the collision, the motion of the two trucks is opposed by a constant horizontal resistance of magnitude R newtons. The trucks come to rest 20 s after the collision.

   (c) Find R. [E]

9. A particle P of mass $1.5\,\text{kg}$ is moving along a straight horizontal line with speed $3\,\text{ms}^{-1}$. Another particle Q of mass $2.5\,\text{kg}$ is moving, in the opposite direction, along the same straight line with speed $4\,\text{ms}^{-1}$. The particles collide. Immediately after the collision the direction of motion of P is reversed and its speed is $2.5\,\text{ms}^{-1}$.

   (a) Calculate the speed of Q immediately after the impact.
   (b) State whether or not the direction of motion of Q is changed by the collision.
   (c) Calculate the magnitude of the impulse exerted by Q on P, giving the units of your answer. [E]

10. Two small steel balls A and B have mass $0.6\,\text{kg}$ and $0.2\,\text{kg}$ respectively. They are moving towards each other in opposite directions on a smooth horizontal table when they collide directly. Immediately before the collision, the speed of A is $8\,\text{ms}^{-1}$ and the speed of B is $2\,\text{ms}^{-1}$. Immediately after the collision, the direction of motion of A is unchanged and the speed of B is twice the speed of A. Find

   (a) the speed of A immediately after the collision,
   (b) the magnitude of the impulse exerted on B in the collision. [E]

Part 7

Moments

Previously we have considered forces acting on objects that can be modelled as particles. The effect of the forces was to move, or tend to move, the particle in a straight line.

If a force acts on a rigid body, eg. a plank or a spanner, the force could cause the body to rotate or tend to rotate.

In this part, all rigid bodies such as planks, beams, and bridges are modelled as rods. A rod is an object whose mass is concentrated along a line. It has length only, its other dimensions being neglected.

A rod is rigid. A plank, for example, would be modelled as a rod although the plank may bend a little.

Other bodies such as people or vehicles are modelled as particles.

A force, or set of forces, may act on a lamina. A lamina is like a thin sheet of card – its thickness is small compared with its other dimensions.

7.1 The moment of a force

Suppose a light rod of length 3 m is hinged at one end H so that it is free to rotate and a force of 40 N is applied perpendicular to the rod at the other end.

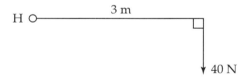

The turning effect of the 40 N force about the hinge H is called its moment about H, which in this case is: $40 \times 3 = 120$ Nm clockwise about H.

- In general, the moment of force F about point P is defined as:

$$\mathbf{F} \times d$$

where d is the perpendicular distance of P from the line of action of F.

7.2 Sum of the moments of more than one force

It is important to consider the sense of rotation of each force, either clockwise or anticlockwise. Moments with the same sense of rotation are added and those with an opposite sense of rotation are subtracted to give an overall moment.

Example 1

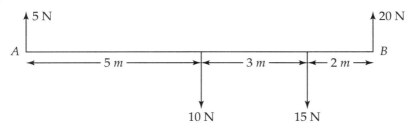

The diagram shows forces applies to a light rod AB. Find the overall moment about point A and its sense of rotation.

Taking moments about A:

5 N force: moment = 5 × 0 = 0 Nm

10 N force: moment = 10 × 5
  = 50 Nm clockwise

15 N force: moment = 15 × 8
  = 120 Nm clockwise

20 N force: moment = 20 × 10
  = 200 Nm anticlockwise

Total clockwise moment = 170 Nm

Total anti-clockwise moment = 200 Nm

Sum of the moments = 200 − 170
  = 30 Nm anticlockwise.

Example 2

A force $5\mathbf{i}$ N acts through a point with position vector $(\mathbf{i} + 3\mathbf{j})$ m and another force $-2\mathbf{i}$ N acts through a point with position vector $(4\mathbf{i} - \mathbf{j})$ m. Find the resultant moment of these forces about the points with position vectors:

(a) $P(3\mathbf{i} + \mathbf{j})$ m

(b) $Q(3\mathbf{i} + 4\mathbf{j})$ m

(a)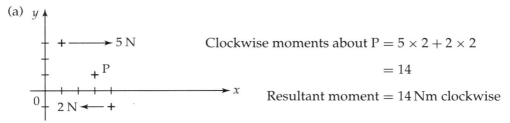

Clockwise moments about P = 5 × 2 + 2 × 2
  = 14

Resultant moment = 14 Nm clockwise

157

(b)

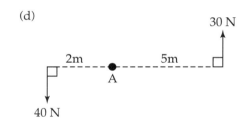

Taking moments about Q:

Clockwise moment $= 2 \times 5 = 10\,\text{Nm}$

Anticlockwise moment $= 5 \times 1 = 5\,\text{Nm}$

Resultant moment $= 10 - 5$

$= 5\,\text{Nm}$ clockwise

Exercise 7A

1. In each of the following find the total moment (or the sum of the moments) about the point A of the forces shown: and state the sense of rotation of each moment.

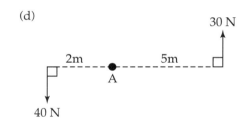

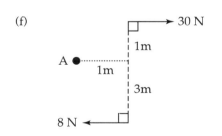

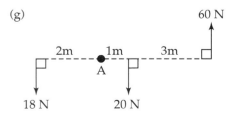

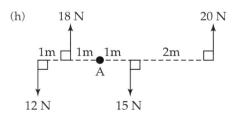

158

2. Find the moment about point P of each of the following forces acting on a lamina. State the sense of rotation.

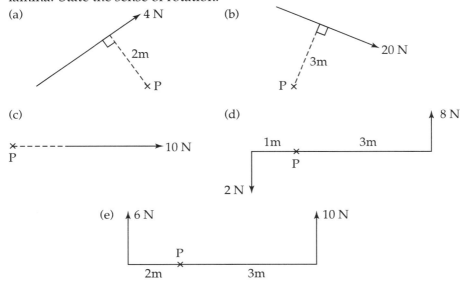

3. A force of 3**j** N is applied at a point P of a lamina. Relative to a fixed origin, the position vector of P is $(4\mathbf{i} + 2\mathbf{j})$ m.

   Calculate the moment of the force about the origin.

4. A force 3**i** N acts through a point with position vector $(2\mathbf{i} + 4\mathbf{j})$ m relative to a fixed origin. Find the moment of the force about the origin.

5. A force of 5**j** N acts at the point P of a lamina, where P has position vector $(2\mathbf{i} + 3\mathbf{j})$ m relative to a fixed origin. Find the moment about a point with position vector 4**i** m.

6. A force of 3**i** N acts at a point P on a lamina where P has position vector $(4\mathbf{i} - \mathbf{j})$ m with respect to an origin O. Calculate the moment of the force:

   (a) about the origin
   (b) about the point with position vector $(2\mathbf{i} - 3\mathbf{j})$ m.

7.3 Uniform and non-uniform bodies

Any rigid body such as a plank or beam which is tending to rotate is modelled as a rod. A rod is rigid so that it does not bend.
We can have light rods which have no weight, or rods which do have weight. In this case we have to consider uniform and non-uniform rods.

(a) Uniform rod.

   The weight of a uniform rod can be considered to act through its centre.

(b) Non-uniform rod.

   The weight of a non-uniform rod does not act through its centre. The point the weight acts through is either given, or will need to be determined.

The point the weight acts through is called the centre of mass.

7.4 Equilibrium of parallel forces acting on a body

A system of parallel forces acting on a body is in equilibrium when there is no resultant force and no turning effect. This means that:

- The resultant force is zero.
- The sum of the moments about **any** point is zero
  [or total clockwise moments = total anticlockwise moments]

Example 1

A uniform rod AB of length 6 m and mass 4 kg is pivoted at C, where $AC = 2$ m. A mass m kg is attached at A so the rod is in equilibrium. Find the mass m and the reaction at the pivot C.

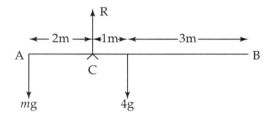

Since the rod is uniform the weight acts through the mid-point of AB. The pivot at C will exert a normal reaction force on the rod.

We can take moments about any point, but it is sensible to take moments about C since this eliminates the unknown force R, which has a zero moment about C.

For force mg: moment about $C = mg \times 2$
$$= 2mg \text{ Nm} \qquad \text{anticlockwise}$$

For force $4g$: moment about $C = 4g \times 1$
$$= 4g \text{ Nm} \qquad \text{clockwise}$$

In equilibrium, anticlockwise moment = clockwise moment
$$2mg = 4g$$
$$m = 2$$

The mass at $A = 2$ kg.

In equilibrium, the forces up = the forces down
$$R = 2g + 4g$$
$$= 6g$$

The reaction at the support $= 58.8$ N

Example 2

A uniform beam AB of length 4 m and mass 20 kg, rests horizontally on supports at A and B. A woman of mass 40 kg stands on the beam a distance of 1m from A. Find the forces exerted on the beam by the supports.

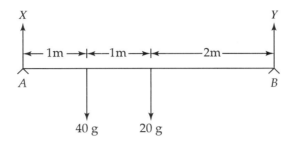

Notice the forces exerted on the rod by the supports will be different due to the position of the woman.

Also the beam is uniform so the line of action of the weight is through the centre of the beam.

Take moments about A:

Sum of the clockwise moments = sum of the anticlockwise moments.

$$40\,g \times 1 + 20\,g \times 2 = Y \times 4$$

$$Y = 196$$

We can now take moments about B or resolve vertically; the latter generally being easier.

Resolving vertically:

$$X + 196 = 40\,g + 20\,g$$

$$X = 392$$

The supporting forces are 392 N at A and 196 N at B.

Example 3

A uniform plank AB of length 4 m and mass 20 kg is supported by two vertical chains attached at B and at a point 1m from A. A mass of 15 kg is placed on the plank a distance 0.5 m from B. Find the tension in each of the chains.

Assume the weight of the chains is negligible.

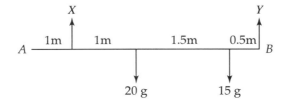

Take moments about B:
$$X \times 3 = 20\,g \times 2 + 15\,g \times 0.5$$
$$X = 665$$

Resolving vertically:
$$665 + Y = 20\,g + 15\,g$$
$$Y = 322$$

The tensions are 665 N and 332 N.

Exercise 7B

1. In the following diagrams the forces are acting on a light horizontal rod which is in equilibrium. Find the forces, P and Q and find also the distance x.

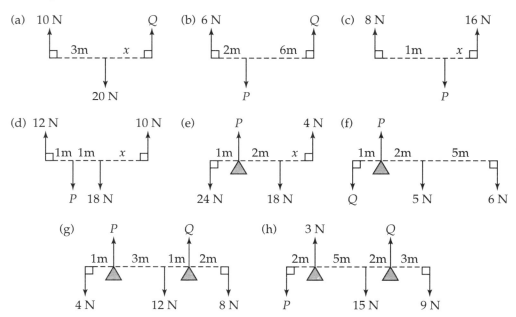

2. The diagram shows a uniform plank AF of mass 40 kg and length 5 m supported on two trestles at B and D. Two men of mass 70 kg and 50 kg are positioned at C and E respectively.

$AB = 1$ m, $BC = 0.5$ m, $DE = 0.5$ m and $EF = 0.5$ m.

   (a) Find the reaction at each support.
   (b) State two modelling assumptions used.

3. A uniform plank AB has length 15 m and weight 250 N. It rests horizontally on two supports at A and B. A man of mass 80 kg stands on the plank 5 m from B. Find the reactions at the two supports.

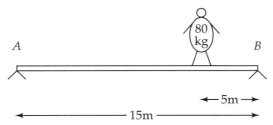

4. A uniform beam AB has length 8 m and weighs 50 N. A weight of 25 N is attached at a point 3 m from A. The beam is held from the roof by two vertical ropes attached to points 1 m from each end so that the beam is horizontal.

   Find the tensions in the two ropes.

5. A straight uniform rigid beam AB of length 8 m and mass 20 kg is supported at its ends A and B and rests horizontally. A load of 60 kg is placed on the beam at point C. Given that the magnitude of the force exerted on the support at A is three times the force at B, find the distance AC.

6. A uniform plank AB has mass 50 kg and length 6 m. It is supported in a horizontal position by two smooth pivots, one at end A and the other 4 m from end A. A man of mass 100 kg stands on the plank, which remains in equilibrium. The magnitude of the reactions at the two pivots are each equal to R newtons.

   (a) Find the value of R
   (b) Find the distance of the man from A
   (c) Write down two modelling assumptions you have made.

7. The diagram shows a uniform rod AB of mass 5 kg and length 8 m, which is supported at point P. A particle of mass 10 kg is attached at B. Find the distance PB.

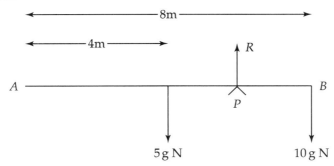

8. A uniform rod AB of mass 6 kg and length 4 m is pivoted at point P where $AP = 1.5$ m. If the rod is in equilibrium when a particle of mass m kg is attached to end A, find m.

163

9. A uniform beam *AB* of length 5 m is supported at its mid-point. If a girl of mass 30 kg sits at end *A*, find how far from end *B* a boy of mass 40 kg must sit if the beam balances horizontally.

10. A uniform rod *AB* has length 8 m and mass 4 kg. It is supported in a horizontal position by two vertical strings attached at *A* and *B*. When a particle of mass 8 kg is placed on the rod *x* m from *A*, the tension in the string at *A* is twice the tension at *B*.

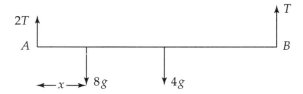

Find (a) the tension in the string at *B* (b) the distance *x*.

11. A uniform beam *AB* of length 6 m and mass 20 kg is suspended by two strings at *A* and *B*. A particle of mass 12 kg is placed on the beam 1 m from *A* and another particle of mass 8 kg is placed on the beam 1.5 m from end *B*.

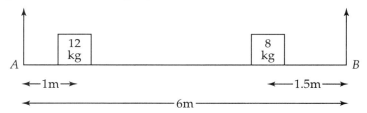

(a) Draw a diagram showing all the forces acting on the beam.

(b) Find the tensions in the two strings.

12. A uniform rod *AB* has mass 3 kg and length 4m. Masses of 6 kg and 3 kg are fixed to ends *A* and *B* respectively. If the rod rests in equilibrium on a support at *C*, find

(a) the reaction at the support (b) the distance *AC*.

13. A uniform beam of length 2 m and mass 30 kg rests horizontally on two supports, one at each end.

A mass of 40 kg is placed 0.5 m from one end of the beam.

Find the reactions at the supports.

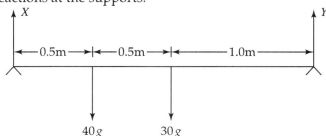

7.5 Tilting

7.5.1 Overlapping plank

If a plank is placed such that it overlaps the edge of a horizontal platform, a downward force F can be applied to one end of the plank so that the plank is on the point of tilting about the edge.

The normal reaction force on the plank will act at the edge of the platform.

Example 1

A uniform beam AB of length 8 m and mass 30 kg rests on a horizontal table with end B projecting 3 m over the end of the table. A mass of m kg is placed on end B. Find the maximum value of m such that the plank remains in equilibrium.

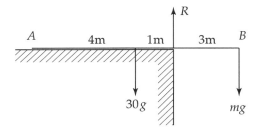

The beam will be on the point of tilting about the edge of the table.

To eliminate R, take moments about the edge of the table.

$$mg \times 3 = 30\,g \times 1$$

$$m = 10$$

The mass $= 10$ kg

7.5.2 Plank on two supports

When a plank is placed on two supports, as shown in the diagram, a downward force can be applied to the end of the plank to make it tilt about support B. Since the plank is tilting about B, the normal reaction at A will be zero.

Example 2

A uniform beam AB of length 8 m and mass 6 kg rests in equilibrium on two supports at C and D, where $AC = 2$ m and $BD = 3$ m. When a mass m kg is placed on the beam at A, the beam is on the point of tilting about C. Find the value of m.

165

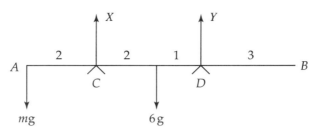

If the beam is on the point of tilting about C, the reaction force Y will be zero. Take moments about C to eliminate the reaction force X.

$$mg \times 2 = 6g \times 2$$

$$m = 6$$

The mass $= 6\,\text{kg}$

Exercise 7C

1. A uniform beam of length 4 m and mass 6 kg has a mass of 2 kg attached to one of its ends. How far could the other end of the beam overhang the edge of a horizontal roof before it toppled.

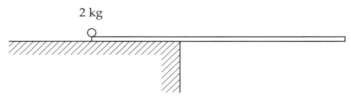

2.

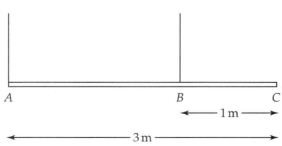

A uniform rod AC has mass 20 kg and length 3 m.

The rod is held horizontally by two strings attached at points A and B as shown in the diagram.

Find the greatest mass which can be fixed to the beam at C so that the rod remains in equilibrium. In this case find the tension in the string at B.

3. A uniform rod has mass 6 kg and length 4 m. It rests on two supports at P and Q shown in the diagram. A particle of mass M kg is placed at B.

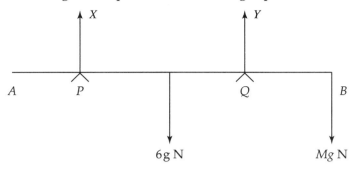

$AP = 1.0$ m, $QB = 1.5$ m

The rod is about to tilt about support Q.

Find the mass M of the particle.

4. A uniform rod AB of mass 3 kg and length 6 m is suspended by two vertical strings attached at points P and Q. When a particle of mass 4 kg is attached, the rod is on the point of turning about P.

Distance $AP = 2.0$ m and $QB = 1.0$ m.

Draw a diagram showing the forces acting on the rod.

Find the distance of the 4 kg mass from the point P.

5. A non-uniform rod AB of mass 15 kg and length 6 m, rests horizontally on two supports, one at A and the other at C, where $AC = 4$ m. If the reaction forces on the rod at A and C are equal, find the position of the centre of mass of the rod.

If an extra weight W newtons is attached at B, find the magnitude of W if

(a) the reaction at C is three times the reaction at A

(b) the rod is just about to tilt.

6. A uniform rod of length 6 m weighs 50 N. 2 m of the rod lies on a table and the rest lies over the edge. A 60 N weight is placed on the end which lies on the table. What is the maximum downward force which can be applied to the other end of the rod without causing it to tilt over?

7. A uniform rod of length 6 m weighs 50 N. 1 m of the rod lies on a horizontal table and the rest lies over the edge.

(a) What downward force must be applied to the end of the rod to just stop it from tilting over?

(b) What is the reaction force of the table on the rod when it is about to tilt? (Hint: the reaction force acts at the edge of the table.)

7.6 Non-uniform rods

Example 1

A non-uniform rod AB of length 4 m and mass 20 kg is pivoted at its mid-point. A mass of 30 kg is placed at A and a mass of 40 kg is placed at B. If the rod remains in equilibrium, find the distance of the centre of mass of the rod from A.

Let the distance of the centre of mass from A be x.

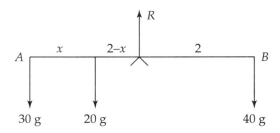

Take moments about the pivot to eliminate R.

$$30\,g \times 2 + 20\,g(2-x) = 40\,g \times 2$$
$$60 + 40 - 20x = 80$$
$$20 = 20x$$
$$x = 1$$

The centre of mass is 1 m from A.

Example 2

A non-uniform beam AB of length 6 m and mass 15 kg rests in equilibrium, horizontally, on two supports at C and D, where $AC = 1$ m and $BD = 2$ m. The centre of mass of the beam is at G where $AG = 2$ m. Find the reactions at the supports.

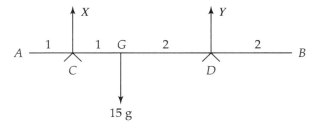

Take moments about D to eliminate Y:

$$X \times 3 = 15g \times 2$$
$$X = 98$$

Resolving vertically:
$$X + Y = 15\,g$$
$$98 + Y = 147$$
$$Y = 49$$

The reactions at X and Y are 98 N and 49 N respectively.

Example 3

A non-uniform plank AB of mass 20 kg and length 5 m is supported horizontally by two supports at C and D, where $AC = 1$ m and $BD = 2$ m.

(a) When a child of mass 30 kg stands on the plank 1 m from B, the plank is on the point of tilting about D. Find the distance of the centre of mass of the plank from A.

(b) The child then stands at a point 2 m from A. Find the magnitude of the reactions at C and D.

(a)
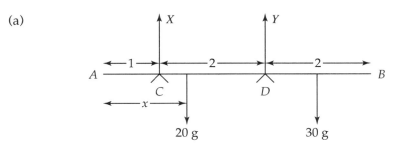

The plank is on the point of tilting about D, so the reaction $X = 0$.

Take moments about D to eliminate Y:

$$20g(3 - x) = 30g \times 1$$

$$60 - 20x = 30$$

$$x = 1.5$$

The centre of mass is 1.5 m from A.

(b)
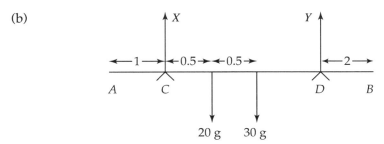

Taking moments about C:

$$20\,g \times 0.5 + 30\,g \times 1 = Y \times 2$$

$$40\,g = Y \times 2$$

$$Y = 20\,g$$

$$= 196$$

Resolving vertically:
$$X + Y = 20\,g + 30\,g$$
$$X + 196 = 490$$
$$X = 294$$

The reactions C and D are 294 N and 196 N respectively.

Exercise 7D

1. A non-uniform rod AB of length 4 m and weight 60 N is supported horizontally by two supports, one at A and the other at B. The centre of mass of the rod is 1.5 m from end A.

   Find the reactions at the supports.

2. A non-uniform rod AB of length 3 m and mass M kg is held horizontally by two strings at A and B. The tension in the string at A is two times the tension at B.

   Find the distance of the centre of mass of the rod from A.

3. A non-uniform plank of mass 20 kg and length 4 m, rests on a pivot at its mid-point. Two children of masses 35 kg and 25 kg are sitting at its ends. The plank is balanced horizontally.

   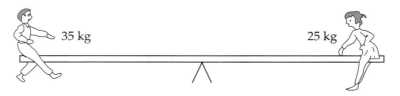

   Determine which side of the pivot the centre of mass of the plank will be and draw a diagram showing all the forces acting on the plank.

   State one modelling assumption regarding the children.

4. A non-uniform rod AB of mass 10 kg and length 5 m is held in equilibrium by two vertical strings attached at A and B.

   If the centre of mass of the rod is 3 m from A, find the tensions in the two strings.

5. A non-uniform beam AB 10 m long rests on the ground. C is a point 1 m from A and D is a point 2 m from B. It is found that the end A can just be lifted off the ground by a force of 90 N applied vertically at C.

   It is also found that the end B can just be lifted off the ground by a vertical force of 60 N at D.

   Calculate the weight of the beam.

Examination Exercise 7

1.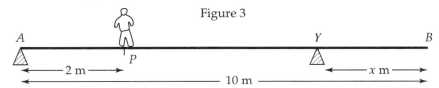

   Figure 2

   A uniform steel girder AB, of mass 150 kg and length 10 m, rests horizontally on two supports at A and B. A man of mass 90 kg stands on the girder at the point P, where $AP = 2$ m, as shown in Fig. 2. By modelling the girder as a uniform rod and the man as a particle,

   (a) find the magnitude of the reaction at B.

   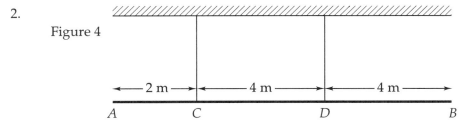

   Figure 3

   The support B is moved to a point Y on the girder, where $BY = x$ metres, as shown in Fig. 3. The man remains on the girder at P. The magnitudes of the reactions at the two supports are now equal.

   Find (b) the magnitude of the reaction at each support,

   (c) the value of x. [E]

2. Figure 4

   A light rod AB has length 10 m. It is suspended by two light vertical cables attached to the rod at the points C and D, where $AC = 2$ m, $CD = 4$ m and $DB = 4$ m, as shown in Fig. 4. A load of weight 60 N is attached to the rod at A, and a load of weight X newtons is attached to the rod at B. The rod is hanging in equilibrium in a horizontal position.

   Find, in terms of X,

   (a) the tension in the cable at C,

   (b) the tension in the cable at D.

   (c) Hence show that $15 \leq X \leq 90$.

   If the tension in either cable exceeds 120 N, that cable breaks. [E]

   (d) Find the maximum possible value of X.

3.

Figure 3

A uniform plank ABC, of length 12 m and mass 30 kg, is supported in a horizontal position at the points A and B, where AB = 8 m and BC = 4 m, as shown in Fig. 3. A woman of mass 60 kg stands on the plank at a distance of 2 m from A, and a rock of mass M kg is placed on the plank at the end C. The plank remains in equilibrium. The plank is modelled as a uniform rod, and the woman and the rock as particles.

Given that the forces exerted by the supports on the plank at A and B are equal in magnitude,

(a) find

   (i) the value of M,

   (ii) the magnitude of the force exerted by the support at A on the plank.

(b) State how you have used the modelling assumption that the rock is a particle. [E]

4.

A large log AB is 6 m long. It rests in a horizontal position on two smooth supports C and D, where AC = 1 m and BD = 1 m, as shown. David needs an estimate of the weight of the log, but the log is too heavy to lift off both supports. When David applies a force of magnitude 1500 N vertically upwards to the log at A, the log is about to tilt about D.

(a) State the value of the reaction on the log at C for this case.

David initially models the log as a uniform rod. Using this model,

(b) estimate the weight of the log.

The shape of the log convinces David that his initial modelling assumption is too simple. He removes the force at A and applies a force acting vertically upwards at B. He finds that the log is about to tilt about C when this force has magnitude 1000 N. David now models the log as a non-uniform rod, with the distance of the centre of mass of the log from C as x metres. Using this model, find

(c) a new estimate for the weight of the log,

(d) the value of x.

(e) State how you have used the modelling assumption that the log is a rod. [E]

5.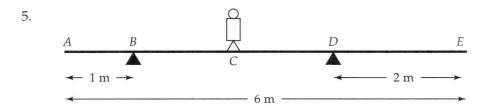

A plank AE, of length 6 m and mass 10 kg, rests in a horizontal position on supports at B and D, where $AB = 1$ m and $DE = 2$ m. A child of mass 20 kg stands at C, the mid-point of BD, as shown in the diagram. The child is modelled as a particle and the plank as a uniform rod. The child and the plank are in equilibrium. Calculate

(a) the magnitude of the force exerted by the support on the plank at B,

(b) the magnitude of the force exerted by the support on the plank at D.

The child now stands at a point E on the plank. The plank is in equilibrium and on the point of tilting about D.

(c) Calculate the distance DF. [E]

6.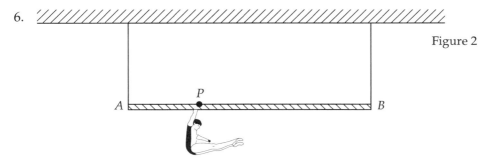

Figure 2

A gymnast of mass 36 kg hangs by one hand from the point P on a bar AB of length 3 m and mass 12 kg. The bar is suspended by two vertical cables which are attached to the ends A and B, and it is hanging in equilibrium in a horizontal position, as shown in Fig. 2. The tension in the cable at A is twice the tension in the cable at B. By modelling the bar as a uniform rod, and the gymnast as a particle,

(a) find the distance AP.

(b) State two ways in which, in your calculation, you have used the model of the bar as a "uniform rod". [E]

7.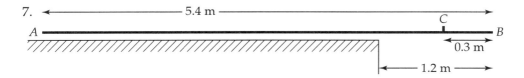

A plank of wood AB has length 5.4 m. It lies on a horizontal platform, with 1.2 m projecting over the edge, as shown in the diagram. When a girl of mass

50 kg stands at the point C on the plank, where $BC = 0.3$ m, the plank is on the point of tilting. By modelling the plank as a uniform rod and the girl as a particle,

(a) find the mass of the plank.

The girl places a rock on the end of the plank at A. By modelling the rock also as a particle,

(b) find, to 2 significant figures, the smallest mass of the rock which will enable the girl to stand on the plank at B without it tilting.

(c) State briefly how you have used the modelling assumptions that
   (i) the plank is uniform,
   (ii) the rock is a particle. [E]

8.

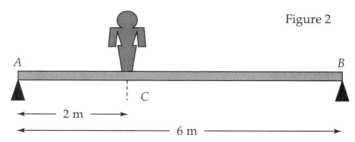

Figure 2

A non-uniform plank of wood AB has length 6 m and mass 90 kg. The plank is smoothly supported at its two ends A and B, with A and B at the same horizontal level. A woman of mass 60 kg stands on the plank at the point C, where $AC = 2$ m, as shown in Fig. 2. The plank is in equilibrium and the magnitudes of the reactions on the plank at A and B are equal. The plank is modelled as a non-uniform rod and the woman as a particle.

Find

(a) the magnitude of the reaction on the plank at B,

(b) the distance of the centre of mass of the plank from A.

(c) State briefly how you have used the modelling assumption that
   (i) the plank is a rod,
   (ii) the woman is a particle. [E]

9. A non-uniform thin straight rod AB has length $3d$ and mass $5m$. It is in equilibrium resting horizontally on supports at the points X and Y, where $AX = XY = YB = d$.

A particle of mass $2m$ is attached to the rod at B. Given that the rod is on the point of tilting about Y, find the distance of the centre of mass of the rod from A. [E]

Part 8

Applications of vectors to mechanics

8.1 Addition of vectors

If we have vectors $\overrightarrow{OA} = 3\mathbf{i} + 4\mathbf{j}$ and $\overrightarrow{AB} = 2\mathbf{i} - \mathbf{j}$, then as we have seen before:
$$\overrightarrow{OA} + \overrightarrow{AB} = 5\mathbf{i} + 3\mathbf{j}$$

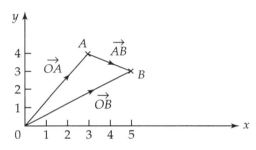

In vector form: $\overrightarrow{OB} = \overrightarrow{OA} + \overrightarrow{AB}$

This means that vector $\overrightarrow{OB}$ is vector $\overrightarrow{OA}$ taken together with vector $\overrightarrow{AB}$ or going from O to B is equivalent to going from O to A and then A to B.

It is very useful to get this relationship. It is not necessary to draw an accurate vector diagram. Any triangle will do provided the arrows are in the right direction.

For example, if we want vector BA and are given vectors OA and OB, then draw a triangle OAB with the arrows in the correct direction.

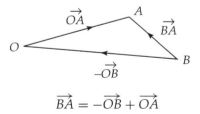

$$\overrightarrow{BA} = -\overrightarrow{OB} + \overrightarrow{OA}$$

8.2 The displacement vector

Displacement is distance measured in a particular direction.

In section 8.1 $\overrightarrow{AB}$ is called a displacement vector. It gives the position of B relative to A.

Vectors $\overrightarrow{OA}$ and $\overrightarrow{OB}$ give the positions of A and B respectively relative to the origin, so these particular displacement vectors are called *position vectors*.

8.3 Relative displacement

r is generally used as a symbol for displacement and position vectors.

If r_A and r_B represent the position vectors of points A and B respectively:

$$\overrightarrow{OB} = \overrightarrow{OA} + \overrightarrow{AB}$$

$$r_B = r_A + \overrightarrow{AB}$$

$$\overrightarrow{AB} = r_B - r_A$$

This gives the relative displacement of B from A or the position of B relative to A.

Note that the position of A relative to B would be given by:

$$\overrightarrow{BA} = r_A - r_B$$

Example 1

The position vectors of two particles A and B are $(4i + 6j)$m and $(8i + 3j)$m respectively. Find:

(a) the position vector of B relative to A

(b) the position vector of A relative to B

(c) the distance AB.

Roughly sketch the positions of O, A and B.

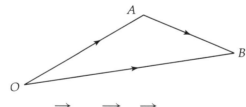

(a) $\quad\overrightarrow{AB} = -\overrightarrow{OA} + \overrightarrow{OB}$

ie. going from A to B is equivalent to going from A to O and then from O to B. Notice $\overrightarrow{AO} = -\overrightarrow{OA}$.

$$\overrightarrow{AB} = -(4i + 6j) + (8i + 3j)$$
$$= (4i - 3j)\,\text{m}$$

(b) $\quad\overrightarrow{BA} = -\overrightarrow{OB} + \overrightarrow{OA}$

$$= -(8i + 3j) + (4i + 6j)$$
$$= (-4i + 3j)\,\text{m}$$

(c) $\quad\text{Distance} = |\overrightarrow{AB}|$

$$= \sqrt{4^2 + 3^2}$$
$$= 5\,\text{m}$$

8.4 The velocity vector

When there is no acceleration and the velocity is constant:

$$\text{Velocity} = \frac{\text{change of displacement}}{\text{time}}$$

$$\text{Speed} = \text{magnitude of velocity}$$

Example 2

Initially ($t = 0$) a particle has position vector $(-2\mathbf{i} + 5\mathbf{j})$ m and 4 seconds later its position vector is $(3\mathbf{i} + \mathbf{j})$ m. Assuming the velocity is constant find:

(a) the velocity of the particle

(b) the speed of the particle

(a)
$$\text{Velocity} = \frac{\text{change in displacement}}{\text{time}}$$
$$= \frac{(3\mathbf{i} + \mathbf{j}) - (-2\mathbf{i} + 5\mathbf{j})}{4} = \frac{5\mathbf{i} - 4\mathbf{j}}{4}$$
$$= (1.25\mathbf{i} - \mathbf{j})\,\text{ms}^{-1}$$

(b)
$$\text{Speed} = \sqrt{1.25^2 + (-1)^2}$$
$$= 1.60\,\text{ms}^{-1}$$

8.5 The acceleration vector

When the acceleration is constant:

$$\text{acceleration} = \frac{\text{change in velocity}}{\text{time}}$$

Example 3

A particle moving with constant acceleration has an initial velocity $(2\mathbf{i} - 2\mathbf{j})$ ms^{-1} and 3 seconds later its velocity is $(8\mathbf{i} + \mathbf{j})$ ms^{-1}. Find:

(a) the acceleration of the particle

(b) the magnitude of the acceleration

(a)
$$\text{acceleration} = \frac{(8\mathbf{i} + \mathbf{j}) - (2\mathbf{i} - 2\mathbf{j})}{3}$$
$$= \frac{6\mathbf{i} + 3\mathbf{j}}{3}$$
$$= (2\mathbf{i} + \mathbf{j})\,\text{ms}^{-2}$$

(b) magnitude of acceleration = $\sqrt{2^2 + 1^2}$

$= 2.24 \text{ ms}^{-2}$

8.6 Constant velocity

This section is about finding displacement or position vectors given that the velocity vector is constant.

At time $t = 0$ a particle is at point A with position vector $\mathbf{r_0}$. After a time t it has moved with a constant velocity $\mathbf{v}$ to point B with position vector $\mathbf{r}$.

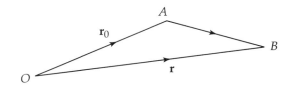

The displacement vector $AB = \mathbf{v}t$

$$\overrightarrow{OB} = \overrightarrow{OA} + \overrightarrow{AB}$$

$$\mathbf{r} = \mathbf{r_0} + \mathbf{v}t$$

This is an important equation. Learn it!

Example 4

A particle with an initial position vector $(3\mathbf{i} + 2\mathbf{j})$ m travels with a velocity $(5\mathbf{i} - 4\mathbf{j})$ ms^{-1}. Find:

(a) the position vector after t seconds

(b) the position vector after 2 seconds

(c) the distance from the origin after 2 seconds.

(a) at time t, $\quad \mathbf{r} = \mathbf{r_0} + \mathbf{v}t$

$\quad\quad = [(3\mathbf{i} + 2\mathbf{j}) + (5\mathbf{i} - 4\mathbf{j})t]$m

(b) after 2 seconds, $\quad \mathbf{r} = (3\mathbf{i} + 2\mathbf{j}) + (5\mathbf{i} - 4\mathbf{j})2$

$\quad\quad = (13\mathbf{i} - 6\mathbf{j})$ m

(c) $|\mathbf{r}| = \sqrt{13^2 + (-6)^2}$

$\quad = 14.3$ m

Example 5

A particle with an initial position vector $(2\mathbf{i} + 5\mathbf{j})$m travels with speed 20 ms^{-1} in the direction of the vector $(3\mathbf{i} + 4\mathbf{j})$. Find the position vector of the particle after 2 seconds.

Velocity of the particle	$\mathbf{v} = k(3\mathbf{i} + 4\mathbf{j})$, where k is a positive constant
Speed	$|\mathbf{v}| = \sqrt{(3k)^2 + (4k)^2} = 5k$
Hence	$5k = 20$
	$k = 4$
Velocity	$\mathbf{v} = (12\mathbf{i} + 16\mathbf{j})$ ms^{-1}
Position vector after 2 seconds,	$\mathbf{r} = \mathbf{r_0} + \mathbf{v}t$
	$= (2\mathbf{i} + 5\mathbf{j}) + (12\mathbf{i} + 16\mathbf{j}) \times 2$
	$= (26\mathbf{i} + 37\mathbf{j})$ m.

8.7 Least distance between two particles

The least distance is found by:

1. obtaining an expression for the relative position vector between the two particles
2. from this obtain an expression for the square of the distance between them
3. minimise this expression by completing the square or by differentiation.

Example 6

At time t seconds the position vectors of particles A and B are:

$$\mathbf{r_A} = [(3 + 2t)\mathbf{i} + 4t\mathbf{j}]\text{m}$$
$$\mathbf{r_B} = [(5 + 3t)\mathbf{i} + (6 + 2t)\mathbf{j}]\text{m}$$

Find the least distance between A and B and the time at which this occurs.

The position vector of B relative to A is:

$$\mathbf{r_B} - \mathbf{r_A} = (2 + t)\mathbf{i} + (6 - 2t)\mathbf{j}$$

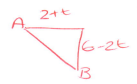

The distance d between A and B is $|\mathbf{r_B} - \mathbf{r_A}|$.

$$d^2 = (2 + t)^2 + (6 - 2t)^2$$
$$= 4 + 4t + t^2 + 36 - 24t + 4t^2 = 5t^2 - 20t + 40$$

Completing the square: $d^2 = 5\left[t^2 - 4t + 8\right]$
$$= 5\left[(t-2)^2 - 4 + 8\right] = 5\left[(t-2)^2 + 4\right]$$

d^2 has a minimum value of 20 when $t = 2$

The least distance $d = 4.47$ m when the time $t = 2$ seconds.

179

Note: This could also be solved by differentiation:

$$\frac{d(d^2)}{dt} = 10t - 20$$

$$= 0 \quad \text{for minimum}$$

$$t = 2$$

Substitute $t = 2$ in the expression for d, etc.

8.8 Collision of two particles

If two particles collide, the position vectors of the two particles are the same at the time of the collision.

Example 7

At time $t = 0$ the position vectors and the velocity vectors of two particles A and B are:

$r_{A0} = (4i - 3j)$m $\qquad v_A = (3i + 6j)$ms

$r_{B0} = (8i + 5j)$m $\qquad v_B = (i + 2j)$ms

Find the position vector of A and of B after t seconds. Show that the two particles collide. Find the time of the collision and the position vector of the point where the collision occurs.

At time t, $\qquad r = r_0 + vt$

Position vector of A: $\qquad r_A = (4i - 3j) + (3i + 6j)t$

Position vector of B: $\qquad r_B = (8i + 5j) + (i + 2j)t$

If a collision occurs: $\qquad r_A = r_B$

$$4i - 3j + 3ti + 6tj = 8i + 5j + ti + 2tj$$

Equating components of **i** and **j**:

$$\mathbf{i}: \quad 4 + 3t = 8 + t$$
$$2t = 4$$
$$t = 2$$

$$\mathbf{j}: \quad -3 + 6t = 5 + 2t$$
$$4t = 8$$
$$t = 2$$

These times are the same, so the particles are in the same place at the same time and therefore collide.

Time of collision is $t = 2$ seconds.

Substitute $t = 2$ into $\mathbf{r}_A$: $\mathbf{r} = 4\mathbf{i} - 3\mathbf{j} + 3t\mathbf{i} + 6t\mathbf{j}$

$$= 4\mathbf{i} - 3\mathbf{j} + 6\mathbf{i} + 12\mathbf{j}$$

$$= 10\mathbf{i} + 9\mathbf{j}$$

Position vector of point of collision = $(10\mathbf{i} + 9\mathbf{j})$m.

Exercise 8A

1. Given the following position vectors of the points A and B, find the vector $\overrightarrow{AB}$.

    (a) $\overrightarrow{OA} = (2\mathbf{i} + 5\mathbf{j})$m, $\overrightarrow{OB} = (6\mathbf{i} + 10\mathbf{j})$m

    (b) $\overrightarrow{OA} = (-3\mathbf{i} + 4\mathbf{j})$m, $\overrightarrow{OB} = (7\mathbf{i} - 2\mathbf{j})$m

    (c) $\overrightarrow{OA} = (5\mathbf{i} - \mathbf{j})$m, $\overrightarrow{OB} = (3\mathbf{i} + 3\mathbf{j})$m

    (d) $\overrightarrow{OA} = (-8\mathbf{i} + 10\mathbf{j})$m, $\overrightarrow{OB} = (-5\mathbf{i} - 4\mathbf{j})$m.

2. Given the following position vectors of the points A and B, find the vector $\overrightarrow{BA}$.

    (a) $\overrightarrow{OA} = (9\mathbf{i} + 5\mathbf{j})$m, $\overrightarrow{OB} = (6\mathbf{i} + 3\mathbf{j})$m

    (b) $\overrightarrow{OA} = (-4\mathbf{i} + 7\mathbf{j})$m, $\overrightarrow{OB} = (8\mathbf{i} - 2\mathbf{j})$m

    (c) $\overrightarrow{OA} = (12\mathbf{i} - 10\mathbf{j})$m, $\overrightarrow{OB} = (-5\mathbf{i} + 6\mathbf{j})$m

    (d) $\overrightarrow{OA} = (-5\mathbf{i} - 4\mathbf{j})$m, $\overrightarrow{OB} = (-8\mathbf{i} - 9\mathbf{j})$m.

3. A particle is initially at the point with position vector $\mathbf{r}_0$. It moves with constant velocity $\mathbf{v}$ and after a time t seconds is at a point with position vector $\mathbf{r}$.

    Find $\mathbf{r}$ when:
    (a) $\mathbf{r}_0 = 2\mathbf{i}$, $\mathbf{v} = 3\mathbf{i} + \mathbf{j}$, $t = 2$
    (b) $\mathbf{r}_0 = 3\mathbf{j}$, $\mathbf{v} = \mathbf{i} + \mathbf{j}$, $t = 3$
    (c) $\mathbf{r}_0 = \mathbf{i} + 2\mathbf{j}$, $\mathbf{v} = \mathbf{i} + 2\mathbf{j}$, $t = 4$
    (d) $\mathbf{r}_0 = -2\mathbf{i} + \mathbf{j}$, $\mathbf{v} = 3\mathbf{i} + \mathbf{j}$, $t = 2$
    (e) $\mathbf{r}_0 = 2\mathbf{i} + \mathbf{j}$, $\mathbf{v} = 4\mathbf{i} - 3\mathbf{j}$, $t = 3$
    (f) $\mathbf{r}_0 = -3\mathbf{i} + 2\mathbf{j}$, $\mathbf{v} = -2\mathbf{i} + 5\mathbf{j}$, $t = 2$
    (g) $\mathbf{r}_0 = -4\mathbf{i} - 3\mathbf{j}$, $\mathbf{v} = 2\mathbf{i} + \mathbf{j}$, $t = 3$

4. A particle is initially at the point r_0 and t seconds later it is at the point r, Find the velocity vector and the speed of the particle, assuming the velocity is constant, when:

(a) $r_0 = 2i$, $r = 12i$, $t = 2$

(b) $r_0 = 2j$, $r = -10j$, $t = 4$

(c) $r_0 = 2i + j$, $r = 8i + 4j$, $t = 3$

(d) $r_0 = -3i$, $r = -2i + 5j$, $t = 2$

(e) $r_0 = 4i - j$, $r = 3i - j$, $t = 0.5$

(f) $r_0 = -3i + 5j$, $r = -i + 3j$, $t = 2$

5. A particle has an initial velocity u ms^{-1} and after t seconds it has velocity v ms^{-1}. Given that the particle moves with uniform acceleration a ms^{-2}, find a when:

(a) $u = 3i$, $v = 9i$, $t = 2$

(b) $u = 6i$, $v = 2i$, $t = 2$

(c) $u = 4i$, $v = 8i + 12j$, $t = 4$

(d) $u = 2j$, $v = 9i + 8j$, $t = 3$

(e) $u = 2i + j$, $v = 10i + 5j$, $t = 4$

(f) $u = 5i - j$, $v = 3i - 5j$, $t = 2$

6. A particle has an initial velocity u ms^{-1}. The particle moves with uniform acceleration a ms^{-2}, and after t seconds it has velocity v ms^{-1}.

Find v when:

(a) $u = 2i$, $a = 3i$, $t = 2$

(b) $u = 3j$, $a = 2i$, $t = 4$

(c) $u = i + j$, $a = 2i + 3j$, $t = 2$

(d) $u = i + 2j$, $a = 3i - 2j$, $t = 3$

(e) $u = -i + 4j$, $a = i - 2j$, $t = 5$

(f) $u = 3i - 2j$, $a = -i + 4j$, $t = 1$

7. At time t seconds a particle has a position vector given by $r = [(2 + 4t)i + (1 + 5t)j]$ m, where the unit vectors i and j are due east and due north respectively.

Find the time, t seconds, when the particle is due north of each point given by position vectors:

(a) $10i$

(b) $20i - 10j$

(c) $6i - 9j$.

8. At times t seconds a particle has a position vector given by
   $\mathbf{r} = [(3 + 4t)\mathbf{i} + (1 + 2t)\mathbf{j}]$ m, where the unit vectors $\mathbf{i}$ and $\mathbf{j}$ are due east and due north respectively.

   Find the time t seconds, when the particle is due east of each point given by the position vectors:

   (a) $5\mathbf{j}$

   (b) $4\mathbf{i} + 9\mathbf{j}$

   (c) $6\mathbf{i} + 15\mathbf{j}$.

9. Find in vector form the velocity of a particle

   (a) moving with speed $3\,\mathrm{ms}^{-1}$ parallel to the positive y-axis.
   (b) moving with speed $20\,\mathrm{ms}^{-1}$ parallel to the vector $3\mathbf{i} + 4\mathbf{j}$.
   (c) moving with a speed $26\,\mathrm{ms}^{-1}$ parallel to the vector $-5\mathbf{i} + 12\mathbf{j}$.

10. Find in each case the speed of a body moving with velocity:

    (a) $(3\mathbf{i} + 4\mathbf{j})\,\mathrm{ms}^{-1}$
    (b) $(5\mathbf{i} - 12\mathbf{j})\,\mathrm{ms}^{-1}$
    (c) $(-7\mathbf{i} - 24\mathbf{j})\,\mathrm{ms}^{-1}$

11. A body moves with constant velocity from A to B in 5 seconds where A and B have position vectors $(2\mathbf{i} - \mathbf{j})$ m and $(22\mathbf{i} - 31\mathbf{j})$m respectively. Find the velocity in the form $a\mathbf{i} + b\mathbf{j}$.

12. A body moves with constant velocity $(2\mathbf{i} - 3\mathbf{j})\,\mathrm{ms}^{-1}$ from A to B in 3 seconds. If the position vector of A is $(2\mathbf{i} + 11\mathbf{j})$ m, find the position vector of B.

13. A body moves from A to B where A and B have position vectors $(3\mathbf{i} + 4\mathbf{j})$m and $(23\mathbf{i} + y\mathbf{j})$m respectively. If the velocity is $(4\mathbf{i} - 3\mathbf{j})\,\mathrm{ms}^{-1}$, find:

    (a) the time to go from A to B
    (b) the value of y.

14. A body has speed $13\,\mathrm{ms}^{-1}$ and its velocity is $(x\mathbf{i} + 5\mathbf{j})\,\mathrm{ms}^{-1}$. Find x given that it is a positive integer.

15. A body has speed $10\,\mathrm{ms}^{-1}$ and its velocity is $(6\mathbf{i} + y\mathbf{j})\,\mathrm{ms}^{-1}$. Find y given that it is a negative integer.

16. A particle has an initial position vector of $(3\mathbf{i} - 4\mathbf{j})$ m. The particle moves with a constant velocity of $(5\mathbf{i} + 2\mathbf{j})\,\mathrm{ms}^{-1}$.

    (a) Find its position vector after 2 seconds.
    (b) Determine whether or not the particle passes through the point with position vector $(38\mathbf{i} + 8\mathbf{j})$ m.

17. A particle has a constant velocity of $(5\mathbf{i} + 4\mathbf{j})\,\mathrm{ms}^{-1}$. After 5 seconds it has a position vector of $(21\mathbf{i} + 22\mathbf{j})$ m. Find its initial position vector.

18. A body has a constant velocity of $(2\mathbf{i} + 7\mathbf{j})\,\mathrm{ms}^{-1}$ and has an initial position vector of $(2\mathbf{i} - 15\mathbf{j})$ m. Find its distance from the origin after 3 seconds.

19. A body has an initial position vector of $(\mathbf{i} - 2\mathbf{j})$ m and has a constant velocity of $(-3\mathbf{i} + a\mathbf{j})$ ms^{-1}. 2 seconds later the body is 13 m away from the origin.

    (a) Write down, in terms of a, the position vector after 2 seconds

    (b) Show that $(2a - 2)^2 = 144$

    (c) Hence find the two possible values of a.

20. At time $t = 0$ a particle has position vector $(2\mathbf{i} - 3\mathbf{j})$ m. It moves with a constant velocity of $(\mathbf{i} + 2\mathbf{j})$ ms^{-1} where $\mathbf{i}$ and $\mathbf{j}$ are unit vector due east and due north respectively.

    (a) Find an expression for the position vector of the particle after t seconds in the form $\mathbf{r} = \mathbf{r_0} + \mathbf{v}t$.

    (b) Find the time at which the particle is due north of the point with position vector $(5\mathbf{i} + 3\mathbf{j})$m.

21. A particle A has an initial position vector $(3\mathbf{i} - 4\mathbf{j})$m and a velocity of $(2\mathbf{i} + 3\mathbf{j})$ ms^{-1}. A particle B has an initial position vector $(6\mathbf{i} + 8\mathbf{j})$m and a velocity $(\mathbf{i} - \mathbf{j})$ ms^{-1}.

    (a) Find the position vectors of A and B after 2 seconds.

    (b) Find expressions for the position vectors of A and B after t seconds.

    (c) Show that A and B collide. After what time does this happen?

22. A particle with an initial position vector $(2\mathbf{i} + 3\mathbf{j})$ m travels with speed 20 ms^{-1} in the direction of the vector $(3\mathbf{i} - 4\mathbf{j})$ ms^{-1}. Find the position vector of the particle after t seconds.

23. At time $t = 0$, a particle P is at a point A with position vector $(2\mathbf{i} + 8\mathbf{j})$ m and is moving with velocity $(\mathbf{i} - \mathbf{j})$ ms^{-1}.

    (a) Find an expression for the position vector of P after a time t seconds.

    (b) Show that the distance d metres, of P from the point with position vector $(\mathbf{i} + 4\mathbf{j})$ m is given by
    $$d^2 = 2t^2 - \cancel{4t + 20}\ \ 6t + 17$$

    (c) Using calculus or by completing the square, find the value of t for which d^2 is a minimum and hence find the least distance of P from A.

24. Initially a ship P is at a point O and a ship Q is at the point with position vector $(5\mathbf{i} + 10\mathbf{j})$ km relative to O, where $\mathbf{i}$ and $\mathbf{j}$ are unit vectors directed due east and due north respectively.

    Ship P is moving with velocity $10\mathbf{i}$ km h^{-1} and ship Q is moving with velocity $(12\mathbf{i} - 5\mathbf{j})$ km h^{-1}.

    Find (a) the position vector of each ship relative to O after time t hours.

    (b) the distance of Q from P when $t = 1$.

    (c) the value of t when Q is due north of P.

25. At noon a boat A has position vector $(4\mathbf{i} + 2\mathbf{j})$ km and velocity $(10\mathbf{i} + 5\mathbf{j})$ km h^{-1}. At the same time boat B has position vector $(7\mathbf{i} + 6\mathbf{j})$ m and velocity $(4\mathbf{i} - 3\mathbf{j})$ km h^{-1}.

    Show that, unless some action is taken, these boats will collide and find the time when this will happen.

26. At time $t = 0$ a particle is at a point with position vector $4\mathbf{j}$ m, relative to a fixed origin O, and is moving with velocity $(2\mathbf{i} - 6\mathbf{j})$ ms^{-1}, where $\mathbf{i}$ and $\mathbf{j}$ are unit vectors directed due east and due north respectively.

    (a) Find the position vector of P after t seconds.

    (b) Find the time at which P is south-east of the origin.

    (c) Show that at time t the distance d metres of P from the origin is given by
    $$d^2 = 40t^2 - 48t + 16$$

    (d) Find the time t when d is a minimum.

27. At time $t = 0$ seconds, a small boat is 10 m east of a point P on the shore. It is moving with a constant velocity of $(4\mathbf{i} + 6\mathbf{j})$ ms^{-1}, where $\mathbf{i}$ and $\mathbf{j}$ are unit vectors due east and due north respectively. At time $t = 10$ seconds another small boat is 10 km west and 30 m south of point P. This boat is moving with a velocity $(5\mathbf{i} + 7.5\mathbf{j})$ ms^{-1}.

    (a) Show that the two boats will collide unless avoiding action is taken.

    (b) Find the position vector of the point of the collision.

28. Relative to a fixed point P, the position vector, $\mathbf{r}$ m, of a particle at time t seconds, is given by
    $$\mathbf{r} = (2t - 3)\mathbf{i} + (t + 4)\mathbf{j}$$

    (a) Find the value of t when the particle is closest to point P.

    (b) Find the least distance of the particle from P.

Examination Exercise 8

1. At noon, two ships A and B have position vectors $(3\mathbf{i} + 2\mathbf{j})$ km and $(-\mathbf{i} + 4\mathbf{j})$ km respectively, referred to an origin O. The velocities of A and B are $(-\mathbf{i} + 5\mathbf{j})$ km h^{-1} and $(2\mathbf{i} + \mathbf{j})$ km h^{-1} respectively. The position vector of A relative to B, at t hours after noon, is $\mathbf{r}$ km. Show that

   (a) $\mathbf{r} = (4 - 3t)\mathbf{i} + (-2 + 4t)\mathbf{j}$,

   (b) A and B are nearest to each other at 12.48 p.m. [E]

2. A particle P of mass 3 kg is moving under the action of a constant force $\mathbf{F}$ newtons. At $t = 0$, P has velocity $(3\mathbf{i} - 5\mathbf{j})$ms^{-1}. At $t = 4$ s, the velocity of P is $(-5\mathbf{i} + 11\mathbf{j})$ms^{-1}. Find

   (a) the acceleration of P, in terms of $\mathbf{i}$ and $\mathbf{j}$,

   (b) the magnitude of $\mathbf{F}$.

   At $t = 6$ s, P is at the point A with position vector $(6\mathbf{i} - 29\mathbf{j})$ m relative to a fixed origin O. At this instant the force $\mathbf{F}$ newtons is removed and P then moves with constant velocity. Three seconds after the force has been removed, P is at the point B.

   (c) Calculate the distance of B from O. [E]

3. Two ships P and Q are moving along straight lines with constant velocities. Initially P is at a point O and the position vector of Q relative to O is $(6\mathbf{i} + 12\mathbf{j})$ km, where $\mathbf{i}$ and $\mathbf{j}$ are unit vectors directed due east and due north respectively. The ship P is moving with velocity $10\mathbf{j}$ km h^{-1} and Q is moving with velocity $(-8\mathbf{i} + 6\mathbf{j})$ kmh^{-1}. At time t hours the position vectors of P and Q relative to O are $\mathbf{p}$ km and $\mathbf{q}$ km respectively.

   (a) Find $\mathbf{p}$ and $\mathbf{q}$ in terms of t.

   (b) Calculate the distance of Q from P when $t = 3$.

   (c) Calculate the value of t when Q is due north of P. [E]

4. At noon, the position vector of a helicopter A relative to a fixed point O is $32\mathbf{i}$ km, and it is moving horizontally with constant velocity $(48\mathbf{i} + 64\mathbf{j})$ km h^{-1}, where $\mathbf{i}$ and $\mathbf{j}$ are unit vectors due east and due north respectively.

   (a) Find the speed of A.

   (b) Find the position vector of A at 1400 hours, and show that A is then north east of O.

   At 1300 hours, a helicopter B leaves O and flies horizontally at a constant speed of 100 km h^{-1} in the direction of the vector $7\mathbf{i} + 24\mathbf{j}$.

   (c) Find the position vector of B at 1400 hours.

   At 1400 hours, B is forced to land. Helicopter A immediately changes course and flies horizontally, at the same constant speed as before, directly to the point C vertically above the point where B has landed.

(d) Find the displacement vector of C from A at 1400 hours.

(e) Find, to the nearest minute, how long it will take after A changes course for A to reach C. [E]

5. A destroyer is moving due west at a constant speed of 10 km h^{-1}. It has radar on board which, at time $t = 0$, identifies a cruiser, 50 km due west and moving due north with a constant speed of 20 km h^{-1}. The unit vectors $\mathbf{i}$ and $\mathbf{j}$ are directed due east and north respectively, and the origin O is taken to be the initial position of the destroyer. Each vessel maintains its constant velocity.

(a) Write down the velocity of each vessel in vector form.

(b) Find the position vector of each vessel at time t hours.

(c) Show that the distance d km between the vessels at time t hours is given by
$$d^2 = 500t^2 - 1000t + 2500.$$

The radar on the cruiser detects vessels only up to a distance of 40 km. By finding the minimum value of d^2, or otherwise,

(d) determine whether the destroyer will be detected by the cruiser's radar. [E]

6. *[In this question the vectors $\mathbf{i}$ and $\mathbf{j}$ are horizontal unit vectors in the directions due east and due north respectively.]*

Two boats A and B are moving with constant velocities. Boat A moves with velocity $9\mathbf{j} \text{ km h}^{-1}$. Boat B moves with velocity $(3\mathbf{i} + 5\mathbf{j}) \text{ km h}^{-1}$.

(a) Find the bearing on which B is moving.

At noon, A is at the point O, and B is 10 km due west of O. At time t hours after noon, the position vectors of A and B relative to O are $\mathbf{a}$ km and $\mathbf{b}$ km respectively.

(b) Find expressions for $\mathbf{a}$ and $\mathbf{b}$ in terms of t, giving your answers in the form $p\mathbf{i} + q\mathbf{j}$.

(c) Find the time when B is due south of A.

At time t hours after noon, the distance between A and B is d km. By finding an expression for $\overrightarrow{AB}$,

(d) show that $d^2 = 25t^2 - 60t + 100$.

At noon, the boats are 10 km apart.

(e) Find the time after noon at which the boats are again 10 km apart [E]

7. *[In this question, the horizontal unit vectors $\mathbf{i}$ and $\mathbf{j}$ are directed due East and North respectively.]*

A coastguard station O monitors the movements of ships in a channel. At noon, the station's radar records two ships moving with constant speed. Ship A is at the point with position vector $(-5\mathbf{i} + 10\mathbf{j})$ km relative to O and has velocity $(2\mathbf{i} + 2\mathbf{j}) \text{ km h}^{-1}$. Ship B is at the point with position vector $(3\mathbf{i} + 4\mathbf{j})$ km and has velocity $(-2\mathbf{i} + 5\mathbf{j}) \text{ km h}^{-1}$.

(a) Given that the two ships maintain these velocities, show that they collide.

The coastguard radios ship A and orders it to reduce its speed to move with velocity $(\mathbf{i} + \mathbf{j})$ km h^{-1}.

Given that A obeys this order and maintains this new constant velocity,

(b) find an expression for the vector $\overrightarrow{AB}$ at time t hours after noon.

(c) find, to 3 significant figures, the distance between A and B at 1400 hours,

(d) find the time at which B will be due north of A. [E]

8. [*In this question, the unit vectors* $\mathbf{i}$ *and* $\mathbf{j}$ *are horizontal vectors due east and north respectively.*]

At time $t = 0$, a football player kicks a ball from the point A with position vector $(2\mathbf{i} + \mathbf{j})$ m on a horizontal football field. The motion of the ball is modelled as that of a particle moving horizontally with constant velocity $(5\mathbf{i} + 8\mathbf{j})$ ms^{-1}. Find

(a) the speed of the ball,

(b) the position vector of the ball after t seconds.

The point B on the field has position vector $(10\mathbf{i} + 7\mathbf{j})$ m.

(c) Find the time when the ball is due north of B.

At time $t = 0$, another player starts running due north from B and moves with constant speed v ms^{-1}. Given that he intercepts the ball,

(d) find the value of v.

(e) State one physical factor, other than air resistance, which would be needed in a refinement of the model of the ball's motion to make the model more realistic. [E]

Specimen M1 paper A   Time $1\frac{1}{2}$ hours

1. Two particles A and B of masses 3 kg and 5 kg respectively, are connected by a light inextensible string which is initially slack. The particles are resting on a smooth horizontal surface. A is projected directly away from B with speed $4\,\text{ms}^{-1}$. When the string jerks tight, find

    (a) the common speed of the particles, **(4)**

    (b) the impulse in the string. **(3)**

---

2. (In this question the unit vectors **i** and **j** are directed due east and due north respectively).

    A particle moving with constant acceleration is initially travelling due east at $6\,\text{ms}^{-1}$. 4 seconds later it is travelling due north at $8\,\text{ms}^{-1}$.

    (a) Write down the initial velocity of the particle as a vector. **(1)**

    (b) Find the acceleration of the particle in the form $(a\mathbf{i} + b\mathbf{j})\,\text{ms}^{-2}$. **(3)**

    (c) Given that the particle starts at the origin, find its position vector after 4 seconds. **(3)**

---

3. A distress flare is fired vertically upwards, with a speed of $35\,\text{ms}^{-1}$ from a small boat which is at rest. Assuming that the flare is fired from a height of 2 m above the sea, find

    (a) the maximum height of the flare above the sea, **(3)**

    (b) the time during which the flare is more than 32 m above the sea. **(5)**

    (c) State one modelling assumption you have used in your calculation. **(1)**

---

4. A non-uniform plank AB, of mass 20 kg and length 4 m, is supported horizontally on two supports at C and D, where $AC = 1$ m and $BD = 1.5$ m.

    When a boy of mass 30 kg stands on the plank 1 m from B, the plank is on the point of tilting about D.

    (a) Find the distance of the centre of mass of the plank from A. **(5)**

    The boy then stands at a point 2 m from A.

    (b) Find the magnitude of the reactions at C and D. **(5)**

5. A straight road runs parallel to a railway track. At time $t = 0$, a train is stopped at a signal when it is passed by a car moving at a constant speed $30\,\text{ms}^{-1}$. After time $t = 40$ seconds the signal changes and the train immediately sets off in the same direction as the car. It takes the train 100 seconds to accelerate uniformly to its top speed of $50\,\text{ms}^{-1}$, after which times it moves with constant speed. The train then overtakes the car at time $t = T$.

   (a) Sketch, on the same diagram, the speed-time graphs for the car and the train. **(3)**

   (b) Find the value of T. **(9)**

6.

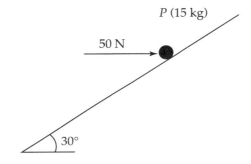

A particle P, of mass $15\,\text{kg}$, lies on a rough plane inclined at $30°$ to the horizontal. A horizontal force of magnitude $50\,\text{N}$ holds the particle in equilibrium. This force acts in a vertical plane through a line of greatest slope of the plane. The particle is on the point of slipping down the plane.

   (a) Draw a diagram showing all the forces acting on the particle. **(2)**

   (b) Find the friction force acting on the particle. **(3)**

   (c) Find the normal reaction of the plane on the particle. **(3)**

   (d) Find the coefficient of friction between the particle and the plane. **(1)**

   (e) If the $50\,\text{N}$ force is removed, find the acceleration of the block down the plane. **(5)**

7.

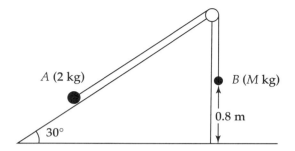

A particle A, of mass 2 kg, rests on a rough plane inclined at 30° to the horizontal. The coefficient of friction between A and the plane is $\frac{1}{3}$. A light inextensible string, which passes over a smooth fixed pulley at the top of the plane, connects particle A to particle B, of mass M kg, which hangs freely 0.8 m above a horizontal floor. The string between A and the pulley lies along a line of greatest slope of the plane.

The system is released from rest with the string taut so that particle A accelerates at $2\,\text{ms}^{-2}$ up the plane. Find

(a) the friction force between A and the plane, (3)

(b) the tension in the string, (3)

(c) the mass of B. (3)

When B hits the floor it does not rebound and A continues moving towards the pulley, which it does not reach. Find

(d) the speed with which B hits the ground. (2)

(e) the distance moved by A after B hits the floor until A comes to rest. (5)

Specimen M1 paper B Time $1\frac{1}{2}$ hours

1. A stone slides horizontally in a straight line across a frozen ice rink. The initial speed of the stone is $12\,\text{ms}^{-1}$ and it moves a distance 24 m before coming to rest. Find

   (a) the deceleration of the stone while it is moving, (2)

   (b) the coefficient of friction between the stone and the ice. (4)

2. A car is moving along a straight road with uniform acceleration. The car passes a point A with a speed of $10\,\text{ms}^{-1}$ and another point B with a speed of $20\,\text{ms}^{-1}$. The distance from A to B is 450 m.

   (a) Find the time taken by the car to move from A to B. (4)

   M is the mid-point of AB.

   (b) Find the speed with which the car passes M. (4)

3. (In this question the unit vectors **i** and **j** are directed due east and due north respectively).

   At time $t = 0$ a particle P is at a point with position vector $4\mathbf{i}$ m relative to a fixed origin O and is moving with velocity $(-\mathbf{i} + 3\mathbf{j})\,\text{ms}^{-1}$.

   (a) Find the position vector of P after a time t seconds. (2)

   (b) Find the value of t at which P is due north of O. (3)

   (c) Show that the distance d metres of P from O is given by
   $d^2 = 10t^2 - 8t + 16$ (3)

   (d) Find the value of t when d is a minimum. (3)

4.

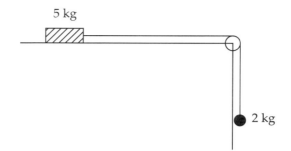

A box of mass 5 kg rests on a rough horizontal table. A light inextensible string, attached to the box, passes over a smooth pulley fixed at the edge of the table and the other end of the string is attached to a ball of mass 2 kg, which hangs freely.

The system is released from rest and the ball descends a distance of 0.6 m in 1 second. Modelling the box and the ball as particles, find

(a) the acceleration of the ball, (3)

(b) the tension in the string, (4)

(c) the coefficient of friction between the box and the table. (5)

(d) State how you have used the fact that the pulley is smooth. (1)

5.

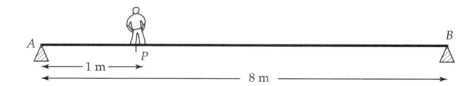

A non-uniform beam, of mass 40 kg and length 8 m, rests horizontally on two supports at A and B. A man, of mass 60 kg, stands on the beam at point P, where $AP = 1$ m. The magnitude of the reaction of the support at A is four times the magnitude of the reaction of the support at B. The beam is modelled as a non-uniform rod and the man as a particle. Find

(a) the magnitude of the reaction at B, (3)

(b) the distance of the centre of mass of the beam from end A. (4)

The support at B is now moved to a point C on the beam, where $AC = x$ metres. The man remains on the girder at point P.

The magnitudes of the reactions at the supports are now equal. Find

(c) the magnitude of the reaction at each support, (2)

(d) the value of x. (4)

6. Two particles A and B are moving directly towards each other. Particle A, of mass 4 kg, is moving with a speed of 1 ms^{-1}. Particle B is moving with a speed of 0.5 ms^{-1}. A and B collide and during the collision B exerts an impulse on A of magnitude 2.8 Ns.

   (a) Calculate the speed of A immediately after the collision. (3)

   (b) State the direction of motion of A immediately after the collision. (1)

   Immediately after the collision the speed of B is 0.9 ms^{-1} in the same direction as A.

   (c) Calculation the mass of B. (4)

   (d) Calculate the time taken after the collision for A and B to be 4 m apart. (3)

---

7. A lift of mass 600 kg, carrying a woman of mass 50 kg, is pulled upwards by a vertical cable. It makes the ascent by accelerating uniformly from rest at 2 ms^{-2} to some maximum speed which it maintains for some time and then it decelerates uniformly at 4 ms^{-2} to rest. Find

   (a) the tension in the lift cable when the lift is accelerating, (3)

   (b) the tension in the lift cable when the lift is decelerating, (3)

   (c) the magnitude of the reaction force exerted on the woman by the lift when it is decelerating. (4)

   (d) the magnitude of the reaction force exerted on the floor of the lift by the woman when the lift is accelerating. (3)

Answers

Exercise 1A   page 6
1. $t = 5\,\text{s}$ 2. $t = 8\,\text{s}$ 3. $v = 8.3\,\text{ms}^{-1}$
4. $2.5\,\text{m}$ 5. $t = 2\,\text{s}$ 6. $a = 3\,\text{ms}^{-2}$
7. $s = 45\,\text{m}$ 8. $45\,\text{m}$ 9. $104\,\text{m}$
10. $1.02\,\text{ms}^{-2}$ 11. $1.5\,\text{ms}^{-2}$
12. $20.6\,\text{ms}^{-1}$ 13. $3\,\text{ms}^{-2}$ 14. $14\,\text{m}$
15. $1\,\text{ms}^{-1}, 4\,\text{s}$ 16. $3\,\text{s}, 11\,\text{ms}^{-1}$
17. $20\,\text{ms}^{-1}, 3\,\text{ms}^{-2}$
18. (a) $20\,\text{ms}^{-1}$ (b) $50\,\text{ms}^{-1}$
    (c) $18\,\text{km}\,\text{h}^{-1}$ (d) $43.2\,\text{km}\,\text{h}^{-1}$
19. (a) $s = 20t + \dfrac{t^2}{8}$ $s = 15t + 2.63t^2$
    (b) $2\,\text{s}$ (c) $91.8\,\text{km}\,\text{h}^{-1}$
20. (a) $4\,\text{s}$ (c) $6\,\text{s}$ (d) $39\,\text{m}$
21. $u = 15\,\text{ms}^{-1}, \quad a = 3\,\text{ms}^{-2}$

Exercise 1B   page 11
1. (a) $0.495\,\text{s}$ (b) $4.85\,\text{ms}^{-1}$
2. $8.85\,\text{ms}^{-1}$ 3. $24.2\,\text{ms}^{-1}$ 4. $2.45\,\text{s}$
5. (a) $0.15\,\text{s}$ $3.93\,\text{s}$ (b) $3.78\,\text{s}$
6. $21\,\text{ms}^{-1}$
7. (a) $h = \dfrac{u^2}{2g}$ (b) $t = \dfrac{2u}{g}$
8. $5.60\,\text{s}$ 9. $1.33\,\text{s}$ 10. $30\,\text{m}$
11. (a) $1.79\,\text{s}$ (b) $15.7\,\text{m}$

Exercise 1C   page 15
1. (a) $4\,\text{ms}^{-2}$ (b) $-2\,\text{ms}^{-2}$ (c) $250\,\text{m}$
2. $4\,\text{ms}^{-2}, 100\,\text{m}$
3. (a) $4\,\text{s}$ (b) $-5\,\text{ms}^{-2}$ 4. $11.1\,\text{ms}^{-1}$
7. (a) $89\,\text{s}$ (b) $111\,\text{s}$
8. (b) $8\,\text{s}$ 9. (b) $178\,\text{s}$
10. (b) $42\,\text{m}$ (c) $58\,\text{m}$ 11. $15\,\text{s}$
12. (a) $9\,\text{ms}^{-1}$ (c) $6.75\,\text{s}$ 13. $23\,\text{s}$

Exercise 1D   page 19
1. (a) $3\,\text{ms}^{-1}$, $0\,\text{ms}^{-1}$, $450\,\text{m}$
   (b) $0\,\text{ms}^{-1}$, $3\,\text{ms}^{-1}$, $450\,\text{m}$
   (c) $3\,\text{ms}^{-1}$, $3\,\text{ms}^{-1}$, $300\,\text{m}$
   (d) $2\,\text{ms}^{-1}$, $3\,\text{ms}^{-1}$, $350\,\text{m}$
   (e) $30\,\text{mph}$, $0\,\text{mph}$, $15\,\text{mph}$, $75\,\text{miles}$

2. (a) $-800\,\text{m}$ (b) $2400\,\text{m}$
   (c) $4.8\,\text{ms}^{-1}$

3. (a) $20\,\text{m}$ (b) $28\,\text{m}$ (c) $3.5\,\text{ms}^{-1}$

5. (b) $4.8\,\text{kmh}^{-1}$ (c) $3.2\,\text{kmh}^{-1}$

Examination Exercise 1   page 21

1. (a) $162\,\text{m}$ (b) 6.2 (c) $0.56\,\text{ms}^{-2}$

2. (a) $138.5\,\text{m}$
   (b) Straight line graph $\Rightarrow$ constant deceleration $\Rightarrow$ constant force.

3. (b) $0.48\,\text{ms}^{-2}$ (c) $250\,\text{s}$ (d) $375\,\text{s}$

4. (b) $42\,\text{ms}^{-1}$ (c) $2.4\,\text{ms}^{-2}$

5. (a) $12\,\text{ms}^{-2}$ (b) $80\,\text{ms}^{-1}$

6. (a) $185\,\text{s}$ (b) $2480\,\text{m}$

7. (a) $0.1\,\text{ms}^{-2}$ (b) $155\,\text{s}$

8. (b) $5400\,\text{m}$ (c) $112\,\text{s}$

9. (b) $200\,\text{s}$ (c) $60\,\text{s}$ (d) $50\,\text{ms}^{-1}$

Exercise 2A   page 31

1. (a) $4\mathbf{i}+6\mathbf{j}$ (b) $-12\mathbf{i}+3\mathbf{j}$
   (c) $-8\mathbf{i}+9\mathbf{j}$ (d) $6\mathbf{i}+2\mathbf{j}$
   (e) $-2\mathbf{i}+4\mathbf{j}$ (f) $8\mathbf{i}+5\mathbf{j}$
   (g) $10\mathbf{i}+\mathbf{j}$ (h) $-2\mathbf{i}-10\mathbf{j}$
   (i) $-10\mathbf{i}+6\mathbf{j}$

2. (a) 5 (b) 13 (c) 25
   (d) 1.41 (e) 5.39 (f) 3.61

3. (a) $45°$ (b) $26.6°$ (c) $71.6°$
   (d) $56.3°$ (e) $117°$ (f) $129°$

4. (a) $\dfrac{1}{\sqrt{2}}(\mathbf{i}+\mathbf{j})$ (b) $\dfrac{1}{\sqrt{13}}(2\mathbf{i}+3\mathbf{j})$
   (c) $\dfrac{1}{5}(3\mathbf{i}+4\mathbf{j})$ (d) $\dfrac{1}{\sqrt{29}}(-2\mathbf{i}+5\mathbf{j})$
   (e) $\dfrac{1}{20}(12\mathbf{i}+16\mathbf{j})$ (f) $\dfrac{1}{10}(-6\mathbf{i}-8\mathbf{j})$

5. (a) 6 (b) 16 (c) 6

6. (a) $18\mathbf{i}+24\mathbf{j}$ (b) $-10\mathbf{i}+24\mathbf{j}$
   (c) $2.8\mathbf{i}-9.6\mathbf{j}$

7. (a) $\mathbf{i}+2\mathbf{j}$ (b) $4\mathbf{i}-3\mathbf{j}$ (c) $4\mathbf{j}$
   (d) $\mathbf{i}-2\mathbf{j}$ (e) $-3\mathbf{i}+5\mathbf{j}$ (f) $6\mathbf{i}-\mathbf{j}$
   (g) $2\mathbf{i}+6\mathbf{j}$

8. $5,\quad 13,\quad 2.24,\quad 3.16$

9. (a) 8.60 (b) $12\mathbf{i}-5\mathbf{j}$ (c) 13

10. (a) $12,\ -15$ (b) $-1,\ 2$
    (c) $5,\ -3$ (d) $6,\ 5$

11. (a) $4\mathbf{i}+5\mathbf{j}$ (b) $10\mathbf{i}-6\mathbf{j}$
    (c) $-2\mathbf{i}+4\mathbf{j}$ (d) $3\mathbf{i}-14\mathbf{j}$

12. (a) $3\mathbf{i}+2\mathbf{j}$ (b) $-12\mathbf{i}+9\mathbf{j}$
    (c) $17\mathbf{i}-16\mathbf{j}$ (d) $3\mathbf{i}+5\mathbf{j}$

Exercise 2B   page 33

1. (a) $18\mathbf{i}+9\mathbf{j}$ (b) $2\mathbf{i}+\mathbf{j}$
   (c) $10\mathbf{i}-2\mathbf{j}$ (d) $28\mathbf{i}+7\mathbf{j}$
   (e) $11\mathbf{i}+2\mathbf{j}$ (f) $\mathbf{i}+4\mathbf{j}$
   (g) $22\mathbf{i}+4\mathbf{j}$ (h) $-20\mathbf{i}+4\mathbf{j}$
   (i) $12\mathbf{i}+6\mathbf{j}$

2. (a) 25 (b) $\sqrt{5}$ (c) 25 (d) 3
   (e) 2 (f) 4

3. 45° 4. (a) $-\dfrac{3}{5}\mathbf{i} - \dfrac{4}{5}\mathbf{j}$ (b) 12

5. (a) $12\mathbf{i} + 9\mathbf{j}$ (b) $24\mathbf{i} - 10\mathbf{j}$
   (c) $14\mathbf{i} + 48\mathbf{j}$ (d) $\dfrac{4}{5}\mathbf{i} + \dfrac{3}{5}\mathbf{j}$
   (e) $-18\mathbf{i} - 80\mathbf{j}$

6. (a) $4\mathbf{i} + \mathbf{j}$ (b) $2\mathbf{i} + 5\mathbf{j}$ (c) $-2\mathbf{i} + 4\mathbf{j}$
   (d) $\mathbf{i} - 3\mathbf{j}$ (e) $-3\mathbf{i} - 4\mathbf{j}$ (f) $5\mathbf{j}$
   (g) $4\mathbf{i} - 4\mathbf{j}$ (h) $-\mathbf{i} - 8\mathbf{j}$

7. (a) 10 (b) 13 (c) $\sqrt{2}$ (d) 5
   (e) 6 (f) $19.2 (= \sqrt{369})$

8. (a) $\sqrt{10}$ (b) $9\mathbf{i} + 2\mathbf{j}$
   (c) $\sqrt{85} (= 9.22)$

9. (a) $\sqrt{34}$ (b) $-4\mathbf{i} - 4\mathbf{j}$
   (c) $\sqrt{32} (= 5.66)$

10. (a) $-\mathbf{a}$ (b) $\mathbf{b} - \mathbf{a}$ (c) $\mathbf{b} - \mathbf{a}$
    (d) $\mathbf{a} - \mathbf{b}$ (e) $2\mathbf{a}$ (f) $\mathbf{a} + \mathbf{b}$
    (g) $\mathbf{a} + \mathbf{b}$ (h) $\mathbf{a} - 2\mathbf{b}$ (i) $2\mathbf{b} - \mathbf{a}$

11. $\dfrac{1}{2}\mathbf{s} - \dfrac{1}{2}\mathbf{t}$ 12. $2\mathbf{x} + 2\mathbf{y}$

Exercise 4A   page 48
1. (a) (i) 8.66 N (ii) 5 N
   (b) (i) 12.9 N (ii) 15.3 N
   (c) (i) 21.2 N (ii) 21.2 N
   (d) (i) 14.7 N (ii) −10.3 N
   (e) (i) −47.6 N (ii) −15.5 N
   (f) (i) −5.20 N (ii) 3.00 N

2. (a) 37.6 N, 13.7 N
   (b) 4.50 N, 5.36 N
   (c) 6.08 N, 34.5 N

3. (a) $P\cos\theta$, $P\sin\theta$
   (b) $-P\cos\theta$, $P\sin\theta$

4. (a) (i) 10.3 N, (ii) 28.2 N
   (b) (i) 37.6 N, (ii) 13.7 N
   (c) (i) 2.50 N (ii) 4.33 N
   (d) (i) 7.25 N (ii) 3.38 N
   (e) (i) 14.7 N (ii) 8.50 N
   (f) (i) 10.4 N (ii) 6 N
   (g) (i) $W\sin\theta$ (ii) $W\cos\theta$
   (h) (i) $P\cos\theta$ (ii) $P\sin\theta$

5. (a) (i) 3.80 N, (ii) 15.2 N
   (b) (i) 30.5 N, (ii) −2.36 N
   (c) (i) −18.2 N (ii) 27.6 N
   (d) (i) 0.340 N (ii) 0.428 N
   (e) (i) −8.39 N (ii) 10.6 N
   (f) (i) 37.8 N (ii) −5.92 N

6. (a) $17.1\mathbf{i} + 47.0\mathbf{j}$ (b) $17.3\mathbf{i} + 10\mathbf{j}$

7. (a) 13 N, 22.6° (b) 10 N, 36.9°
   (c) 22.4 N, 26.6° (d) 28.3 N, 45.0°
   (e) 16.6 N, 25.0° (f) 5.66 N, 45.0°

8. (a) 2.45 N, 71.8° (b) 7.87 N, 69.5°
   (c) 5.82 N, 23.4° (d) 16.1 N, 67.0°

9. (a) 2.61 N, 1.54° (b) 9.61 N, 37.3°
   (c) 11.4 N, 19.5°

10. (a) $F\cos 30° = 15\cos 60°$
        $F = 8.66$
    (b) $R = 9.32$ N

11. 5 N, 53.1°

12. 9.43 N, 32.0°

13. (a) $12\mathbf{i} + 10\mathbf{j}$, 15.6 N, 39.8°
(b) $6\mathbf{i} - 2\mathbf{j}$, 6.32 N, 18.4°
(c) 2.24 N, 63.4° $-\mathbf{i} + 2\mathbf{j}$, 2.24 N, 116.6°

14. $a = 5$, $b = -12$

Exercise 4B page 58

1. (a) $P = 3.26$ N $Q = 2.23$ N
(b) $P = 8.21$ N $Q = 12.0$ N
(c) $P = 8.66$ N $Q = 5$ N
(d) $P = 28.2$ N $Q = 36.8$ N

2. (a) 10 N   36.9°   (b) 25 N   73.7°
(c) 10.3 N   60.9°

3. (a) $X = 19.7$ N $Y = 10.4$ N
(b) $X = 19.9$ N $Y = 12.0$ N

4. (a) $a = 2$ $b = -4$
(b) $a = -8$ $b = 4$
(c) $a = -2$ $b = 2$

5. $T = 7.42$ N $W = 11.4$ N

6. (a) 30°   (b) 173 N

7. (a) 2.52 N   (b) 3.92 N

8. (b) 56.6 N   (c) 28.3 N   (d) light

9. (a) $p = -4, q = 2$ (b) 4.47 N
(c) 26.6°

10. (b) 7050 N   (c) 7510 N

11. (a) 55.5°   (b) 87.1 N

12. $T = 26.6$ N, $W = 67.4$ N

13. (b) 75 N   (c) 45 N

14. 20.1 N,   15.6 N

15. (b) 88.0 N,   65.2 N

Exercise 4C page 66

1. (a) 15 N, at rest   (b) 19.6 N, at rest
(c) 19.6 N, accelerate

2. (a) 7 N   (b) 24.5 N   (c) 14.7 N

3. 0.25

4. (a) 0.4   (b) 6 N   (c) 20 N

5. (a) 146 N   (b) 86.6 N   (c) 0.593

6. (b) $R = 10g - P\sin 40°$
$F = P\cos 40°$
(c) 38.3 N

7. (a) 22.1 N   (b) 22.4 N

8. (a) 14.7 N   (b) 14.5 N   (c) 20.5 N

9. 70.3 N

Exercise 4D page 76

1. (a) 18.9 N   (b) 13.7 N
(c) 14.9 N   (d) 29.4 N

2. (a) 17.3 N   (b) 20.0 N

3. 21.0 N

4. (a) 49 N   (b) 30°   (c) 84.9 N

5. (a) 26.6 N   (b) 12.4 N   (c) 0.466

6. 0.173   **7.** 8.0 N   **8.** 48.2 N

9. (a) (i) 9.06 N (ii) 4.23 N
   (b) (i) 15.3 N (ii) 12.9 N
   (c) (i) 14.8 N (ii) 2.60 N
   (d) (i) 23.0 N (ii) 19.3 N
10. (a) 6.04 N (b) 19.2 N (c) 5.98 N
    (d) 21.4 N (e) 6.04 N (f) 25.1 N
11. (a) 18.3 N (b) 25.7 N (c) 22.0 N
    (d) 44.8 N (e) 17.7 N (f) 32.8 N
12. (a) 35.0° (b) 56.2 N
13. (a) 1.95 N   not limiting
14. (a) 9.89 N (b) 27.9 N
15. (a) 66.5 N (b) 95.0 N (c) 0.700
16. (b) 160 N (c) 214 N
17. $7.35\,\text{N} \le P \le 41.5\,\text{N}$ 18. 79.5 N
19. (a) 45.2 N (b) 15.0 N
20. (a) 1.70 N
    (b) 1.96 N, motion occurs

Examination Exercise 4   page 82
1. 11.0 N
2. (a) 63° (c) 4.47 N
3. (a) $p = 2$ $q = -6$
   (b) 6.32 N (c) 18°
4. (a) 77.8 N (b) 59.6 N
5. 0.444
6. (a) 43° (b) 53 N   7. (b) $\dfrac{4}{7}$

8. (b) $\dfrac{2\,mg}{11}$
   (c) Friction force acts down the plane.
9. (a) 2.7 N (b) 10.6 N   10. 0.262
11. (a) 0.450 (b) 1.44 N
    (c) Not in equilibrium.
12. (a) 88.3 N (b) 74.8 N

Exercise 5A   page 93
1. (a) 20 N (b) 45 N (c) 59 N
   (d) 39 N (e) 15 N (f) 17 N
2. (a) $2\,\text{ms}^{-2}$ (b) $1.5\,\text{ms}^{-2}$
   (c) $2.4\,\text{ms}^{-2}$ (d) $2\,\text{ms}^{-2}$
3. $1.5\,\text{ms}^{-2}$ 4. 3 kg
5. (a) $2\,\text{ms}^{-2}$ 1000 N
6. (a) $-400000\,\text{ms}^{-2}$ (b) 4000 N
7. 800 N   8. 1500 N   9. 2 s
10. 142 N   11. 43.3 N   223 N
12. 0.316   13. 0.0765   14. 500 N
15. $3.43\,\text{ms}^{-2}$ 16. 19.5 N
17. $X = 293\,\text{N}$, $Y = 224\,\text{N}$ 18. 575 N
19. $1.08\,\text{ms}^{-2}$ 20. $\mu = 0.189$
21. (a) 2.99 N (b) $1.73\,\text{ms}^{-2}$
22. (a) 36.5 N (b) 5.10 m
23. 1.68 N   24. 7800 N   25. 5000 N
26. (b) 918 N   (c) 918 N
27. (a) 2360 N (b) 7670 N
28. (a) 1560 N (b) 5070 N

Exercise 5B page 101
1. (a) 44.4 N (b) 4.14 ms^{-2}
   (c) 12.4 ms^{-1}
2. (a) 5.62 ms^{-2} (b) 6.70 ms^{-1}
3. 30°
4. (a) 34.5 N (b) 10.5 N (c) 39.4 N
   (d) $\theta = 60°, a = 3.51$ ms^{-2}
5. (a) (i) 44.4 N (ii) 10.7 N
       (iii) 0.241
   (b) (i) 46.0 N (ii) 15.7 N
       (iii) 0.341
   (c) (i) 40.1 N (ii) 10.1 N
       (iii) 0.252
   (d) (i) 67.4 N (ii) 12.8 N
       (iii) 0.190
6. 5.4 ms^{-2}
7. (a) 1.5 ms^{-2} (c) 0.559
8. (a) 101 N (b) 13.8 N (c) 122 N
9. (b) 25.3 N (c) 10.1 N
   (d) 2.48 ms^{-2}
10. (a) 2.25 ms^{-2} (b) 0.463
11. (a) 8.85 N (b) 1.47 ms^{-2}
12. (a) 3.10 m, (b) coin moves down
13. (a) 2.08 ms^{-2} (b) 0.332
14. (a) 3.20 ms^{-2} (b) 5.66 ms^{-1}

Exercise 5C page 109
1. (a) 4 ms^{-2} (b) 12 N
2. (a) 1.55 ms^{-2} (b) 12 N
3. (a) 3000 N (b) 1000 N
   (c) 1200 N (d) 400 N
4. -0.5 ms^{-2}; 200 N; thrust
5. (a) 3.75 ms^{-2} (b) 5500 N
6. (b) 9200 N; 66700 N
7. (a) (i) 150 N (ii) $X = 400$ N
   (b) 0.212 ms^{-2}, 309 N
8. (a) 53100 N (b) 17700 N, 35400 N
9. (a) 0.325 ms^{-2} (b) 788 N
10. 1.74 ms^{-2}; 5770 N; light and inextensible.
11. (a) 86.1 N, (b) 49.2 N
12. 58.8 N, 88.2 N
13. 147 N, 343 N
14. (a) 2.37 ms^{-2} (b) 2840 N

Exercise 5D page 116
1. (a) 2.45 ms^{-2} (b) 36.8 N
   (c) both particles have same velocity and acceleration
   (d) tension same throughout the string
2. (a) 3.27 ms^{-2} (b) 4.43 ms^{-1}
   (c) 52.3 N
3. (a) 3.92 ms^{-2} (b) 3.96 ms^{-1}
   (c) 4.8 m
4. (a) 4.2 ms^{-2} (b) 8.4 m
   (c) 8.4 ms^{-1} (d) 1.71 s

5. (a) $2.67\,\text{ms}^{-2}$ (b) $35.7\,\text{N}$
   (c) ~~2.68 kg~~ $2.86\,\text{kg}$

6. $3.27\,\text{ms}^{-2}$

7. (c) $1.63\,\text{ms}^{-2}$ (d) $24.5\,\text{N}$
   (e) $34.6\,\text{N}$

8. (b) $4.31\,\text{ms}^{-2}$ (c) $3.22\,\text{ms}^{-1}$
   (e) $3.92\,\text{ms}^{-2}$ (f) $1.32\,\text{m}$

9. (b) $26.5\,\text{N}$

10. (a) $5.44\,\text{ms}^{-2}$ (b) $3.30\,\text{ms}^{-1}$
    (c) $0.910\,\text{s}$
    (d) smooth pulley, string light, string inextensible, masses are particles.

Exercise 5E page 124

1. (a) $0.98\,\text{ms}^{-2}$ $17.6\,\text{N}$
   (b) $3.00\,\text{ms}^{-2}$ $38.4\,\text{N}$

2. (a) $1.4\,\text{ms}^{-2}$ (b) $2.05\,\text{ms}^{-1}$

3. (a) $17.8\,\text{N}$ (b) $7.12\,\text{N}$
   (c) $2.80\,\text{ms}^{-2}$ (d) $21.0\,\text{N}$

4. (a) $4.57\,\text{ms}^{-2}$ (b) $30.6\,\text{N}$

5. (a) $2.23\,\text{ms}^{-2}$, $52.4\,\text{N}$
   (b) $0.437\,\text{ms}^{-2}$, $28.1\,\text{N}$

7. $17.0\,\text{kg}$, pulley smooth, string light, string inextensible.

8. (b) $39\,\text{N}$ (c) $31.4\,\text{N}$ (e) 0.238

9. (a) weight acts through a point and body does not rotate,
   (b) weight of string not in equation of motion,
   (c) speed and acceleration same for both particles,
   (d) tension same throughout the string

10. (a) $0.706\,\text{ms}^{-2}$ (b) $1.68\,\text{ms}^{-1}$
    (c) $6.11\,\text{ms}^{-2}$ (d) $2.23\,\text{m}$

11. (a) $1.76\,\text{ms}^{-2}$ (b) $0.801\,\text{m}$

12. (b) $50\,\text{N}$ (c) $58.3\,\text{N}$
    (d) $62.5\,\text{N}, 0.933$

13. (b) $50\,\text{N}$ (c) $30°$ 14. $1.54\,\text{ms}^{-2}$

Exercise 5F page 130

1. $(10\mathbf{i} + 4\mathbf{j})\,\text{N}$ 2. $(4\mathbf{i} - 3\mathbf{j})\,\text{ms}^{-2}$

3. $(4\mathbf{i} + \mathbf{j})\,\text{ms}^{-2}$

4. (a) $3.61\,\text{ms}^{-2}$ (b) $33.7°$
   (c) $13\,\text{ms}^{-1}$

5. $(9\mathbf{i} - 4\mathbf{j})\,\text{N}$

6. (a) $(-2\mathbf{i} + 3\mathbf{j})\,\text{ms}^{-2}$
   (b) $(-24\mathbf{i} + 36\mathbf{j})\,\text{ms}^{-1}$
   (c) $(-144\mathbf{i} + 216\mathbf{j})\,\text{m}$

7. (a) $(-11\mathbf{i} - 4\mathbf{j})\,\text{N}$ (b) $(-5\mathbf{i} + 4\mathbf{j})\,\text{N}$

Examination Exercise 5 page 130

1. (a) $2.45\,\text{ms}^{-2}$ (b) 0.25

2. (a) $1.51\,\text{ms}^{-2}$ (b) $3.01\,\text{ms}^{-1}$
   (c) $1.51\,\text{ms}^{-2}$

3. (a) $0.7\,\text{ms}^{-2}$ (b) $960\,\text{N}$

4. 500 N

5. (a) $4.50\,\text{ms}^{-2}$ (c) $1.51\,\text{ms}^{-2}$

6. (a) 22.8 N (b) $m = 1.9$ (c) 45.6 N
   (d) tension is the same throughout its length

7. (a) 15.7 N (b) 0.624

8. (a) $t = 2$ (b) 1.76 N
   (c) 0.259 (d) 2.5 N

9. (a) inextensible string
   (b) $5.88\,\text{ms}^{-2}$ (c) 1.8 h

10. (a) $\dfrac{3\,mg}{2}$ (b) $\dfrac{1}{2}$

11. (a) $3.2\,\text{ms}^{-2}$ (b) 5.28 N (c) 0.751
    (d) same acceleration for A and B

12. (a) 10.1 N (b) 153.4°

13. (a) $(9\mathbf{i} - 3\mathbf{j})$ N (b) 108.4°
    (c) $(3\mathbf{i} - \mathbf{j})\,\text{ms}^{-2}$ (d) $4.12\,\text{ms}^{-1}$

14. (a) $0.4\,\text{ms}^{-2}$ (b) 720 N
    (c) $0.09\,\text{ms}^{-2}$, decreases

15. (b) $I = 7$ (d) 2360 N
    (e) 688 N

Exercise 6A page 138

1. (a) $640\,\text{kg ms}^{-1}$
   (b) $50000\,\text{kg ms}^{-1}$
   (c) $3750000\,\text{kg ms}^{-1}$
   (d) $200\,\text{kg ms}^{-1}$

2. $30000\,\text{kg ms}^{-1}$ 3. $45000\,\text{kg ms}^{-1}$

4. $12\,\text{kg ms}^{-1}$, 12 Ns

5. 4.5 Ns 6. $5\,\text{ms}^{-1}$ 7. 1.6 s

8. $m = 16$ 9. $20\,\text{ms}^{-1}$ 10. 10 Ns

11. (a) $6.26\,\text{ms}^{-1}$ (b) $5.42\,\text{ms}^{-1}$
    (c) 2.34 Ns

12. 375 N

Exercise 6B page 142

1. (a) $3.2\,\text{ms}^{-1}$ (b) $2\,\text{ms}^{-1}$
   (c) $2\,\text{ms}^{-1}$ (d) $4\,\text{ms}^{-1}$
   (e) $2\,\text{ms}^{-1}$ (f) 18 kg
   (g) $1.2\,\text{ms}^{-1}$ (h) 0.4 kg

2. $3\,\text{ms}^{-1}$ 3. $2\,\text{ms}^{-1}$ 4. $9\,\text{ms}^{-1}$

5. $1\,\text{ms}^{-1}$ 6. $3.2\,\text{ms}^{-1}$ 7. $9\,\text{ms}^{-1}$

8. (a) 2.5 kg (b) 1.5 kg

9. $2.4\,\text{ms}^{-1}$

10. (a) $12.5\,\text{ms}^{-1}$ (b) $15.5\,\text{ms}^{-1}$
    (c) $6.5\,\text{ms}^{-1}$ (d) $5\,\text{ms}^{-1}$

11. $1.33\,\text{ms}^{-1}$, direction reversed.

12. $\dfrac{1}{3}u$, direction reversed

Exercise 6C page 145

1. $6\,\text{ms}^{-1}$ 2. $188\,\text{ms}^{-1}$

3. (a) $-2.5\,\mathbf{i}\,\text{ms}^{-1}$ (b) $-10\,\mathbf{i}\,\text{ms}^{-1}$

4. B and C $2\,\text{ms}^{-1}$, B $6\,\text{ms}^{-1}$, C $2\,\text{ms}^{-1}$ reversed

Exercise 6D page 146

1. $1\,\text{ms}^{-1}$, 5 Ns

2. $4.5\,\text{ms}^{-1}$, 3 Ns 3. $1\,\text{ms}^{-1}$

Exercise 6E   page 148
1. $10.8\mathbf{i}\,\text{ms}^{-1}$
2. $-40\mathbf{i}\,\text{N}$
3. $(5\mathbf{i}+10\mathbf{j})\,\text{N}$
4. speed $= 19.8\,\text{ms}^{-1}$
5. $(3.75\mathbf{i}-3.75\mathbf{j})\,\text{N}$

Exercise 6F   page 149
1. $m=16$
2. $0.8\,\text{ms}^{-1}$ to the left,   24 Ns
3. (a) $0\,\text{ms}^{-1}$ (b) $0.048\,\text{Ns}$
4. $1.75\,\text{ms}^{-1}$
5. $10\,\text{ms}^{-1}$,   particles coalesce
6. $\frac{1}{5}u\,\text{ms}^{-1}$, to the left; $6mu$ Ns
7. (a) $0.25\,\text{ms}^{-1}$ (b) direction reversed (c) $12.5\,\text{Ns}$
8. $\frac{u}{3}$; $4mu$
9. (a) $2000\,\text{kg ms}^{-1}$
10. (a) $5\,\text{ms}^{-1}$ (b) $4.5\,\text{ms}^{-1}$ (c) $3.6\,\text{Ns}$
11. $1\,\text{ms}^{-1}$, direction unchanged; $12m$ Ns
12. (b) $3.92\,\text{ms}^{-1}$ (c) $7060\,\text{N}$
13. $1\,\text{ms}^{-1}$, $5\,\text{Ns}$
14. (a) $4\,\text{ms}^{-1}$ (b) $12000\,\text{Ns}$ (c) $1250\,\text{N}$
15. (a) $6.26\,\text{ms}^{-1}$ (b) $5.89\,\text{ms}^{-1}$ (c) $57.8\,\text{ms}^{-1}$ (d) $4910\,\text{N}$
16. (a) $2.69\,\text{ms}^{-1}$ (b) $10400\,\text{Ns}$ (c) $R=1180$

Examination Exercise 6   page 153
1. (a) $1.75\,\text{ms}^{-1}$ (b) $0.75\,\text{Ns}$
2. $4\,\text{ms}^{-1}$
3. (a) $2\,s$ (b) $2.4\,\text{m}$ (c) $0.3\,\text{ms}^{-1}$ (d) $0.06\,\text{Ns}$
4. (b) $2250\,\text{Ns}$ (c) $0.149\,\text{m}$
5. (b) $5.2\,\text{ms}^{-1}$ (c) $8100\,\text{N}$ (d) $0.16\,\text{m}$
6. (a) $\dfrac{6u}{5}$ (b) $\dfrac{14mu}{5}$
7. $0.6\,\text{ms}^{-1}$, direction reversed
8. (a) $4.8\,\text{ms}^{-1}$ (b) $43200\,\text{Ns}$ (c) 3600
9. (a) $0.7\,\text{ms}^{-1}$ (b) unchanged (c) $8.25\,\text{Ns}$
10. (a) $4.4\,\text{ms}^{-1}$ (b) $2.16\,\text{Ns}$

Exercise 7A   page 158
1. (a) 30 Nm anticlockwise
   (b) 80 Nm clockwise
   (c) 55 Nm clockwise
   (d) 230 Nm anticlockwise
   (e) 100 Nm anticlockwise
   (f) 54 Nm clockwise
   (g) 256 Nm anticlockwise
   (h) 71 Nm anticlockwise
2. (a) 8 Nm clockwise
   (b) 60 Nm clockwise (c) 0
   (d) 26 Nm anticlockwise
   (e) 18 Nm anticlockwise

3. 12 Nm   4. 12 Nm   5. 10 Nm

6. (a) 3 Nm   (b) 6 Nm

Exercise 7B   page 162
1. (a) 10 N, 3 m   (b) 8 N, 2 N
   (c) 24 N, $\frac{1}{2}$ m   (d) 4 N, 2 m
   (e) 38 N, 1 m   (f) 63 N, 52 N
   (g) 4 N, 20 N   (h) 2 N, 23 N

2. (a) 658 N, 518 N
   (b) assume men are particles and the plank is a rod

3. 386 N, 648 N

4. 41.7 N, 33.3 N

5. 1.33 m

6. (a) 735 N   (b) 1.5 m
   (c) the man is a particle, the plank is a rod.

7. 1.33 m   8. $m = 2$ 9. 0.625 m

10. (a) 39.2 N   (b) 2 m

11. (b) 176 N, 216 N

12. (a) 118 N   (b) 1.5 m

13. 441 N, 245 N

Exercise 7C   page 166
1. 2.5 m   2. 10 kg   294 N

3. $M = 2$ 4. 0.75 m

5. 2 m from A;
   (a) 13.4 N   (b) 73.5 N

6. 17.5 N   7. (a) 100 N   (b) 150 N

Exercise 7D   page 170
1. 37.5 N, 22.5 N   2. 1 m

3. right, children are particles.

4. 39.2 N, 58.8 N   5. 129 N

Examination Exercise 7   page 171
1. (a) 911.4 N   (b) 1176 N
   (c) 2.25 m

2. (a) $90 - X$ (b) $2X - 30$
   (d) 75 N

3. (a) (i) 7.5   (ii) 478 N

4. (a) 0   (b) 3750 N
   (c) 3125 N   (d) 1.6 m
   (e) AB remains straight

5. (a) 131 N   (b) 163 N
   (c) 0.5 m

6. (a) 0.833 m
   (b) bar remains straight, weight acts through centre

7. (a) 30 kg   (b) 3.6 kg
   (c) (i) weight acts at centre
       (ii) weight acts at A

8. (a) 735 N   (b) $3\frac{2}{3}$ m
   (c) (i) plank remains straight
       (ii) weight of woman acts at C

9. $\frac{8}{5}d$

Exercise 8A   page 181

1. (a) $4\mathbf{i} + 5\mathbf{j}$ (b) $10\mathbf{i} - 6\mathbf{j}$
   (c) $-2\mathbf{i} + 4\mathbf{j}$ (d) $3\mathbf{i} - 4\mathbf{j}$

2. (a) $3\mathbf{i} + 2\mathbf{j}$ (b) $-12\mathbf{i} + 9\mathbf{j}$
   (c) $17\mathbf{i} - 16\mathbf{j}$ (d) $3\mathbf{i} + 5\mathbf{j}$

3. (a) $8\mathbf{i} + 2\mathbf{j}$ (b) $3\mathbf{i} + 6\mathbf{j}$
   (c) $5\mathbf{i} + 10\mathbf{j}$ (d) $4\mathbf{i} + 3\mathbf{j}$
   (e) $14\mathbf{i} - 8\mathbf{j}$ (f) $-7\mathbf{i} + 12\mathbf{j}$ (g) $2\mathbf{i}$

4. (a) $5\mathbf{i}$, $5\,\text{ms}^{-1}$ (b) $-3\mathbf{j}$, $3\,\text{ms}^{-1}$
   (c) $2\mathbf{i} + \mathbf{j}$, $2.24\,\text{ms}^{-1}$
   (d) $0.5\mathbf{i} + 2.5\mathbf{j}$, $2.55\,\text{ms}^{-1}$
   (e) $-2\mathbf{i}$, $2\,\text{ms}^{-1}$ (f) $\mathbf{i} - \mathbf{j}$, $1.41\,\text{ms}^{-1}$

5. (a) $3\mathbf{i}$,   (b) $-2\mathbf{i}$ (c) $\mathbf{i} + 3\mathbf{j}$
   (d) $3\mathbf{i} + 2\mathbf{j}$ (e) $2\mathbf{i} + \mathbf{j}$ (f) $-\mathbf{i} - 2\mathbf{j}$

6. (a) $8\mathbf{i}$,   (b) $8\mathbf{i} + 3\mathbf{j}$ (c) $5\mathbf{i} + 7\mathbf{j}$
   (d) $10\mathbf{i} - 4\mathbf{j}$ (e) $4\mathbf{i} - 6\mathbf{j}$ (f) $2\mathbf{i} + 2\mathbf{j}$

7. (a) 2 s   (b) $4\frac{1}{2}$ s   (c) 1 s

8. (a) 2 s   (b) 4 s   (c) 7 s

9. (a) $3\mathbf{j}\,\text{ms}^{-1}$ (b) $(16\mathbf{i} + 12\mathbf{j})\,\text{ms}^{-1}$
   (c) $(-10\mathbf{i} + 24\mathbf{j})\,\text{ms}^{-1}$

10. (a) $5\,\text{ms}^{-1}$ (b) $13\,\text{ms}^{-1}$ (c) $25\,\text{ms}^{-1}$

11. $(4\mathbf{i} - 6\mathbf{j})\,\text{ms}^{-1}$ 12. $(8\mathbf{i} + 2\mathbf{j})\,\text{m}$

13. (a) 5 s   (b) -11 14. 12

15. -8 16. (a) 13 i m   (b) No

17. $(-4\mathbf{i} + 2\mathbf{j})\,\text{m}$ 18. 10 m

19. (a) $-5\mathbf{i} - (2 + 2a)\mathbf{j}$ (b) $7, -5$

20. (a) $\mathbf{r} = \begin{pmatrix} 2 \\ -3 \end{pmatrix} + \begin{pmatrix} 1 \\ 2 \end{pmatrix} t$
    (b) 3 s

21. (a) $(7\mathbf{i} + 2\mathbf{j})\,\text{m}$ $(8\mathbf{i} + 6\mathbf{j})\,\text{m}$
    (b) $\mathbf{r}_A = \begin{pmatrix} 3 \\ -4 \end{pmatrix} + \begin{pmatrix} 2 \\ 3 \end{pmatrix} t$
    $\mathbf{r}_B = \begin{pmatrix} 6 \\ 8 \end{pmatrix} + \begin{pmatrix} 1 \\ -1 \end{pmatrix} t$
    (c) 3 s

22. $\begin{pmatrix} 2 \\ 3 \end{pmatrix} + \begin{pmatrix} 12 \\ -16 \end{pmatrix} t$

23. (a) $\mathbf{r} = \begin{pmatrix} 2 \\ 8 \end{pmatrix} + \begin{pmatrix} 1 \\ -1 \end{pmatrix} t$
    (c) 1.5 s   12.5 m

24. (a) $\mathbf{r} = \begin{pmatrix} 10 \\ 0 \end{pmatrix} t$
    $\mathbf{r} = \begin{pmatrix} 5 \\ 10 \end{pmatrix} + \begin{pmatrix} 12 \\ -5 \end{pmatrix} t$
    (b) 8.60 m   (c) 2 s

25. 1230

26. (a) $\begin{pmatrix} 0 \\ 4 \end{pmatrix} + \begin{pmatrix} 2 \\ -6 \end{pmatrix} t$
    (b) $t = 1$ (d) $t = 0.6$

27. (b) $(90\mathbf{i} + 120\mathbf{j})\,\text{m}$

28. (a) $t = 0.4$ (b) 24.2 m

Examination Exercise 8   page 186

2. (a) $(-2\mathbf{i} + 4\mathbf{j})\,\text{ms}^{-2}$
   (b) 13.4 N
   (c) 35 m

3. (a) $\mathbf{p} = 10t\mathbf{j}$
   $\mathbf{q} = 6\mathbf{i} + 12\mathbf{j} + (-8\mathbf{i} + 6\mathbf{j})t$
   (b) 18 km (c) $\frac{3}{4}$ h

4. (a) 80 km h^{-1} (b) $(128\mathbf{i} + 128\mathbf{j})$ km
   (c) $(26\mathbf{i} + 96\mathbf{j})$ km
   (d) $-(100\mathbf{i} + 32\mathbf{j})$ km (e) 79 min

5. (a) $\mathbf{V}_D = -10\mathbf{i}$ $\mathbf{V}_C = 20\mathbf{j}$
   (b) $\mathbf{r}_D = -10t\mathbf{i}$
   $\mathbf{r}_C = -50\mathbf{i} + 20t\mathbf{j}$
   (d) $d = 44.7$ km
   Not detected

6. (a) 031°
   (b) $\mathbf{a} = 9t\mathbf{j}$
   $\mathbf{b} = (-10 + 3t)\mathbf{i} + 5t\mathbf{j}$
   (c) 1520 (e) 1424

7. (b) $\overrightarrow{AB} = (8 - 3t)\mathbf{i} + (-6 + 4t)\mathbf{j}$
   (c) 2.83 km (d) 14.40 hours

8. (a) 9.43 ms^{-1}
   (b) $(2\mathbf{i} + \mathbf{j}) + (5\mathbf{i} + 8\mathbf{j})t$
   (c) 1.6 s (d) 4.25 ms^{-1}
   (e) allow for friction so velocity not constant; allow for vertical component of velocity for motion of ball.

Specimen M1 paper A page 190

1. (a) 1.5 ms^{-1} (b) 7.5 Ns

2. (a) $6\mathbf{i}$ ms^{-1} (b) $(-1.5\mathbf{i} + 2\mathbf{j})$ ms^{-2} (c) $(12\mathbf{i} + 16\mathbf{j})$ m

3. (a) 64.5 m (b) 5.15 seconds (c) air resistance is neglected

4. (a) 1.75 m (b) $R_C = 196$ N, $R_D = 294$ N

5. (b) $T = 225$ seconds

6. (b) 30.2 N (c) 152 N (d) 0.199 (e) 3.21 ms^{-2}

7. (a) 5.66 N (b) 19.5 N (c) 2.5 kg (d) 1.79 ms^{-1} (e) 0.566 m

Specimen M1 paper B page 193

1. (a) $3\,\text{ms}^{-2}$ (b) 0.306

2. (a) $30\,\text{s}$ (b) $15.8\,\text{ms}^{-1}$

3. (a) $(4-t)\mathbf{i} + 3t\mathbf{j}$ (b) $t = 4$ (d) 0.4

4. (a) $1.2\,\text{ms}^{-2}$ (b) $17.2\,\text{N}$ (c) 0.23
   (d) same tension in string on both sides of the pulley

5. (a) $196\,\text{N}$ (b) $2.5\,\text{m}$ (c) $490\,\text{N}$ (d) $x = 3.2$

6. (a) $0.3\,\text{ms}^{-1}$ (b) A moves in the same direction as before collision
   (c) $2\,\text{kg}$ (d) 6.67 seconds

7. (a) $7670\,\text{N}$ (b) $3770\,\text{N}$ (c) $290\,\text{N}$ (d) $590\,\text{N}$

Index

Acceleration vector	177
Acceleration-time graph	14
Application of vectors	175
Bead	57
Coefficient of friction	62
Collisions in vector form	180
Connected particles	104
Conservation of momentum	140
Constant acceleration	1
Displacement	2
Displacement vector	175
Displacement-time graph	18
Dynamics	87
Equilibrium of forces	53
Force, definition	88
Force diagrams	36
Forces on an inclined plane	69
Forces, types of force	35
Friction	62
Gravity, acceleration due to	8
Impulse	136
Inclined plane	69, 98
Jerk in a string	145
Kinematics	1
Least distance in vector form	179
Mathematical modelling	111, 159
Moments	156
Momentum	136
Newton's laws of motion	87
Non-uniform body	159, 168
Particles	111
Pulleys	111
Resolving forces	42
Resultant forces	44
Ring	57
Rod	159
Speed-time graph	12
Statics	42
Strings	111
Tilting	165
Uniform body	159
Vectors, applications of	175
Vectors, basics of	24
Vectors in dynamics	128, 147
Vectors in statics	47, 57
Velocity vector	177
Velocity-time graph	1, 12
Weight	88